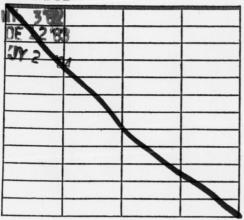

POLITICS AND
THE WARREN COURT

Da Capo Press Reprints in

AMERICAN CONSTITUTIONAL AND LEGAL HISTORY

GENERAL EDITOR: LEONARD W. LEVY

Claremont Graduate School

POLITICS AND
THE WARREN COURT

By Alexander M. Bickel

DA CAPO PRESS • NEW YORK • 1973

Library of Congress Cataloging in Publication Data

Bickel, Alexander M.
  Politics and the Warren Court.

  (Da Capo Press reprints in American constitutional
and legal history)
  Includes bibliographical references.
  1. United States. Supreme Court. 2. Law and
politics. I. Title.
KF8748.B53   1973   347'.73'26   73-398
ISBN 0-306-70573-7

Published by Da Capo Press, Inc.
A Subsidiary of Plenum Publishing Corporation
227 West 17th Street, New York, New York 10011

Politics
and the
Warren
Court

Also by Alexander M. Bickel

The Least Dangerous Branch (1962)

The Unpublished Opinions of
Mr. Justice Brandeis (1957)

POLITICS AND THE WARREN COURT

Alexander M. Bickel

Harper & Row, Publishers

New York

This book is for
my father

Contents

Preface   ix

I. THE RACES IN THE PUBLIC SCHOOLS
1. *The Decade of School Desegregation*   3

II. CIVIL RIGHTS: A NEW ERA OPENS, 1960–1962
2. *Preview: The Presidency and Civil Rights*   49
3. *Review: The Kennedy Record at Mid-term*   56
4. *More on the Kennedy Judges*   69

III. THE NEGRO PROTEST MOVEMENT AND THE CIVIL RIGHTS ACTS OF 1964 AND 1965
5. *Civil Rights and Civil Disobedience*   77
6. *The Civil Rights Act of 1964*   92
7. *The Limits of Effective Legal Action*   109
8. *The Voting Rights Act of 1965*   116

IV. THE WARREN COURT: DEFENSES AND CRITIQUES
9. *Chief Justice Warren and the Presidency*   133
10. *The Law Clerks*   139

vii

11. *Curbing the Union*   146
12. *New Troops on Old Battlegrounds*   162
13. *Supreme Court Fissures*   168

V. REAPPORTIONMENT AND LIBERAL MYTHS

14. *First Round:* Baker v. Carr   175
15. *Congress*   191
16. *One Man, One Vote, More or Less*   196

VI. RELIGION AND THE SCHOOLS

17. *Federal Aid to Education*   201
18. *The School Prayer Cases*   205

APPENDIX

The Original Understanding and the   211
Segregation Decision

Notes   263

Index   293

Preface

ABOUT THE THEME of this book there is nothing novel. What I have tried to contribute is development and variation. The theme is the interaction in our affairs of politics and the Constitution. Sooner or later, as de Tocqueville remarked, and in one fashion or another, the Constitution is likely to intrude on much of our politics. And the Constitution, being in a phrase of Felix Frankfurter, "not a literary composition, but a way of ordering society," defies understanding outside the context of politics. It is the political process that realizes in American life constitutional rules and principles enunciated by the Supreme Court. The Court's major pronouncements are subjected to the stresses of politics. Thus—and not by some mystic process of self-validation—do they become ways of ordering society, rather than mere literary compositions.

A government of laws and not of men—this formula is our ancient pride. It enjoins upon us principled government, responsive to a continuous and coherent tradition. But only a government of men can ensure responsiveness to present needs and desires. Only a government of men is self-government. A government of laws *and* of men, principled *self*-government—such is the true description of our system. Seen in the large, it is of course a working system, and stable, but in tension. It is the tension that interests me in this volume, and the failures we risk when we imagine something else, when we fall in with the illusion that laws alone, or even alone the men of laws who constitute the Supreme Court, can govern effectively. Nothing of importance, I believe, works well or for long in this country unless widespread consent is gained for it by political means. And there is much that must be left to processes of political and even private ordering, without benefit of judicially enforced law. The Court must not overestimate the possibilities of law as a method of ordering society and containing social action. And society cannot safely forget the limits of effective legal action, and attempt to surrender to the Court the necessary work of politics.

And so in this book I assess the impact of the Equal Protection Clause of the Fourteenth Amendment on our public schools, and with equal emphasis the impact of political conditions, North and South, on the rule of desegregation that is derived from the Equal Protection Clause, and on the possible further applications of that rule. An Appendix considers—against the background of the politics of Constitution-making that produced the Fourteenth Amendment—the process by which the Court evolved the rule of desegregation. I then observe the unfolding of the constitutional principle of equal treatment of the races as it is creatively translated from legal doctrine into political policy, and pressed gradually but steadily by executive action, by extralegal direct action in the streets, by legislation, and by all three methods all over again. Nothing so well illustrates as does this historic development the play of the political and legal processes upon each other, the possibilities and limits of law, and the dangers of sole reliance on law.

If our Constitution is a way of ordering society rather than a literary composition, it is a way of ordering society that thrusts statecraft upon judges in an utterly singular fashion, known just so to no system of government but ours. It is essential, therefore, not to be content merely to take a view, from the outside, of the action of the Court upon society and of the political process upon the Constitution, but to acquire also a sense of the judges, of their institution and of the process *they* engage in. I approach this aspect of my subject, and try to direct attention inward, in light of three external events of the past troubled decade in the Court's history. Speculation in 1955-56 about a possible presidential nomination for Chief Justice Warren leads me to examine the paradox of a judicial process which is incompatible with political involvement precisely because it is inextricably involved in politics. Attacks on the Justices' law clerks as being dangerous *éminences grises* are the occasion for a discussion of the Court's relationship with the bar and the law schools, and of the significance of the Justices' professionalism. Finally, some radical constitutional amendments proposed in recent years to curb the power of the Court—amendments that badly miss any conceivably proper target and often any target at all—provide the opportunity for opening up certain lines along which criticism of the Court's decisions might legitimately and fairly run.

I then offer comments on the *new* Warren Court, so to speak, which has been emerging since the retirement of the late Justice Frankfurter in 1962, and which may not be quite what it seems or, at any rate, may not be it for long. The following chapter consists of a detailed critique of the Court's reapportionment decisions. Here, I believe, the Court has intervened unwisely, beyond the limits of effective legal action, into the necessary work of politics. A last chapter returns full circle to the schools, to consider the political possibilities of the constitutional principle of the separation of church and state in the American system of education.

This volume derives in large part from work that I have published in magazines of general circulation and in law journals over the past ten years. But it is far from being a collection of this work, and it is not intended merely as a selection from it. Most of the papers and articles in question have been substantially recast for inclusion here, in the hope of sharpening their address to the central theme. Prior publication of portions of the chapters of this book, or of earlier versions of them, has been as follows: Parts of Chapter I appeared as an article in 64 *Columbia Law Review* 193 (February, 1964); earlier versions of all three sections of Chapter II, portions of the section entitled "Civil Rights and Civil Disobedience" in Chapter III, and earlier versions of the sections entitled, "The Voting Rights Act of 1965," in Chapter III, "Chief Justice Warren and the Presidency," "New Troops on Old Battlegrounds," and "Supreme Court Fissures" in Chapter IV, "Congress," and "One Man, One Vote, More or Less" in Chapter V, and "Federal Aid to Education" in Chapter VI, were published in *The New Republic* in the issues, respectively, for October 31 and November 21, 1960, December 15, 1962, June 8 and October 26, 1963, May 9, 1964, February 20, March 27 and April 3, 1965, January 23, 1956, March 16, 1963, July 11, 1964, February 29, 1964, July 27, 1964, and March 20, 1961; the sections entitled "The Civil Rights Act of 1964," in Chapter III, and "First Round: *Baker v. Carr*," in Chapter V appeared in earlier versions in *Commentary* for August, 1964, and June, 1963, respectively; the sections entitled "The Limits of Effective Legal Action," in Chapter III, and "The Law Clerks," in Chapter IV appeared in somewhat different form in the *New York Times Magazine*, respectively, of August 9, 1964, and April 27, 1958; and the paper published here as an appendix first appeared in 69 *Harvard Law Review* 1 (November, 1955).

I wish to thank the editors and publishers of the journals just mentioned for their kind and ready cooperation. I am additionally grateful to my friend Gilbert A. Harrison, editor in chief of *The New Republic,* for support, stimulation, and encouragement over many years—in short, for being a great editor.

The index was prepared with high competence by Mrs. Meira G. Pimsleur.

A.M.B.

Hamden, Conn.
May, 1965

Constitutional law . . . is not at
all a science, but applied politics,
using the word in its noble sense.
—FELIX FRANKFURTER

THE RACES
IN THE
PUBLIC SCHOOLS

I

The Decade
of School
Desegregation

1

IN THE LONG VIEW, which the historian of our troubles will one day take, the mid-1960's will appear as the time when school desegregation was finally accepted and began to work in earnest in the South, when, therefore, the racial problem in our public schools took on a national aspect, when it was first seen as essentially the same problem of imbalance South and North, as differing not so much in accordance with region and past histories of legal segregation, but from big cities everywhere to smaller ones, from urban to rural districts, and as being ultimately soluble only when the larger problem of renewing the quality and universality of public education in America and the even larger problems of poverty and of the obsolescence of cities themselves approach solution.

But that is the long view. More immediately, at the opening of the second decade since the *School Segregation Cases* of 1954 and 1955,[1] there are abroad in the land, by and large, two sets of attitudes (Southern disaffection to the side, of course). One large body of opinion, while avoiding complacency, feels on the whole encouraged by progress achieved and by prospects for further progress. Another, no doubt smaller but highly articulate groups is outraged by the passage of a decade during which we have witnessed in the South little more than token compliance with the law declared by the Supreme Court; a decade, moreover, which has seen in the country as a whole the merest beginnings of any effort to grapple with the cognate problems of *de facto* school segregation, *de facto* housing segregation, and *de facto* employment discrimination. In the words of the song from which James Baldwin borrowed the title of his famous best seller, and with all the urgency and all the alarm bordering on despair that those words connote in Baldwin's usage, many people feel: "No more water, the fire next time!"

I should like to declare myself as sharing both sets of attitudes. Both, I think, proceed from an accurate view of reality. But the reality of the Negro condition in the United States is very large indeed, and endlessly ramified. Most of us are quite unable to see it whole, at least not without hopeless blurring of detail and even of outline. It is only natural, therefore, that we should from time to time observe different parts of this total condition, and it is then more than natural that we should respond with different attitudes formed by our different impressions. Yet if we would observe for any purpose other than simply enriching the literature of protest or preserving the results in a storage house of private bitterness, we must, while attempting to see the existing situation, at the same time keep in focus the modes and possibilities of legal and other orderly social action, by which the Negro condition can be altered. We see differently, and not necessarily less feelingly, when our field of vision includes those additional realities as well.

Public education for the Negro is a problem that has at least two distinct aspects. One, the immediate aspect in the South and in a limited number of places in the rest of the country, is desegregation. Another is integration. It is no novelty to suggest that the two are very substantially different matters. The failure to see them not perhaps separately but distinctly accounts in part, I believe, for the attitude of unrelieved alarm to which I have referred. Moreover, the chief method of attack on the problem of desegregation, and until very recently also on the problem of integration, has been legal; more particularly, judicial. This method has its ineluctable limitations. A certain impatient failure to appreciate what Roscoe

Pound nearly fifty years ago called the limits of effective legal action[2] is a second factor, in my judgment, accounting for a mood of frustrated urgency. Legal action also has two, certainly not separate but somewhat distinct, aspects. One is the establishment of law, which sometimes in our system means more than merely announcing a rule; it means, sometimes, following through on the announcement with an effort, essentially political in nature and not necessarily assured of success, to generate consent to the rule in principle. Another aspect of legal action is administration of the law, which includes enforcement. If, for the moment, one is prepared to examine the problem of desegregation by itself, on the premise that its solution must precede any process of integration in the South; and if one perceives that the first step had to be the firm establishment of desegregation as a rule of law, then one can find the basis for a modest sense of achievement and for a tolerably sanguine feeling about the future.

The statistics of desegregation have shown dramatic improvement beginning in the fall of 1963. There were then 3,029 biracial districts in a formerly segregated seventeen-state Southern region; that is, 3,029 districts with both white and Negro pupils. Of these 3,029 districts, as of December, 1963, 1,141 had desegregated. Of these 1,141 districts, in turn, some 161 desegregated for the first time in 1963. This compares with 46 desegregating for the first time in 1962, and 31 in 1961. (It compares also with 200 desegregating in 1956—a figure to whose significance I shall presently draw attention.) Moreover, of the 161 districts desegregating for the first time in 1963, 141 did so voluntarily, without awaiting the compulsion of a court decree. Quite evidently, the pace was quickening. The number of newly desegregating districts was about the same again in the fall of 1964—upwards of 160, including four in Mississippi. And all but 25 desegregated voluntarily. These figures are probative, although they cannot be precise indicators, if for no other reason than that the number of school districts surveyed will vary from year to year; consolidation of districts seems to have reduced the total number of biracial school districts in the seventeen-state region to 2,950 in 1964, some 79 fewer than in 1963. But there is another set of relevant statistics, and they show at least as dramatic a trend. At the opening of school in 1964, the number of Negro children actually attending classes with whites in the eleven Southern states (excluding, that is, the Border) was double that of the year before. There are nearly 3 million Negro school children in Alabama, Arkansas, Florida, Georgia, Louisiana, Mississippi, North Carolina, South Carolina, Tennessee, Texas, and Virginia. Of these, 34,105, or just over 1 per cent, were in schools with whites in 1963. In 1964 there were 63,881, over 2 per cent. In the entire seventeen-state region the Negro enrollment is over 3½ million, and the percentage of Negroes in school with whites was 10.8 in 1964, having risen from 9.2 the previous year.

These are impressive figures, and yet it is possible to view them as disastrously bad. The number of desegregated districts is still under half the total number of biracial districts. Moreover, the greater part even of this unsatisfactory sum of desegregated districts is in Border states and in Tennessee and Texas, where the tides of change had begun their work before 1954. Again, a district is counted into this sum even if it has merely declared a policy of desegregation, although only one Negro child, or even none, actually attends school with whites. While not many of these districts have succeeded in passing muster with an abstract declaration and no more, the extent of real desegregation is very meager, indeed, in quite a few. The figures on Negro children attending schools with whites are similarly deflatable. The 2 per cent figure for the eleven Southern states is, to begin with, laughable. Besides, it is beefed up by the showings in Texas (7.26 per cent), Tennessee (5.33 per cent), and Virginia (5.07 per cent). The percentage in Alabama is .032; in South Carolina it is .100; even in North Carolina it is only 1.42, and even, again, in Florida only 2.65. And since the eleven Southern states have 85 per cent of the Negro enrollment in the entire seventeen-state region, the statement that 10.8 per cent of the 3½ million Negro children in the region attend schools with whites loses a good bit of significance.[3]

Such a gloomy view has its validity. Yet it leaves out of account the possibilities of ordered social action, which are never limitless and are also part of the reality, so long at least as we insist on achieving our goal without abandoning existing principles and institutions of government that we deem fundamental and otherwise satisfactory; so long, that is, as our goal remains integration, not disintegration. We must, then, consider a more immediate and more complex standard by which to judge these figures good, bad, or indifferent.

Obviously, the first standard to which we should repair in search of a standard is the Supreme Court's own "all deliberate speed" decree.[4] The standard stated in that decree is relatively simple and straightforward, and the figures given above do not look particularly good or promising when measured against it, either. The lower courts, said the Supreme Court, will require "a prompt and reasonable start toward full compliance"[5] with the Supreme Court's judgment of desegregation. Once such a start has been made, but by plain implication not before, the lower courts might consider reasons why additional time should be allowed to carry out the judgment in an effective manner. The Supreme Court proceeded to list relevant reasons of this sort. They had to do with

problems related to administration, arising from the physical condition of the school plant, the school transportation system, personnel, revision of school districts and attendance areas into compact units to achieve a system of determining admission to the public schools on a non-racial basis, and revision of local laws and regulations which may be necessary in solving the foregoing problems.[6]

It should go without saying, the Court also remarked, taking care not to let it go, "that the vitality of these constitutional principles cannot be allowed to yield simply because of disagreement with them."[7] It really went without saying, however, that the problems listed as relevant by the Court were not the only ones, and perhaps not even the major ones; although they were real and relevant and undoubted occasions of delay. It went without saying also that while the vitality of constitutional principles as reflected in specific court orders ought, to be sure, not be allowed to yield simply because of disagreement with them, disagreement is legitimate and relevant and will, in our system, legitimately and inevitably cause delay in compliance with law laid down by the Supreme Court, and will indeed, if it persists and is widely enough shared, overturn such law.

Others, saying what the Court had left unsaid, filled in the meaning of "all deliberate speed," and I shall offer three rather extensive quotations. The late Aubrey Williams, a Southerner certainly to be counted not only as a man of good will but as one of progressive, liberal outlook, said, in February, 1956, addressing the National Lawyers' Guild, which is itself no collection of reactionaries, and which yet does not appear to have hooted him down:

Now I favor this Supreme Court decision. . . . But I think the Court was absolutely right when it postponed for a year its discussion of implementation, and it was right in its position that it would take as good faith a move toward carrying out the mandate of the Court. There's going to have to be some time given here. We're going to have to back away and give these people some time to get out of the hysteria that they're in. I don't know if they will ever get out of it.[8]

At about the same time, Robert Penn Warren published an interview with himself:

Q. Are you for desegregation?
A. *Yes.*
Q. When will it come?
A. Not soon.
Q. When?
A. When enough people, in a particular place, a particular county or state, cannot live with themselves any more. Or realize they don't have to.
Q. What do you mean, don't have to?
A. When they realize that desegregation is just one small episode in the long effort for justice. It seems to me that that perspective, suddenly seeing the business as little, is a liberating one. It liberates you from yourself.

.   .   .   .

Q. Are you a gradualist on the matter of segregation?
A. If by gradualist you mean a person who would create delay for the sake of delay, then no. If by gradualist you mean a person who thinks it will take time, not time as such, but time for an educational process, preferably a calculated one, then yes. I mean a process of mutual education for whites and blacks. And part of this education should be in the actual beginning of the process of desegregation. It's a silly question, anyway, to ask if somebody is a gradualist. Gradualism is all you'll get. History, like nature, knows no jumps. Except the jump backward, maybe.[9]

Finally—and for obvious reasons I shall quote this at greatest length—here are Thurgood Marshall and Robert L. Carter, special counsel and assistant counsel to the NAACP Legal Defense Fund, in an article published in 1955 and entitled "The Meaning and Significance of the Supreme Court Decree":

While the Court's solution differed from that proposed by counsel for the Negro litigants, chiefly in regard to the fixing of a deadline for compliance, the formula devised is about as effective as one could have expected. The net result should be to unite the country behind a nationwide desegregation program, and if this takes place, the Court must be credited with having performed its job brilliantly. . . .

The decision has opened the door for Negroes to secure unsegregated educational facilities if they so desire. . . . Certainly, on the surface at least, a time limit would have afforded a sense of security that segregation would end within a specific number of years. We fear, however, that such security would have been fed on false hopes.

Some states—Missouri, Maryland, West Virginia, Kentucky seem to fall in this category—would have taken official steps to comply with whatever formula the Court devised. Pressure skillfully applied in a few other states would have resulted in the adoption of a similar policy. While desegregation could be successfully undertaken in many areas of the deep South tomorrow, little will be done for the most part unless Negroes demand and insist upon desegregation. In states such as Georgia and Mississippi, it looks as if desegregation will be accomplished only after a long and bitter fight, the brunt of which will have to be borne by Negroes. In short, we must face the fact that in the deep South, with rare exceptions, desegregation will become a reality only if Negroes exhibit real militancy and press relentlessly for their rights. And this would have been the situation no matter what kind of decision the Court had handed down.

. . . Great responsibility has been placed at the local level [on the federal judges] where it belongs, and where it would have been exercised in any event.

. . . Delays may be occasioned by various devices. This would result in any case. We can be sure that desegregation will take place throughout the United States—tomorrow in some places, the day after in others, and many, many moons hence in some, but it will come eventually to all.[10]

These passages unite in an appreciation of the Southern reality that is at once sensitive and hardheaded, and an assessment of the possibilities of judicial law that is at once confident and down-to-earth. These passages have probative value, therefore, not merely, like certain exceptions to the hearsay rule, by virtue simply of having been made, thus indicating states of mind, vintage 1954; they are given also as evidence of the truth of the matter asserted. By way of rather stark contrast, let me cite a later opinion, which I know has come to be rather widely held. In a study of reactions and developments in South Carolina, Professor H. H. Quint, who had taught in the state but left it before publication of this work in 1958, says that the first judgment of the Supreme Court stunned public and official opinion. Moderate voices in the state remained quiet rather than incur risks by coming to the Court's support, because they relied on the Court itself and on its authority to make the judgment effective. The year's delay that followed and the further delay implicit in the deliberate-speed formula allowed time for opposition to gather. "Had the Court ordered immediate integration, compliance might well have been forthcoming since at the time there was no alternative course of action."[11] This view proceeds from a radically different assessment of the Southern situation and from a radically different, if wholly silent, premise about the role and possibilities of law. If this view is accepted, the judgment that we must pass today is simple and unavoidable. The law has almost succeeded in snatching defeat from the very jaws of its own victory.

Quint's premise, and the premise of many other laments—toward which I intend no disrespect, for they are in almost every instance the product of a fine inability to suffer the scandal of social injustice —must be that when the Supreme Court lays down a rule of constitutional law, that rule is put into effect just about instantly, in just about the totality of the real-life situations to which it is applicable. As the Court itself was pleased to say in *Cooper v. Aaron*,[12] the Little Rock case, it becomes the duty of all persons affected, and especially of government officials, state or federal, to implement the Court's law. For officials at all levels of government are subordinate officers, oath-bound to effectuate the Court's will. Very often that is how things work, and the practice then seems to confirm this theory. Most often, when the Court's law affects limited interests and when the Court's prestige is sufficient to obtain general acquiescence in its will, that is how things work. But that has never been how things have worked on occasions when the Court's judgments have been directed at points of serious stress in our society, and on such occasions that is not the way things should or conceivably could work. The basis of all our law—rules of conduct, whether legislative, judicial, or administrative in origin, behind which is the coercive power of the state—is consensual. We are willing and ought to be willing to pay a limited price only in coercing minorities, and whenever, therefore, a minority is sufficiently large or determined or strategically placed we are not quite in a position to have law on whatever the subject may be on which the minority is constituted and situated as I have described it. We resort, then, to other methods of social action—methods other than law, methods of persuasion and inducement, by appeal not only to reason but to interests, not only to material but to political interests, rather than methods of attempted coercion. It is especially true of judge-made constitutional law, and ought to be, as I have argued more extensively elsewhere,[13] that both its basis and its effectiveness are essentially consensual.

This is no mere theory. As Marshall and Carter were so well aware and made so completely clear, it is built into the very mechanics of the system. The general practice—I shall recur to this point in more detail later—is to leave the enforcement of judge-made constitutional law to private initiative. It is also the general practice to enforce judge-made constitutional law prospectively only, so that no penalties attach to failure to abide by it prior to completion of a judicial proceeding seeking enforcement. This means that generally no one is under an obligation to carry out a rule of constitutional law announced by the Court until someone else has conducted a successful litigation and obtained a decree directing him to do so. Any rule of constitutional law, therefore, that is not put into effect voluntarily by officials and other persons who acquiesce in it, or that is not taken up by legislation and thus made at least somewhat more effective by administrative or noncoercive means, is not in our system an effective rule of law, for in such circumstances of widespread nonobservance the resources neither of private litigating initiative nor of the judicial process are equal to making it effective. This is not to suggest that there isn't opposition from dissenting or antisocial minorities to virtually all law or that our system abhors or ignores the necessity for occasional coercion.

Nor do I mean to suggest that enforcement is not in itself a method of persuasion, and indeed almost always an essential one, for there are always those whose acquiescence cannot be obtained if resistance is free of cost. Nor, again, do I have any quantitative knowledge of just how big and determined a minority needs to be before it can render judicial law, or before it can render legislative law, ineffective. But I do know that it can do so, and that it can render judicial law ineffective much more easily than it can render legislative law ineffective. It is thus never true, to use Quint's words, that there is "no alternative course of action." There always is, when feelings run strong; namely, inaction, on the one hand, and political action in opposition to the Court's law, on the other.

But *should* these alternatives to compliance be open, or is this merely, in a couple of Holmesian phrases, law washed in the cynical acid, the badman's view of the law—and thus a brand of realism that perceives too little and too narrowly, and that in any event, like some behavioral science or other, represents a sterile concentration on what is, with no regard for the ought? Yet the view is accurate, so far as it goes; Marshall and Carter were not for a moment lulled into believing they had won any more than this, or could have won more, when they obtained a favorable judgment in *Brown v. Board of Education*. No doubt, though accurate, this view is partial. Marshall and Carter also knew that in many places, where feelings did not run so deep or where political power is differently distributed than it is in the South, they had won something more immediate; in such places, the good or the indifferent man's view of the law—the unwashed law—was the accurate one, and the mere pronouncement of the Court's new rule had palpable effect. There are two realities, and neither must be allowed to block out the other. As to the ought, the badman we are talking about is a dissenter against a command that comes to him not from the political institutions in whose formation he plays his part and to whose deliberations he has access, but from an insulated, unrepresentative court. The dissenter may, for all we know, be a majority, or be in a position to form one. The coherence of the social order demands that he obey decrees specifically addressed to him. But should there not be the opportunity and the means to reject and to alter the rule of law handed down from above? If there weren't,

I for one would find it extremely difficult to defend the Supreme Court's function as ultimately consistent with democratic self-rule. There ought to be, and there is. This is the meaning of the dissenter's option to wait for litigation. He waits to see how intensely others are concerned to have the rule enforced; the speed and extent of litigation will reveal that, and litigation is thus itself something of a process of balancing interests and of measuring strength. (Little will be done, observed Marshall and Carter, "unless Negroes demand and insist upon desegregation.") He waits to assess the reaction, in the interstitial area left to them to react in, of the Supreme Court's first constituency—the lower federal and state judges. And he waits to allow time for the agitation of public opinion, since he knows that if he turns out to be in the majority or to feel intensely where all others are merely indifferently acquiescent he can change the law, or make it a dead letter, without recourse to the extremely cumbersome process of amendment. In such circumstances he ought to be able to change the law, even aside from the undoubted fact that ultimately, in a government where all the physical and money power is in representative hands, nothing can keep him from doing so. In principle, moreover, as suggested, if he feels intensely enough and there are enough of him, even if he is in a minority and even if the command comes to him from the representative institutions, he ought not to be coerced, at least not forthwith. He—he at large, his entire number and his political leadership—ought rather to be brought around in time; and it gives rise to no contradiction, merely to some untidiness, to hold also that in the meantime, while the issue is in doubt and subject to settlement by political means, coercion does also take place, as litigation succeeds and produces specific decrees. This much of enforcement is part of the process of political settlement.

The course of opposition to the Court's law that I have described, calling for inaction and for political action inconsistent with the law, and embodying what is loosely called disobedience of the law of the land on the part of both private and official persons—this course was widely pursued, for example, after the Court declared minimum-wage legislation unconstitutional in 1923, in *Adkins v. Children's Hospital*,[14] until it succeeded fourteen years later with a judicial retreat in *West Coast Hotel Co. v. Parrish*.[15] It was pursued with respect to released-time programs for religious instruction in public schools, which the Court held unconstitutional in *Illinois ex rel. McCollum v. Board of Education*,[16] and succeeded within five years, with quite as real a judicial retreat in *Zorach v. Clauson*.[17] It is being widely followed now in the wake of the Court's recent *School Prayer Cases*,[18] and it may well succeed. It was followed, with the greatest of vigor, shrewdness, and determination, in opposition to the *School Segregation Cases*, and it has failed. That is one measure of a decade's progress and of the Court's triumph.

It was not to be expected that the principle of school desegregation should be accepted and implemented forthwith in the South, as it was in Pennsylvania and New Jersey and Kansas, in New Mexico and Arizona, or under the federal government's immediate authority in the District of Columbia. The deliberate-speed formula was a candid recognition of this fact. The system would have worked no differently in any event, no matter what the form of the Supreme Court's decree. It is illusion to think otherwise, as was demonstrated, for example, by the history of desegregation in higher education, which began without any express deliberate-speed qualification over a generation ago.[19] A realistic objective, as of 1954-1955, was, Aubrey Williams said, to draw white Southerners "out of the hysteria that they're in." Aside from the South, and as a crucial factor in the process of extracting it from its hysteria, the task was, as Marshall and Carter put it, "to unite the country behind a nationwide desegregation program." For two years after the initial judgment there was considerable desegregation along the border, and a scattering in the South proper. I have noted that the high figure of 200 desegregating districts was reached in 1956, pursuant to decisions made in various localities a year or more earlier. The South was assessing the courses of action and inaction open to it. Then for about six years, from 1956 onward (March 11, 1956, the day the Southern Congressional Manifesto[20] was issued, is a convenient starting date), there was a pitched political struggle over the validity of the ultimate goal of desegregation, and for a good while the issue was in doubt, especially because during the Eisenhower administration, while the President kept his own counsel, the substantial nationwide majority favoring the Court's judgment was left without political leadership. In 1957 and 1958 the South miscalculated badly. The use of bayonets to keep Negro children out of Central High School in Little Rock, and the subsequent school closings in Arkansas and Virginia, caused Northern opinion to coalesce and harden—although during these crises also the President would not lead, even as, at Little Rock, he finally acted. Eisenhower never once said that he considered the Court's decisions right. This inveterate preacher never preached on the morality of desegregation. Responsible political leadership was, however, assumed in the 1960 presidential campaign and after, and it can now be said that the country is united behind the general outlines of a desegregation program. The hysteria of the deep South has been mastered in state after state—Virginia, Arkansas, Louisiana, Georgia, South Carolina. It is in train of being mastered under exceptionally adverse conditions even in Alabama. The "process of mutual education for whites and blacks," which Robert Penn Warren foresaw and of which "the actual beginning of . . . desegregation" is an essential part—this process is under way. Mississippi alone now stands, emotionally but not altogether in practice, where it stood, say, in 1957. It cannot long maintain such a posture entirely alone.

This is, in my judgment, an enormously important achievement; without it, nothing else would have been possible. No doubt, a resisting minority may yet have to be dealt with—for example, in Mississippi, and perhaps in Black Belt counties in other states as well. Nor does it follow that progress in other areas can now be expected to be entirely voluntary, although voluntary compliance is plainly on the rise and may be expected to increase further as Negro communities and the federal government exert pressure. Yet many lawsuits are still in prospect. The law of desegregation is established, but it still needs to be administered on a broad front.

On the basis of decided cases and other communiqués from the front lines, so to speak, I propose now to attempt a more concrete statement of the present status of school desegregation. I will rely heavily on the developing case law, of course, for the cases set the pace; they build models that are then voluntarily followed; they are a form of art widely imitated by life. Yet a good deal also happened before there was any case law, notably massive desegregation in Baltimore, St. Louis, Louisville, and Washington, D.C., not to speak of Arizona, New Mexico, and other more isolated areas in the North and West. These models from real life have, in their turn, exerted their influence on the case law.

It is not accurate to say that the federal courts at any stage, even the earliest, led the way toward tokenism, as it has come to be called. It is quite true, however, that for a season the federal courts accepted what might be called "genuine tokenism," when it was more or less voluntarily offered. At the same time, the attitude of the courts was quite different when they were faced with complete inactivity, with total resistance. The leeway provided by the deliberate-speed formula enabled the courts to react flexibly and politically in accordance with their assessment of local situations, and to feel their way toward the kind of decree which in this place or in that would be most likely to strengthen influences working toward ultimate compliance. In North Carolina, where the hysteria of massive resistance never took hold, the Court of Appeals for the Fourth Circuit as early as 1956 settled on a course of accepting a limited number of transfers of highly selected Negro children into a few white schools.[21] Beneath this outer show the schools remained segregated, just as they had always been. But this outer show did signify acceptance in principle of the law of desegregation at a time when it was being violently resisted on a last-ditch basis in other places. Plainly, the Fourth Circuit decided to wait in North Carolina, and to allow the impetus of a start toward desegregation to have a chance to develop on its own.[22]

The overshadowing issue in the Fourth Circuit was the massive resistance of Virginia, to which the judicial reaction was quite different. North Carolina managed its tokenism through a pupil placement statute setting forth criteria (relating to school administration, educational policy, and the health, welfare, and safety of pupils) for the assignment of individual pupils to available schools. Virginia also enacted such a statute, differing, to be sure, in detail but differing chiefly in that it was not being administered at all, in that it reeked with the rhetoric of massive resistance, and in that it was tied to a wholly defiant school closing law. The North Carolina statute was allowed to stand, but the Virginia statute was struck down.[23] School closings followed briefly in Virginia by order of the governor, but the federal court, happily joined by the state Supreme Court of Appeals, declared the school-closing law unconstitutional.[24] This hard judicial attitude achieved what had quite evidently been its aim. By early 1959 it had broken the back of massive resistance. The Fourth Circuit then assimilated Virginia, which enacted a new pupil placement statute and began to administer it, to North Carolina.

There was, however, one notorious exception in Virginia—Prince Edward County, where particularly determined, resourceful and, incidentally, peaceable resistance combined with misfortunes of litigation to create a unique situation. Under a Virginia statute making the maintenance of public schools a matter of local option, the county ceased appropriating money or levying taxes for its schools, and closed them as of the fall of 1959, thus becoming, and until 1964 remaining, the only county in the United States without a public school system. A segregated private school for whites was set up and supported entirely on private funds in 1959-60. Subsequently tuition grants were provided to parents by both state and county, and the white "private" school continued more comfortably in operation. The Negroes, after going without any education at all in the county for four years, also opened a private school in 1963-64. It wasn't until May, 1964, that the twisting paths of litigation finally converged in the Supreme Court, which held, in an opinion by Justice Black, that the county had to reopen its public schools, since to close them for the sole purpose of preventing their desegregation was unconstitutional.[25] At this late date, the decision presented no doctrinal difficulties, and came as no surprise.*
The public schools were reopened, but they were virtually all-Negro, most whites continuing in the "private" school with the aid of their tuition grants. Then in December, 1964, the Court of Appeals for the Fourth Circuit held that "private" schools born in

---

* Some eyebrows were raised, however, by Justice Black's direction to the district court to order the county officers, if necessary, to levy school taxes. It did not in fact come to this. But such an order by a federal court—enforceable by contempt proceedings—would not have been unprecedented. In a different context, more than a generation ago, the Supreme Court held that federal judicial authority to issue such an order is not lacking. Hendrickson v. Apperson, 245 U.S. 105 (1917). And in 1918, in Virginia v. West Virginia, 246 U.S. 565, a celebrated and extended donnybrook, the Court threatened to hand down a decree requiring the West Virginia legislature as such, not just a county supervisor, to levy taxes. If this was felt to be coercion, thoughtfully remarked Chief Justice Edward D. White, a Louisiana ex-Confederate, the answer was that the issue had been settled by the Civil War.

such circumstances and supported by the state in this fashion are in fact transparently public. The Court directed that the county be enjoined from paying tuition grants for pupils attending the "private" school in Prince Edward County so long as it remained segregated, or for pupils attending "any other segregated school that is, in effect, an extension of the public school system." And the Court issued a similar order in somewhat similar circumstances in Surry County, Virginia.[26]

Further south, the Court of Appeals for the Fifth Circuit had no occasion to accept tokenism on the North Carolina model, for none was brought into litigation. On the narrowest of grounds, the Court declined to strike down the Alabama pupil placement statute, although not the merest token of desegregation had taken place under it.[27] But this was at a time when the outlook in Alabama might have seemed ambiguous; Alabama was in any event not yet writhing in the grip of massive resistance, and it happened to be the moment when the crises in both Arkansas and Virginia were at their height. This was a peak of the political struggle, and the Court, not unnaturally, was holding its breath. It is also to be remarked that Negro pressure in Alabama was not then intense. Earlier in the Fifth Circuit, a Louisiana pupil placement statute, which was accompanied by a constitutional amendment reaffirming segregation, was struck down, as, in due course, was a school-closing law.[28] Somewhat later, in Houston and Dallas, a form of tokenism which, unlike the North Carolina variety, flaunted a purpose substantially to continue segregation, and flaunted it explicitly, right on its face, was disallowed. Houston and Dallas had proposed so-called "salt-and-pepper" plans, providing an integrated school for those, white and Negro, who wanted it, but otherwise continuing the segregated system intact.[29] In Florida the Fifth Circuit made it clear that a mere proffered readiness to administer a pupil placement statute was no defense to a desegregation suit.[30] Tokenism itself was merely a promise, and the Fourth Circuit was accepting it as such. But a promise to promise would not do.

In the Eighth Circuit the problem of Arkansas was dominant. The federal district court assumed a role in meeting massive resistance, as did its counterpart in Virginia, by striking down the school-closing law,[31] although, unlike the Virginia federal court, it lacked the support of the state Supreme Court.[32] But before the crisis in Little Rock Arkansas had somewhat resembled North Carolina, and in the aftermath of the crisis it acted very much like Virginia. Both before and after, therefore, being offered tokenism in the form of palpable symbols, the Eighth Circuit accepted it, as did the Fourth.

Delaware in the Third Circuit and Tennessee in the Sixth went their own rather different ways, on which I shall touch presently; but what has been summarily described here represents, I believe, the main lines along which litigation moved in the first five or six years. It seems not too much of a generalization to say, despite some variant cases, that tokenism was allowed where the local authorities were prepared to symbolize their acceptance of the principle of desegregation by the actual physical introduction of Negro pupils into white schools. It was allowed, that is, where it resulted in action that might hopefully be regarded as carrying a forward momentum. Not otherwise. Administration of the law at this relatively early stage was geared to the process of establishment; the courts accepted a palpable symbol of acquiescence, but also exerted rigid pressure when nothing concrete was forthcoming voluntarily. This, I believe, is the sense of the cases, and in this sense they are coherent. Doctrinally, however, the law was in some conflict and disarray.

In the Fourth Circuit the doctrine developed to fit the North Carolina situation, to which Virginia was soon assimilated. The Court held that no class actions seeking fuller desegregation would be entertained so long as selected Negro students were admitted to white schools under the pupil placement statutes. The Court thus foreclosed itself from noticing the continuation, formal or informal, of essentially segregated school systems. It allowed only individual Negro plaintiffs to litigate, each for himself, and only after exhaustion by each plaintiff of the administrative remedies provided by the pupil placement statutes.[33] It was open to an individual Negro plaintiff to prove that he personally had been denied a transfer to a white school for explicitly or necessarily racial reasons,[34] unmixed with other plausible reasons, such as residential zoning, overcrowding in the white school, or the pupil's lack of aptitude as revealed by various tests. Such plausible reasons were rather indulgently regarded. The upshot of litigation would every now and

then be that the transfer of an additional Negro child or two would be ordered, but no comprehensive plan was put into operation by the federal courts.[35] In the rest of the circuit, West Virginia was proceeding mainly on its own with substantial desegregation, and there was no movement whatever in South Carolina, nor much pressure; the litigation in Clarendon County, South Carolina, which was one of the five original *School Segregation Cases,* was allowed to lag by plaintiffs.[36] Both states, for their diametrically opposed reasons, were therefore not significantly in litigation.

In the Fifth Circuit pupil placement statutes were held to be no defense to a class action to desegregate the schools, and the Court of Appeals entertained such actions without requiring individual Negro plaintiffs to exhaust their state administrative remedies.[37] This was squarely in conflict with the doctrine in the Fourth Circuit. The Eighth Circuit fudged the doctrine, but made it explicit that only the North Carolina model of palpable tokenism would be accepted. School districts, the Court of Appeals said, must take steps "publicly to disestablish segregation,"[38] and at least one district court went to great lengths, indeed, to see to it that the steps taken were public and real. Tokenism, it was clear, requires a token.[39]

All this was not administration of compliance with the law, but administration marking time and seeking to assist in the establishment of law. This phase is now over, and the cases show it, if not yet quite uniformly. In the Fourth Circuit the rule against class actions and the requirement that individual plaintiffs must exhaust the remedies provided by pupil placement statutes are no longer operative. In both North Carolina and Virginia the Court has pierced the veil of tokenism, looked beneath at continued biracial zoning, and demanded more comprehensive action. In May, 1962, in *Green v. School Board of the City of Roanoke, Virginia,*[40] the Fourth Circuit had before it a system under which Negro pupils were assigned to Negro elementary schools without regard to geographic zoning, and then fed to Negro junior high and high schools. Under the pupil placement statute, however, nine Negro children (of thirty-nine applying) were admitted to white schools. Twenty-eight who failed to obtain a transfer sued to enjoin the school board from continuing this essentially segregated system of tokenism. They did not bother to exhaust further remedies under the pupil placement statute. And the Court did not require them to do so. The pupil assignment practices of Roanoke were "infected," the Court said, with racial discrimination. Such practices were tolerated in earlier cases "as interim measures only," but their day was now done.[41] The Court ordered submission of a plan for full compliance. Soon thereafter, in similar circumstances, the Court took even stronger action with respect to Charlottesville, Virginia.[42] And in two further cases, one from Caswell County, North Carolina,[43] a rural county with a Negro majority among its school children, the other from Durham,[44] the Court again heard class actions and issued broad and demanding decrees. The new mood in the Fourth Circuit has been carried forward in more recent cases, including one ordering the district court for the Eastern District of South Carolina to hear a class suit filed in behalf of Negro pupils in Clarendon County, South Carolina.[45]

The Sixth Circuit, embracing Tennessee, did not have early occasion to express itself on the doctrinal problem of individual suits and exhaustion of remedies that bedeviled the Fourth Circuit's transition from an acceptance of tokenism to the administration of compliance. But in a suit from Memphis, a city oriented to Arkansas and Mississippi, decided in March, 1962, the Sixth Circuit brushed aside the Tennessee pupil placement statute, under which, by August, 1961, thirteen Negro children had been admitted to white schools. The Court noted that Memphis still maintained "dual area zone maps, one for white schools and one for Negro schools," and held that "the admission of thirteen Negro pupils . . . is not desegregation, nor is it the institution of a plan for a non-racial organization of the Memphis school system."[46] The judgment, expressed by a writer in the *Columbia Law Review* in 1962, that pupil placement statutes and the tokenism they produced are obsolescent seems correct.[47] And yet, paradoxically, these statutes enjoyed something of a finishing canter in the Fifth Circuit, where their career had never amounted to anything in the past.

The Fifth Circuit's actions in the summer of 1962 were quite in line with those of the Fourth Circuit at about the same time, exhibiting an equally businesslike mood. In a case from Pensacola, Florida,[48] the Court declared itself unsatisfied with the operation of a pupil placement plan which had resulted in the admission of thirteen Negro children to white schools. In the latest phase of the New Orleans case,[49] the Court held that maintenance of racial zoning was unconstitutional, and that the unconstitutionality was not cured by selective assignments under a pupil placement scheme of some Negro children to white schools. Not long thereafter, in a case from Fort Worth, and in February, 1964, in three Mississippi cases, the same Court made short shrift of the argument, proceeding from the now-abandoned Fourth Circuit doctrine, that class actions circumventing state administrative proceedings should not be allowed.[50] But the summer of 1963 saw three regressive actions.

In September, 1961, Atlanta had put into effect a graduated transfer plan approved by the federal district court. It provided for use of the pupil placement statute to select Negro children for transfer to white schools. By the time the case reached the Court of Appeals, some fifty-four Negro pupils had been so transferred. But the initial assignment system was unchanged; Negroes went to Negro schools, whites to white. This is the classic method of tokenism. The Fifth Circuit, like the Fourth and Sixth, had rejected it in Pensacola and in New Orleans, as has been shown. But it now, in 1963, gave it its blessing in Atlanta.[51] The Court's opinion was by Judge Griffin B. Bell, a Kennedy appointee. It was concurred in by Judge Lewis of the Tenth Circuit, sitting by designation, who doubtless did not feel himself competent, on an *ad hoc* basis in a divided court, to be the one to spur a Southern city on to greater efforts. Judge Rives of Alabama, the third member of the panel, dissented, citing the prior decisions in the circuit. Shortly thereafter two other panels of Fifth Circuit judges were faced with extraordinary action in Alabama. In Birmingham, District Judge Lynne accepted the Alabama pupil placement act as an adequate desegregation plan, and held that no class actions would be entertained and that individual plaintiffs would be allowed to sue against discriminatory application of the statute only after having exhausted appropriate state administrative remedies. Thus he flew in the face of all applicable authority in his own circuit, and by now in other circuits as well. In Mobile, in a case filed in March, 1963, seeking to desegregate the schools for the fall term, Judge Thomas, on June 24, set the case for trial in November, with a view to working out a plan for the fall term of 1964. In both cases the Court of Appeals, no doubt feeling that by July, when the cases reached it, its hands had been tied by the delay and, in the Birmingham case one can surely say, obstruction below, ordered only that actual administration of the pupil placement statute begin by September, 1963.[52] And so it was on this basis of old-fashioned tokenism that desegregation began in both Birmingham and Mobile.

Begin it did, however, and it remained characterized by its initial tokenism for one year only. Having considered the Birmingham and Mobile cases once again, more at leisure, the Court of Appeals, on June 18, 1964, held that class actions were appropriate and would be entertained regardless of whether or not the plaintiffs had exhausted their administrative remedies under the pupil placement statute. And the Court ordered acceleration of the grade-a-year plans, so that complete desegregation would be achieved in six years. "The dual or bi-racial school attendance system," the Court continued, "that is, any separate attendance areas, districts or zones, shall be abolished as to each grade to which the plan is applied and at the time of the application thereof to such grades, and thereafter to additional grades as the plan progresses."[53] Meanwhile, in the Atlanta case, in which the Supreme Court had granted certiorari, the school board indicated at the argument before the Supreme Court that it had voluntarily undertaken to proceed beyond mere administration of the pupil placement statute. Thus it saved Judge Bell's 1963 decision from reversal. The Supreme Court sent the case back to the Fifth Circuit for reconsideration in light of the school board's new action.[54]

It seems plain—fitting this recital into the larger context set forth earlier—that it is the consensus of the judges on the firing line, so to speak, that one phase in the administration of the law—the establishment phase, characterized by permissive tokenism, by a sort of minimal judicial holding of the line while the political process did the main job of establishment—has been closed out. The resistant minority has been politically reduced to manageable numbers and to a manageable temper, and it is now time for another phase, that of enforcement in earnest. To be sure, there are what might be called opposition judges, willing in varying degrees to give effect to their feelings whatever the risk of reversal. There have been such judges all along—one of them, in the Savannah, Georgia, case,[55] recently set out expressly to overrule *Brown v. Board of Education*—and there are, unfortunately, some new ones. But the consensus I speak of is broadly based. This consensus, articulated in a sufficient number and variety of cases, provides a foundation for the Supreme Court to grant a group of certioraris and to lay down some new guidelines for the new phase, superseding the very sketchy ones of nearly a decade ago. It will be beneficial if the Court gives a new and unified sense of direction to the lower judges, and it will, incidentally, also be helpful if the Court exerts itself to keep the few opposition judges in line.

There are signs that the Supreme Court may intend to do just that. In a dictum in the Memphis Parks case of 1963[56] the Court went out of its way to indicate that the time had come to raise the speed limit. The Court at the same time also struck down a device that had been permitted by the Court of Appeals for the Sixth Circuit in Tennessee in connection with plans for fairly massive desegregation through nonracial residential zoning. The Sixth Circuit had allowed a provision under which students finding themselves in a racial minority in a school to which they had been newly assigned could request a transfer to a school in which they were in a racial majority. Quite obviously, the effect of this was to allow white children who found themselves zoned into a previously Negro school to escape. As an expedient making a massive desegregation plan more palatable, the device, no doubt, served its purpose. However, at this late date the Supreme Court struck it down as unconstitutionally based on a racial criterion, which in practice, in a city formerly segregated by law, it plainly is.[57] The upshot may be to discourage residential zoning plans of desegregation and encourage free choice plans, but in any event, as applied in Tennessee, which has come a long way, the result is to obtain more actually mixed schools than would have been possible before. The Court's action must be read in context of the general speed-up trend.

  The Court ought to address itself squarely to the problem of pupil placement tokenism. There is no longer good reason why newly desegregated places like Atlanta, or Mobile and Birmingham, and others that will come along, should be treated as they would have been had they desegregated five or six years ago. Tokenism, superimposed on an essentially segregated system, which the courts no longer tolerate elsewhere, should not be allowed anywhere. It is time for the Court so to hold, and make official, as it were, recognition of the law's firm establishment. No doubt there are pockets in the South where the establishment has not been achieved. But they are not isolated or insulated pockets. What happens in Memphis has its effect in Mississippi, and what happens in Charleston has its effect on Clarendon County, and so forth. The deepest, most backward pockets gain time from the fact that their own Negro communities are exerting pressure very mildly; that is, they gain time before litigation brings the matter to a point. But when it has come to a point, it would seem late in the day to reward such communities for the length of time they took and treat them as if they were North Carolina in 1956. No premium must be placed on massive resistance. Nothing can be plainer than the Fourth and Fifth Circuits' awareness of this in the late fifties, as demonstrated by the different initial treatment of North Carolina and Virginia. We must not now relax and forget it.

It is time also for an authoritative word on the grade-a-year plans. It has been fairly general practice in the Fourth, Fifth, and Sixth Circuits to allow either free-choice or nondiscriminatory residential zoning plans to be put into effect on a grade-a-year basis, so that system-wide desegregation will often not take place till well into the nineteen-seventies.[58] Even the Atlanta pupil placement plan operated on a grade-a-year basis, and oddly enough from the top down at that. Sometimes lateral transfers in grades not covered are provided for, sometimes not. The reason for allowing this form of gradualism is clear. It is the reason for insisting on, but also accepting, palpable tokenism, of which these plans are an extension, though differing substantially in kind. It made good sense to allow Houston, for example, or New Orleans to make a relatively slow but real start, and indeed a start embodying the very method of ultimate full desegregation. But does it continue to make sense to allow the slow pace to proceed now? A number of grade-a-year plans, new and old, have been speeded up by the lower courts. One sensible criterion for new plans, which has received mention in the cases, is the stage reached by surrounding or otherwise comparable communities. If Dallas has by now desegregated up to a certain grade, there is no reason why Fort Worth should be allowed additional time to get there. If Nashville has desegregated through the fourth grade, there is no reason why Davidson County right outside should start all over again at grade one.[59] Other criteria are harder to define. It remains true, as the Solicitor General advised the Supreme Court in 1955, that deadlines are unwise, if for no other reason than that "maximum periods tend to become minimum periods."[60] Still, the Supreme Court could require the lower courts to examine existing grade-a-year plans, to put the burden of proof on the school authorities to demonstrate their continuing need for more time, and to disallow whatever cannot fairly be supported.

It is not to be expected, however, that the Supreme Court can, by speaking out now on problems that seem soluble, solve all remaining problems. One of the most perplexing of these, now barely emerging into litigation,[61] is the problem of Negro teachers and administrative personnel. Another, even more forbidding, problem is whether and to what extent the Constitution condemns not only segregation by law but also racial imbalance that is not the product of law nor even of any school board's conscious act. To put it differently, does the Constitution merely forbid segregation or does it also command some measure of integration? At this point, of course, the problems of North, West, and South merge.

I have freely used the term "desegregation," and it is given some content by the cases reviewed. Now it should be defined more clearly with the aid of other materials. Presumably, what most of us visualize as the end result of desegregation is a school system in which there is residential zoning, either absolute or modified by some sort of choice or transfer scheme, and in which, in any event, children are assigned without regard to their race. This may be a good enough abstraction. But it is no statement of what such a system really looks like, nor of how to get there from a system that has for decades been organized on a segregated basis. Sometimes the way of getting there may be simple. If a school district having few Negro children had no Negro school itself, but bused its Negro children to a neighboring segregated school, then it could be ordered —and no doubt should be ordered—to admit its Negro children forthwith to its previously all-white school and stop busing them elsewhere. Indeed, such an order need not rest on *Brown v. Board of Education.* It can rest on the earlier higher education cases, which hold almost exactly this.[62] But if a school district, as is typically true in cities, for example, did have Negro and white schools, what must it now do? Simply rezoning geographically may not be easy, for the schools were not located initially on the basis of straight residential zoning but on the basis of segregated zoning, and so they may not be suitably placed. Moreover, is a school board required to send white children to formerly Negro schools, which may be substandard? Obviously, it ought to improve the Negro schools both physically and educationally, but it cannot do that overnight, nor is there any way for a federal court to produce the resources and the skills needed to do it. Indeed, under present conditions, without massive federal financial help, a school board may not be able to do it at all; the entire school system may be in a state of decline.

The problem is alleviated somewhat—without being in any degree brought nearer to solution—by a measure of inertia not unexpectedly to be found in the Negro community. In the South, and more than we like to admit in the North as well, segregation has been the habit of both races for quite some time. And so a school board may wipe out all former racial zoning lines, unify the system, and either (a) proceed also to wipe out all residential lines, and institute a free choice plan, under which parents simply present their children at the school of their choice, and the children are accepted so long as there is room; or (b) zone residentially without regard to race, and where a zone contains both a formerly all-white and a formerly all-Negro school, allow a free choice between them to children in the zone. When space problems arise, detailed residential criteria, with particular regard for traffic conditions, or criteria relating to the special circumstances of a given child, such as a physical disability or the need or desire for special courses not offered elsewhere, must decide which of several children wishing to register in a given school is to be allowed to do so. But there can be no special tests imposed on Negro children to which white children are not subjected.[63] There can now be no special transfer provisions in effect allowing white children to transfer out of predominantly Negro schools for that reason and no other, thus officially encouraging resegregation.[64] And courts must be on the lookout for the tendency, natural in communities with a history of legal segregation and not unheard of elsewhere, to gerrymander zones so as to produce all-Negro, if not also all-white, schools.[65] Perhaps it is possible also to require, as Judge Kaufman did in New Rochelle, New York,[66] that all requests to transfer out of a Negro school be granted subject only to space limitations or, as was done in Delaware,[67] merely that no Negro child desiring a transfer from a colored to an integrated or white school should be denied it on the ground that the Negro school is nearer to his home. But in the cities, at any rate, space limitations are not trivial. Perhaps in some circumstances it is possible finally, as was also done in Delaware,[68] to erect a rebuttable presumption that any all-Negro school surrounded by all-white attendance areas has been gerrymandered. All such conditions having been met, however, it is difficult to see what alternative a court has to accepting a plan of the kinds I have described. It is plans of this sort that border cities have used in desegregating voluntarily. And it is this sort of arrangement that generally prevails in the North and West. No other models are readily available.

What, then, happens under such plans? Most white children continue to present themselves at formerly all-white schools, great numbers of Negro children continue to present themselves at formerly all-Negro schools, and a number of Negro children are admitted to white schools. Some few white children go to Negro schools; most who would otherwise be required to do so flee to other homes or out of the public school system altogether. In time there is a settlement into conditions of substantial *de facto* segregation, alleviated by a number of successful integrated situations. In other words, essentially Northern conditions. I do not say such conditions have been achieved throughout the South. I do say this is the likely —and anticlimactic—outcome of all the litigating and all the striving.

St. Louis, Missouri, desegregated in 1954-55. The city was rezoned geographically, without regard to racial considerations. According to a thoughtful and thorough report to the United States Civil Rights Commission by a disinterested observer, the transition was "solidly conceived and brilliantly carried off." The result as of 1962?

Roughly 70 percent of the Negro secondary students in St. Louis last year attended high schools whose student bodies were 90 to 100 percent Negro. The same was true with respect to approximately 85 percent of the Negro elementary pupils. Only about 15 of the 136 elementary schools were significantly integrated.[69]

Louisville, Kentucky, desegregated in 1956. For elementary and junior high schools, it rezoned residentially, but also allowed free transfer to any pupil, limited only by the availability of space. Again according to an excellent report made in 1962 to the United States Civil Rights Commission:

There is no apparent gerrymander of boundary lines . . . but nevertheless almost one-half of the [elementary] schools are almost all white or all Negro. . . . [The figure may be lower than in St. Louis, but so is the ratio of Negro to white pupils.] Seventy percent of all Negro junior high school students go to the three Negro schools.[70]

Louisville high schools are not zoned. Students have a free choice among six high schools.

Seventy-three percent of the Negro students attend one high school, Central, the predesegregation Negro high school. . . . There was one white student in this high school in 1961-62.[71]

Baltimore desegregated in September, 1954, instituting a free choice plan. But in 1960 over 50 per cent of all schools were attended entirely by one or the other race. Most pupils tend to choose the neighborhood school. Baltimore did decrease the percentage of one-race schools in the next four years. Yet taking into account schools that are nearly all-Negro, and the addition of a substantial number of new schools to the system, the Civil Rights Commission reported in 1964 that "in fact proportionately there were more segregated Negro schools [in Baltimore] in 1963-64 than in 1953."[72]

And so on. In New York City—all boroughs—as of 1962, 197 of 578 elementary schools have 90 per cent or more Negro and Puerto Rican students, and 118 have 90 per cent or more white. In Chicago some 87 per cent of Negro elementary school pupils attend virtually all-Negro schools. In Philadelphia 14 per cent of all public schools have a Negro enrollment of *over* 99 per cent, while 24 per cent of elementary schools have 90 per cent or more Negro, and 28.5 per cent of elementary schools 90 per cent or more white pupils.[73] Is there a legal remedy? If there has been a gerrymander, there should be a judicial remedy in New Rochelle, New York,[74] or Hillsboro, Ohio,[75] as well as in Fort Worth, Texas,[76] or in the Rose Hill-Minquadale school district in Delaware,[77] and the courts have so held. But as the cases also show, proof of a discriminatory motive may not be as easily forthcoming as in the New Rochelle case,[78] which was a remarkably ill-conducted litigation from the school board's point of view—and not that proof was all that easy, even so. In the Hillsboro case the thing was objectively obvious beyond the possibility of explanation.[79] This will not happen often. Elsewhere, even the presumption set up by the district court in Delaware, to which I have referred, may turn out to be rebuttable. Again, if a school board achieves segregation by allowing white children, but not Negro, to escape to other schools in the system, that ought to be, and has been, stopped in New Rochelle as well as in Charlottesville[80] and Lynchburg, Virginia,[81] or Knoxville, Tennessee.[82] Other transfer policies which, though fair on their face, are discriminatorily applied can also be policed.[83] Finally, as the Supreme Court has indicated, perhaps federal courts ought to hear class actions in the North, even where there is no history of legal segregation, without requiring exhaustion of state administrative remedies.[84] This had not been uniform policy in the lower federal courts outside the South[85] before the Supreme Court's recent decision in the *McNeese* case, and one may question its wisdom as a uniform policy, having regard to difficulties of proof, to what is, as we shall see, the limited range of remedies available to a federal court, and to the greater, though also not unlimited, effectiveness of administrative remedies and the efforts of school authorities in some states to apply them.

Proof of sophisticated Northern discrimination may be hard to come by; and perhaps the incidence of such intentional, if covert, discrimination is rarer than some commentators have supposed. But what is not at all difficult to prove in myriad places, large and small, is that *de facto* segregation, or, if you will, substantial racial imbalance exists. The statistics just cited shout the fact. Despite intimations to the contrary, however, by three federal district judges in cases coming from Springfield, Massachusetts, and from two Long Island communities,[86] racial imbalance resulting from otherwise disinterested neighborhood zoning is not unconstitutional. There is no Supreme Court decision directly on point, but a number of lower federal courts have so held, and Congress evidently takes this view. When, in the Civil Rights Act of 1964, Congress authorized the Attorney General to bring suit in school cases, and empowered the federal Commissioner of Education to extend technical and financial assistance to desegregating school districts, it limited the authority of both officers to cases involving "desegregation," which Congress defined as

the assignment of students to public schools and within such schools without regard to their race, color, religion, or national origin, but "desegregation" shall not mean the assignment of students to public schools in order to overcome racial imbalance.[87]

Congress also expressly disclaimed any intention to

empower any official or court of the United States to issue any order seeking to achieve a racial balance in any school by requiring the transportation of pupils or students from one school to another or one school district to another in order to achieve such racial balance.[88]

These provisions have a negative effect only. They indicate Congress' view of the present state of constitutional law on the subject, and make plain the desire of Congress to go no further than the courts have gone up to now and to put no pressure on the courts to go further. But Congress' view of constitutional law is conclusive on no one, certainly not on state courts which may operate under applicable provisions of their own statutes and constitutions, and certainly not on boards of education, which may wish, on their own authority, to do what Congress has disclaimed any intention of requiring federal courts to do. The Commissioner of Education quite clearly and the Attorney General almost surely are bound by the limitation Congress has imposed on their functions. But nothing in this statute will prevent federal courts from holding, if they ever think it wise to do so, that substantial racial imbalance in public schools is unconstitutional, no matter how innocently or accidentally it came about, so far as a given school board and its predecessors are concerned. And—most emphatically—nothing in this statute prevents state and local authorities from doing something about racial imbalance, including, in the words of the statute, "the transportation of pupils or students from one school to another."

No inclination is noticeable at present, however, on the part of federal courts to take the initiative in the matter of racial imbalance by way of constitutional decisions. In the 1961-62 school year, Gary, Indiana, housed 43,090 students in forty schools. Some 53 per cent of these students—23,055—were Negroes, of whom well over half attended 12 schools that were 99 to 100 per cent Negro and another 7,000 went to five schools that were 77 to 95 per cent Negro. Four schools had a pretty good racial balance (from 13 to 37 per cent Negro). Five schools had a negligible Negro population, and 14 schools, accommodating 10,710 pupils were all-white. This situation, the Court of Appeals for the Seventh Circuit held late in 1963, is not unconstitutional. Nothing in the federal Constitution, the Court said,

requires that a school system developed on the neighborhood school plan, honestly and conscientiously constructed with no intention or purpose to segregate the races [an attempt to prove the contrary had failed to satisfy the trial judge], must be destroyed or abandoned because the resulting effect is to have a racial imbalance in certain schools where the district is populated almost entirely by Negroes or whites.[89]

A year later the Court of Appeals for the Tenth Circuit similarly declined to interfere with racial imbalance in Kansas City, Kansas, resulting from the normal workings of neighborhood and feeder school policies.[90]

For the time being, at any rate, that is that. A plausible contrary constitutional argument can well be made, and the difficulties it raises in the present state of Fourteenth Amendment law are soluble.[91] If *de facto* segregation is less invidious than *de jure*, the difference is one of degree only, and the presumed damage—to the child in the educational setting, of which we know perhaps too little, and to society as a whole, which suffers in later years the divisive and embittering consequences of the habits of apartness, misunderstanding, misinformation, and distrust formed in children who never encounter each other across the racial barrier—the damage is scarcely much less. Moreover, even though *de facto* school segregation may not be chargeable to the conscious act of any official, it is everywhere the result of residential patterns most often fostered or at least encouraged by local authorities at one time or another, and residential patterns, at that, which far surpass in rigidity anything this country has ever seen or still retains by way of nationality ghettos. The Court in the Gary, Indiana, case referred to "innocently arrived at school attendance districts," but there cannot be many American communities that truly think themselves innocent of the housing and economic conditions of their Negroes, and these conditions in turn are the direct cause of *de facto* school segregation.

The reason, possibly, why such a constitutional argument has not prevailed and shows no sign of soon prevailing is not that it is inherently untenable, but that the courts are well aware of their inability to remedy the situation which they might plausibly enough find unconstitutional. If segregation is ordained by law, the law can be struck down and the local school authorities can be required to organize a school system on the free choice or the zoning principle without regard to race, which we know well enough is feasible. If segregation was achieved indirectly, by gerrymandering, by other than innocent site selection, or by discriminatory transfer policies, the courts can in some measure make their remedy follow the wrong. They can undo the gerrymander, order institution of a different transfer policy, and police the selection of future sites. Even when all this is judicially ordained, however, what can we expect to happen?

Judge Kaufman in New Rochelle ordered free transfers from the effectively segregated Lincoln School to other schools where space was available. The result was something, to be sure. Lincoln school went from 94 per cent Negro to 88 per cent. As to the transferees, in one school they found a very different socioeconomic group from their own, and performed rather poorly. Another school in which transfers were accepted already had a considerable Negro enrollment, and, with some whites fleeing to private schools, soon threatened to become another Lincoln. Nevertheless, the judicial remedy worked, in the sense that it did some good—as we conceive the good in terms of integration. But it worked, in the degree that it did, in New Rochelle, a relatively small community of 77,000, of whom 14 per cent are Negroes, with a school system which, as the consequences of Judge Kaufman's decree tend to show, must have been relatively healthy and not overly crowded. And even in New Rochelle the remedy could work in the long run only because a reconstituted school board proceeded to implement its spirit with administrative imaginativeness. Lincoln School was eventually closed, and Judge Kaufman modified his order to permit the school board to carry out a program of active racial dispersal throughout the system.[92]

No such judicial remedy could conceivably work any wonders, not even small ones, for example, in New York, Chicago, or Philadelphia. The Negro populations of all three cities are large and densely concentrated residentially. In Manhattan nearly 75 per cent, and in New York City as a whole 40 per cent, of grammar and junior high school students are Negro or Puerto Rican, and the trend is upward.[93] In Chicago, 40 per cent of all elementary school pupils are Negro, and it is estimated that by 1970 the public elementary schools will be predominantly Negro. In Philadelphia Negroes constitute 49 per cent of the school population.[94] In St. Louis 58.5 per cent of elementary and 55.4 per cent of all public school students are Negro. The figures in 1955 were, incidentally, 38.4 per cent for elementary and 31.2 per cent for high schools.[95] Other, even more striking figures, such as those for Washington, D.C., are well known, and what they mean is obvious. A schoolteacher in New York, speaking no doubt prematurely, is reported to have said: "There is nobody left to integrate with."[96] In Philadelphia, given distances to outlying white areas, it is estimated that "the 120,000 Negroes in the school system could be integrated with no more than 50,000 to 60,000 white children."[97]

Can a court, in such circumstances, bring itself to forbid continuation of the neighborhood school policy, which rests on numerous considerations having nothing to do with race? Can a court order the adoption of a school-pairing (Princeton) plan, which competent educators may deem unsuitable in a given city for reasons not related to race? Is a court qualified to order large-scale busing to distant areas, or to estimate—as may be unavoidably, if regrettably, necessary—the tipping point at which a desegregated school will resegregate? A court may step in with some confidence to undo what was done, not in the exercise of professional judgment but for an ulterior and unlawful purpose. Surely, however, the questions just posed involve genuine and close professional judgments. Perhaps it will be said that guesses are the only answer anyone can give, and perhaps that is true. At any rate, such judgments or guesses will not, and ought not, be accepted from courts. Ultimately, as has been well said, "the schools must be better [and more integrated] in order to make the community better, but the community must be better in order to provide better schools. This is a familiar but by no means impossible American paradox."[98] Yet it is an impossible paradox from the point of view of a judicial remedy. What courts do not know how to remedy they are in a poor position to hold unconstitutional—at least, as caution leads one to add, for the time being.

To say that something is not unconstitutional, however, is merely to say that it is no concern of the courts. It is not to say that it is good—it is indeed not to say much more than that it is not utterly intolerable, if my double negatives are still comprehensible; it is not to say that others ought not to concern themselves with the situation or that they may not experiment with, and find, ways to improve it. The paradox that sets the American school and the American community to chasing each other on a circular race track toward betterment may be formidable as well as familiar, and it may not be susceptible to judicial resolution. The facts may further require one to recognize that the problem will not yield to any prompt or radical solution, and to none certainly that comes from school authorities alone. But it is equally true that an ultimate cure will be hastened and made easier, that the total problem will be made more tractable by transitional efforts at amelioration now, no matter how pitifully insufficient such efforts may often appear. The degree to which the problem will yield at all varies from place to place, and even the neighborhood school policy is not everywhere sacrosanct in all circumstances. Any given neighborhood is, after all, an arbitrary construct, the trace at some time of somebody's pencil on a map, and nobody has a vested right in it. There can be no true amelioration of conditions without the expenditure of new effort and new money to improve the quality of schools that are subjected to reshuffling. All that can be achieved otherwise is mere motion and turmoil, with probable resegregation as the end result, and the kind of equality in the meantime that brings everyone down to the less equal level of some. But if the resources and the effort are adequate, then no matter how arduous, cumbersome, and initially disruptive the operation may be, and no matter if everyone knows that the larger problem remains unsolved and in the immediate aspect virtually untouched, rescuing the future of a hundred or a dozen children, or of one, by bringing them from a poor school situation into a better one, is in itself a sufficient reward. And when the courts decline to involve themselves in the problem of racial imbalance, they do not thereby absolve local school authorities or the political institutions, state and federal, from responsibility in the premises. On the contrary, that is where they return the responsibility.

Beginning with an initiative by the New York Board of Regents in 1960, numerous communities, large and small, in the North and West and in the Border states, have been studying and implementing measures to ameliorate racial imbalance in their schools.[99] Often such measures are undertaken under pressure of Negro demonstrations, which may well be expected to continue. While results have been far from spectacular, a movement of sorts may be said to be afoot, and it has raised a legal issue of its own. The courts, as we have seen, have imposed no over-all obligation to cure conditions of racial imbalance. But will they, on the other hand, limit or in any fashion restrict the discharge by school officials and political institutions of their own responsibility? Here attention turns more to state than to federal courts. The answer so far is generally no. The leading cases come from the highest courts of New Jersey[100] and New York,[101] which have held that the amelioration of racial imbalance is a proper consideration in the formulation of zoning and general educational policies.

In the New Jersey case, which originated in Montclair, a junior high school with a population some 90 per cent Negro had been closed, and its pupils given a free choice to attend any of the other three junior high schools. White parents complained that their children, who remained assigned to the schools of their zones and had no free choice of other schools, were being discriminated against. But no one has a right to insist on the perpetuation of any given zoning or educational policy, and different treatment of different pupils, who in the judgment of competent authorities should be differently treated for good and sufficient educational or social reasons, is a commonplace. The federal Constitution cuts across such professional judgments in so far as their effect may be to enforce a separation of the races, which is held to be invidious, harmful to the largest purposes of our society, and, in the judgment of many, immoral. Otherwise, judges normally defer to the discretion of the competent authorities, and that is what the New Jersey court did. This was the result also in the New York case, in which the zoning of a new junior high school in Brooklyn was attacked on the ground that it changed old neighborhood lines in order to achieve a racially balanced student body. So also an intermediate appellate court in New York upheld an order of the state commissioner of education to the authorities in Malverne, Long Island, to remedy a 75 per cent imbalance by converting two schools to a K-3 attendance, and assigning grades four and five to the previously unbalanced school.[102] Another New York judge approved the pairing of two elementary schools, five blocks apart in Long Island City, which had previously been, respectively, 87 per cent white and 78 per cent Negro.[103] And a federal court in New Jersey declined to interfere with strong dispersal measures taken in Englewood, which included establishment of a city-wide sixth-grade school.[104]

The upshot is that courts, which will not substitute their own judgment for that of professional educators by dictating policies of integration, will also not second-guess a professional judgment that a given policy of racial dispersal is neutral or beneficial from an educational point of view. As the New York intermediate court said in the Malverne case:

> On application of the conventional test, we find the Commissioner's decision to be neither arbitrary nor capricious. When there is found to be a rational basis for the administrative determination, the judicial function is exhausted and the administrative agency, not the court, is the final arbiter.[105]

This is as it should be, although there lurks in these cases a difficulty of constitutional logic, since school boards that act to cure racial imbalance may be thought to be using—however benevolently—the proscribed racial criterion for assigning pupils, and although it is impossible to be quite certain that no state or federal court, especially no court of first instance, will be found to give ear to complaints of white parents, and at least temporarily interfere with a plan for racial integration.

As already indicated, care was taken in the drafting of the Civil Rights Act of 1964 not to engage federal administration in the task of integrating legally desegregated schools. One may doubt that this attempt to wash the federal government's hands can long succeed. The pressures that have been exerted against *de facto* segregation must in the end reach Washington. For much the same reasons that argue against the feasibility of a judicial remedy, it will be seen that no coercive federal measure of any sort—attempting to enforce this or that scheme of pupil dispersal—is possible. The federal government will have to induce rather than coerce, to help rather than do. Yet it cannot avoid its responsibilities. Presidential exhortation, identifying the problem as one of national concern, and defining some minimum national goal on the long road to its solution—such leadership from the White House will be demanded and will be required. Presidential neutrality on matters of race relations—whatever they be, from school questions to marches on Montgomery or Washington—is no longer possible. From the White House, when issues become acute, there can be only leadership that defines legitimate Negro demands or opposition to such demands as they come up. Moreover, massive federal financial assistance toward raising the quality of the public schools generally is plainly in the offing. Administrative ingenuity and flexibility will eventually have to be applied in using federal moneys to induce, at the least, some experimentation with pupil dispersal techniques. And the federal government—presumably the United States Office of Education—will find itself called upon to lead in the invention and validation of new educational policies, which might conduce to integration without sacrificing the values attributed to the standard neighborhood school, and in gaining professional acceptance for them. It is illusory to expect federal administrative neutrality and abstention. There can be no such thing. Neutrality is not neutral, for racial imbalance is not static in growing and evolving school systems, whether they evolve toward improvement or deterioration. When the federal government helps, it cannot help helping either further to entrench and unbalance racial imbalance or to ameliorate it. These are the alternatives, and no other.

Such is the nature of the federal involvement that looms ahead, in a future that may be more or less distant. In the shorter run, the Civil Rights Act of 1964 confers important functions on federal administrative agencies in expediting and completing school desegregation in the seventeen-state Southern and Border region. The Commissioner of the Office of Education is authorized under Title IV to help any school board or larger jurisdiction with technical assistance in preparing and implementing desegregation plans.[106] For the first time, school districts will thus be able to inform themselves, from a source both official and professional, about practices and experiences elsewhere. The Commissioner is also authorized to make available personnel especially trained to assist in coping with desegregation problems.[107] Finally, he is authorized to finance and arrange special teacher-training programs with a view to solving problems to which desegregation gives rise—chiefly the need to devote special attention to children who might be transferred from substandard Negro schools to better white schools.[108] Energetic and imaginative execution of these Title IV powers by the Commissioner of Education could achieve startling results.

Even more striking and immediate results could be obtained from the combined operation of Title VI of the Civil Rights Act of 1964 and President Johnson's Elementary and Secondary Education Act of 1965. Title VI, although it makes no specific mention of schools, requires all federal agencies administering any grant-in-aid program to ensure that there will be no discrimination, by way of exclusion, segregation, or otherwise, in the activity receiving the federal assistance. As to schools, the effect of Title VI is greatly heightened by the Education Act, which will pump over a billion dollars into the school system, with the lion's share going to low-income areas such as the deep South. This constitutes quite an inducement to abide by federal standards of nondiscrimination. Since this is new money, it can and will be withheld until, at the very least, a school district promises to desegregate. Funds already in the pipeline under existing programs continue to be disbursed while compliance is sought or while a statutorily prescribed process of hearing and review winds its way toward a possible cut-off.

In May, 1965, Commissioner Francis Keppel of the Office of Education issued an excellent "General Statement of Policies," which set forth the kind of desegregation plan a school district must promise to adopt if it is to receive federal funds. What is acceptable according to this statement, aside from nonracial residential zoning, which not many deep South districts are likely to opt for, is a free choice plan that gives full opportunity—with notice—to parents to choose the school they want; disregards the restrictive transfer criteria of pupil-placement statutes; provides for assignment of a pupil, regardless of race, to the school nearest his home, in case he has made no choice or has chosen a school that is oversubscribed; eliminates segregation in services and facilities affiliated with the schools, such as busing; provides for assigning teachers and administrators without regard to race, and, as to teachers and administrators previously assigned on a racial basis, makes a start at desegregation, at least to the extent of providing for joint faculty meetings. By 1967 the measures just outlined should have been taken throughout the school system administered by a given district, and a promise to meet the target date must be made now. Meanwhile, as of the fall of 1965, at least four grades should be desegregated, namely, at least the first elementary school grade, the lowest grade of junior high school, if any, and the first and last high school grades. Every system must thus promise to graduate a desegregated class in 1966 and at all three possible levels take in desegregated classes in 1965. Compliance reports are required.

Commissioner Keppel's statement follows the best and most recent of the Fourth and Fifth Circuit cases. But it does not supersede other existing court orders, some of which are less admirable, and it provides that in case of a variance between a desegregation plan approved by the Commissioner and a subsequent final court order, the latter shall govern. Hence the developing case law continues in large measure to set the pace. But the statement should help make the statistics for the school year 1965-1966 better than ever, and by a substantial margin. And yet the millennium is not here, and part of the reason is that the Office of Education does not have nearly the staff—and possibly the intensity of will—necessary for effective administration of either Title VI or Title IV.

When a district has made the required promise, its application under the Education Act of 1965 is approved, and the money goes out. And the district is on its own. If, in perfect good faith, it doesn't quite know how to proceed with application in its own particular circumstances of the general policy it has subscribed to, if it lacks the staff and skills it suddenly finds it needs, there is too little help from the Office of Education. And if a district evades or fudges its promise or sits by while community pressure keeps 100 per cent of the Negro pupils—as a matter now of "free choice"—bottled up in the same Negro school, all the small staff in the Office of Education can do is await an inadequate compliance report or a complaint. Then there will have to be lawsuits. Results will be achieved, to be sure. But any spectacular leap forward would require the presence in the field of a goodly number of federal professionals, working out of regional offices, to guide, help, and monitor compliance.

Not Title VI, not Title IV, and not seven more titles and Civil Rights Acts can quite undo, just like that, the decades of segregation and decay in the deep rural South. But the point has now been reached where progress can come at different rates of speed, and where these rates are, in some measure, determined by conditions not in the South but in Washington. That is the case with the administration of Titles VI and IV. More money and more people could make a difference. The amounts in question are relatively paltry, and one would think the President could find them.

Quite aside from litigation to enforce promises under Title VI, the act also provides in Title IV that the Attorney General may bring suit to desegregate schools in the name and at the expense of the United States. Before he may do so he must determine that neither the persons concerned nor interested organizations—meaning, chiefly, the NAACP—are able to bear the expense of the litigation, and, secondly, he must determine that "the institution of an action will materially further the orderly achievement of desegregation in public education."[109] This provision raises serious problems on several levels. It is obviously an effort to alter those mechanics of the system to which I referred earlier, and which ensure that a rule of constitutional law will become effective only when it is widely assented to. Of course, nothing is likely altogether to alter the system. Given the judicial resources that are available, and given, indeed, the resources that can conceivably be made available to the Attorney General himself, it is still out of the question that desegregation can be achieved wholly or even chiefly through litigation; it is still impossible that desegregation can be achieved if people are not moved by political action to achieve it voluntarily, because it is morally right and because it is, on balance, in their political and material interest. Yet the intention is to achieve more coercion more promptly.

If the system were to be altered in this fashion across the board, as was seriously proposed while the act was under consideration in the House;[110] if, that is, the Attorney General were empowered to enforce all existing constitutional rights, and to seek from the courts declaration of new rights, then surely one would be entitled to the gravest of misgivings, because then the nice adjustment between authoritarian judicialism and government by consent would be significantly altered. Not only would the process of private litigation, which is in its totality something of a political process of measuring the intensity and strength of interests affected by a judicial rule— not only would this process be circumvented, with the result that judicial power would be potentially enhanced quite out of proportion to what it now is or ought to be. The Attorney General would gain and share with the courts, at his option, powers entirely free of the imprecise safeguards that are implicit in our present reliance on private litigating initiative. It would be the Attorney General, in the exercise of a discretion for whose control no machinery exists or is easily conceived, who would choose to make existing rules of constitutional law effective, or explore the possibility of new ones, for he would elect from time to time to concentrate on enforcement in this or that area of constitutional law. This would be quite a revolutionary change. I hope that, in some appropriately old-fashioned words of Justice McKenna, "it is something more than timidity, dread of the new, that makes me fear that it is a step from the deck to the sea—the metaphor suggests a peril in the consequences."[111] Attorney General Robert Kennedy, one was encouraged to note, resisted being decorated with any such broad powers.

But this is an argument at wholesale. The Attorney General already exercises by statute authority to enforce a great deal of law which, in the legislative judgment, needed enforcement beyond what could be expected from private initiative. And so do other administrative officers. There is a difference of more than just degree when the law to be enforced is constitutional rather than statutory. But it can be argued that when Congress passes a statute authorizing the Attorney General to enforce a given rule of constitutional law, the source of that rule is no longer exclusively in the judiciary. And that is so, so long as Congress closely defines what it wishes to see enforced. This is the view that prevailed when the Attorney General was given the authority that he now possesses to enforce the Fifteenth Amendment's guaranty of an equal vote. There is also a limited criminal statute under which the Attorney General can enforce constitutional rights. But the authority under this statute has been most cautiously and circumspectly limited by the courts, so as to encompass only well-defined and thoroughly established rules of constitutional law.[112] As for the right to vote, there are very special circumstances that make private litigation for its enforcement extremely difficult, indeed almost certainly beyond any private resources. The power to litigate to desegregate public facilities and accommodations, also conferred by the statute, though not unqualifiedly, is again a special and different matter. First, the source of the right to be asserted is at most only partly constitutional; essentially, the Attorney General is to enforce, on the basis of specific substantive provisions, something not unlike the Wages and Hours Act. Secondly, the private interest involved is so diffuse, and in any individual case so slight, that the incentive to undergo the ordeal of litigation is in this instance at a minimum, and yet the collective feeling on the subject is known, in the most concrete way, to be quite intense. In school cases private litigation is a going concern. No superhuman efforts at collecting data fit for a census bureau and in any event not likely to be readily obtained from local officials—no such unusual efforts, which characterize voting cases, are required here. What is perhaps most important, no statutory definition of the sort of school segregation—*de jure* and, in some instances of gerrymandering or other covert discrimination, *de facto*—that Congress may wish to see most efficiently abolished is proposed. Congress, of course, could not be brought to agree on such a definition. Nor is there a definition of remedies. With voting and with public accommodations it is otherwise. Both the objectives and the ways of attaining them are relatively clear, and Congress has stated them. The power conferred with respect to schools is, therefore, much more far-ranging and much more independent.

If it is conceded that there is a general presumption against executive power to litigate constitutional rights, and that exceptions must justify themselves, then I believe that the argument I have offered suffices. Still, it is a question of judgment, and there is yet more to be said, even if somewhat cumulatively. How is the Attorney General to decide that this or that case will "materially further the orderly achievement of desegregation in public education."? To put the matter quite concretely, when is school desegregation to start in this or that Black Belt county? And is any *de facto* segregation to be attacked, and if so, where? And when? As things now stand, private parties, parents locally, local Negro lawyers, if any, the NAACP and its corresponding counsel, and whatever other leadership is present and effective in the Negro community nationwide somehow make the decision. The lawyer in charge of the suit in Clarendon County, South Carolina, for some years opted not to push it. Then one day he decided that the time had come. He may not be able to articulate the grounds for that decision, and it may be right or wrong as we view it afterwards. If we substitute the Attorney General as the decision maker, must we not expect from him some more orderly, rational, and articulable process? For his decision will have been made at the expense of a dozen other places which pressed their claims on his resources—the resources of government, to which in principle all are equally entitled. It will be said that we do not displace the private decision makers by empowering the Attorney General to bring suit, and on the face of things that is no doubt true. But in practice, if the Attorney General is given the necessary resources and makes energetic use of his authority, private initiative is bound to be chilled and the flow of private funds is bound to be discouraged and diverted elsewhere, where the help of the federal government is not available. When a private suit is brought, it will come inevitably to be regarded somewhat suspiciously by the courts and by public opinion, and will inevitably be treated as of secondary importance. It will, after all, by hypothesis be a suit that does not necessarily "materially further the orderly achievement of desegregation in public education."

It would be a different matter if the business of desegregation were seriously taken in hand in administrative fashion. That is, it would be a different matter if the Office of Education, for example, or the Civil Rights Commission were given adequate statutory standards to formulate plans of desegregation, were then required to hold hearings where there was opposition to the plans proposed, and were authorized to issue orders at the conclusion of those hearings, and to go to court to enforce such orders. In some measure, this sort of more responsible and methodologically different displacement of private and local responsibility will occur under Title VI, but it is to be regretted that Congress has not dealt more specifically and more in detail with the school problem, and that it has scattered administrative authority in a number of federal agencies. However, the authority Congress has conferred in Title VI is inducing—not coercing—authority, and it has surrounded even that with significant procedural safeguards, in addition to requiring direct presidential approval of administrative regulations.

Quite aside from statutory authorization, there is considerable federal litigating power not subject to the misgivings I have voiced. Since before the famous 1895 case of *In re Debs*,[113] the Attorney General has been allowed to go into the courts of the United States in special circumstances to protect not only its material but its functional interests.[114] There was some language in *In re Debs* that was more sweeping than it needed to be, but on its facts the objection to that case is that the courts were asked to do—and did— something they were not fit to do, at anyone's behest, not that the Attorney General was an improper party to initiate the suit.[115] Just what a definable functional interest of the United States may be which does not include everything is hard to say. But the point of this line of cases is that occasional authority exists in limited circumstances. In each case some special federal responsibility must be shown.[116] And so long as this is the rule, it may be expected that the decision to exercise inherent litigating power, being rare, will be made responsibly, at the highest executive level. And no derogation of private litigating initiative need be feared, for no announced federal undertaking to litigate is in play, and there can be no expectations. Before there was a Civil Rights Act of 1964, the government tried some desegregation suits against impacted-area school districts that receive federal funds, and against airports and hospitals that also receive federal funds, with results that were not clear, but certainly not negative.[117] There was better than a good chance that inherent power to sue in such circumstances would be confirmed by the Supreme Court. These and other suits that fall somewhere in the traditional category could have been prosecuted to good purpose without raising the difficulties that inhere in broader statutory authority.

CIVIL RIGHTS:
A NEW ERA
OPENS,
1960-1962

II

Preview:
The Presidency
and
Civil Rights

2

THE PRINCIPLE OF A SELF-STARTING, creative and expansive discharge of the presidential office was one of the most insistent themes in John F. Kennedy's 1960 campaign. The theme recurred with particular frequency in his discussions of civil rights. In his second television debate with Richard Nixon, Kennedy said that some civil rights objectives could be achieved by unaided executive action, and he emphasized, quoting F.D.R., that the Presidency is "above all, a place of moral leadership." But just what exactly, as of 1960, were the powers of the President affecting civil rights?

There is always a tendency to exaggerate what one man in the White House can possibly direct, or even know. There is, indeed, as Thomas Reed Powell once wrote in another connection, a certain "unwarranted animism" in the use of the phrase "the Administration." This much it is necessary to say by way of caution. But the President *can* generally summon great, immediate, and effective power, provided two things are true. One, that the President conceives it to be one of his missions, domestically as well as internationally, to initiate policy and to carry it into effect on his own responsibility, and to reach out boldly until he is stopped by the retaining wall of a countervailing power, such as Congress. Retaining walls there are, and there are, God knows, enough of them; a President need not begin by worrying that he will be allowed to go too far without being stopped. Kennedy certainly so conceived the office in his campaign, and Nixon professed to also. Eisenhower, with a few exceptions (viz., the so-called inflation issue in 1958-59) did not, as Taft and Harding and Coolidge and Hoover before him had not. Two, it must be true that the President is willing, for a time at least, to devote a disproportionate share of his total effort to a domestic problem on which he wishes to exert the full reach of his power and influence. The decisions and the leadership that are called for cannot be delegated. The sources of the authority and of the drive that are both necessary cannot be separated. What is involved is not administration but creative work on the frontiers of power, and the President must be willing to immerse himself in it for a time. He cannot do so with respect to many matters at once.

If these two conditions are met, the opportunities are great. In attempting to analyze them as they bear on civil rights and as they opened up for John Kennedy in 1960, one may put to one side two distinct presidential functions: (1) recommending legislation to Congress and (2) executing authority specifically conferred by Congress. The one is generally well understood, though there was reason to doubt sometimes that Eisenhower quite grasped its significance. The other is delegable and is indeed often delegated by Congress itself to Cabinet officers and the like, acting under the direction of the President. Kennedy justly complained in campaign speeches that only six suits were started by the Eisenhower administration under the Civil Rights Acts of 1957 and 1960, which deal with the right to vote. The Civil Rights Division of the Department of Justice was organized tardily and poorly, and run without distinction. Its record under Eisenhower was laughable when compared, for example, with that of the same department's Antitrust Division. This was in part owing, perhaps, to certain hostile attitudes in Congress that manifested themselves in regard to both appropriations and nominations. It was owing in the largest part to complacent administration. The cure lay in the appointment of vigorous, dedicated men at Cabinet and sub-Cabinet levels. It did not demand the exertion of much more presidential leadership than that.

There was something, however, that the President and only the President could do about the subject matter of the 1957 and 1960 acts. He was uniquely in a position to draw attention to the problem of voting rights, not by comfortable homilies but by pointing to specific, glaring abuses until the whole nation blushed. And he could heighten the importance and prestige of the Civil Rights Commission, created and given investigative powers by the 1957 act, by associating it in the public mind with his own person and office. Eisenhower took an unconscionable time making the necessary appointments to the Commission after Congress had created it, and he pretty much ignored it afterward. When the Commission met with defiance in the South, the government's law officers in due course vindicated it in court. That was as it should be. But the President did not react, as he could have, by appealing to public opinion on his own and indicating that it was not some miscellaneous bureaucrats who had been flouted but the President's trusted appointees and delegates.

President Eisenhower's failure to react in this fashion is worth stressing because it was attributable not only to temperament but to an aspect of the conception of the passive Presidency which was of particular importance with respect to civil rights. At least until 1964 basic civil rights policy was constitutional and therefore judge-made. Eisenhower generally took the position that it is not for the President to have public views on matters that are in process of being decided by the courts, and also, as in the instance of the school segregation decision, that it is no less improper for the President to speak his own mind after the courts have acted. This is the mechanistic view of the doctrine of separation of powers, the view, to borrow a witticism of Chief Justice Taft's, that the machinery of government is really machinery. It was not the attitude of Theodore Roosevelt or even of President Taft, both of whom felt free to have convictions about the meaning of the Sherman Antitrust Act and about the constitutionality of an income tax before and after the courts announced their opinions. It was not Franklin Roosevelt's conception, as it had not been Jackson's. And it was not Lincoln's, who had a few public thoughts about the *Dred Scott* case.

The President, of course, must take the lead in obeying, and in urging and in the end enforcing obedience to judicial decrees. But, as Lincoln pointed out long ago, it is one thing—and quite inadmissible—to resist a specific court decision. It is quite another to reject it (or to accept and support it) as what he called a "political rule," governing the behavior of the other branches of the government on cognate matters.[1] This is a distinction crucial to a true view of the doctrine of separation of powers. It follows that a President, while obliged to enforce, was free to deplore the Supreme Court's decisions on schools or on the investigative powers of the Civil Rights Commission. If so minded, however, he was free also to accept such decisions, and to use his "place of moral leadership," and exploit his unique access to the minds and hearts of the American people, in order to support the Court's actions. If so minded, moreover, he had the power to make the principle underlying the Court's decisions the "political rule" of his administration. John Kennedy was so minded. This was his conception of the office of President. He was prepared, it seemed, to make of the principle of equal protection a "political rule," but would he find it possible to devote the necessary disproportionate share of his energies to its effectuation?

In planning for the first few months of 1961, the first choice that had to be made was between unaided executive action, on the one hand, and executive activation of the legislature, on the other. Both would be necessary in the longer run. But immediately? This was going to be a time, to be sure, of heightened—yet not limitless—energies, and a peak time of executive effectiveness in legislative leadership. But it would be also a short and crowded time of competing priorities, all high; and the risk to the quantity and quality of the total legislative program that would inhere in asking immediately for civil rights legislation was obvious and familiar.

To have assessed this risk was not to conclude the choice. But it happened also that a number of immediate needs could be met by the President acting on his own; and that meeting them vigorously and imaginatively would amount to a fresh start on civil rights, a hopeful and it might be even a spectacular start. Moreover, and this was most important, it was reasonable to expect that the assumption of presidential responsibility would alter the shape and posture of things so as vastly to enhance the chances of far-reaching Congressional action when the time for that did come.

Assuming, then, that no new legislation would be sought initially, and that an attempt would be made to exert executive power to the fullest, what actions were open to President Kennedy as his administration began? The initial step in the assumption of presidential responsibility could fittingly be issuance soon after inauguration not of one or more executive orders—though they also would be needed —but of a Proclamation. We have not ceased to live by symbols, and it would not be purposeless thus to call to mind the grandest traditions of the office and the boldest actions of its great occupants. The President could review the history of Negro rights (and wrongs) since Lincoln's Proclamation: the Civil War Amendments, the largely ineffectual Reconstruction Civil Rights Acts, the forward movement in modern constitutional litigation to the climax of the segregation cases of 1954 and their progeny, and the Civil Rights Acts of 1957 and 1960. He could then proclaim his purpose to protect and defend, to apply and to extend recent legislative and judicial policies throughout the realm of executive power. And he could announce that he proposed, in the language of the Constitution, to "take care that the laws be faithfully executed" as follows:

Public education. The Civil Rights Commission, in its 1959 report, noted that many school districts attempting to evolve a desegregation plan had "no established and qualified source to which to turn for information and advice." The Commission proposed that it be given statutory authority to act as a clearinghouse for such information and advice, and also to act as a mediation and conciliation service helping school boards work out plans.[2] A bill by Senator Paul H. Douglas, of Illinois, would have given similar authority to the Department of Health, Education and Welfare. But the Office of Education in that department dates back to a statute of 1867, and the description of its duties makes remarkable reading. The office is "to collect statistics and facts showing the condition and progress of education in the several States . . . to diffuse such information respecting the organization and management of schools . . . and shall . . . promote the cause of education throughout the country."[3]

The authority was there for the President to use. He could direct the Office of Education to extend technical assistance to districts seeking to desegregate their schools, and, beyond that, to "promote the cause of education" by working out desegregation plans for districts that had taken no initiative of their own. The Office could collect and make readily available the lessons of experience on such matters as the maintenance of scholastic standards, social relationships in schools, utilization of Negro teachers, and Negro-white community cooperation. It could also, as a conciliating agency, suggest the application of these lessons to local conditions. In carrying out its conciliation function, the Office could have available on a continuous basis the counsel and assistance of the Civil Rights Division of the Department of Justice. Senator Douglas' bill would also have authorized the Attorney General to go to court and enforce integration plans worked out by the Office of Education. But the President could send his law officers to court not as enforcement officials but as friends of the court, which was the way they did enter the original school cases, and later the Little Rock case.

The suggestion was made at a Conference on Civil Rights at Notre Dame University early in 1960 that the President could refuse to grant any federal aid to a college or university that discriminates in selecting its student body. The President would wish to give an opportunity for compliance rather than laying down a flat rule, and he would grant hearings (though not personally, of course) in cases where the facts were in dispute. But otherwise, as Father Hesburgh of Notre Dame indicated, the only thing lacking was the will.[4]

Housing. The President had—and in the course of the campaign promised to exercise—the power to follow another 1959 recommendation of the Civil Rights Commission[5] and establish a policy of nondiscrimination in federally aided housing. It could, no doubt, again not be a flat rule, for that might deprive Negroes as well as others of any new housing in areas where it was worst needed. But the authority to exert pressure was available, and it could be employed with most fruitful immediacy, perhaps, in the North. The Housing and Home Finance Agency, the Federal Housing Administration, the Veterans Administration, the Public Housing Administration, and the Urban Renewal Administration could work out policies to encourage the growth of racially integrated neighborhoods, or at least prevent the perpetuation of segregated ones. Consultation with local authorities was advisable, of course, but the federal policy would ultimately be enforced as a condition upon the receipt of federal funds and assistance.

Government building, employment, and contracts. It was common ground all around that the President could, if he wished, enforce the principle of equal protection in the employment practices of the government and its contractors, and thus incidentally cover a considerable segment of the economy. President Eisenhower indeed declared a policy of nondiscrimination by executive order, and delegated to a Committee on Government Contracts, headed by Vice-President Nixon, the authority to effectuate it. And that was all he did, except to complain to Congress that the Committee could do its job better if it was put on a statutory basis. The problem was—and remains—complex, involving as it does, for one example, labor union practices, and it is even larger than it is complex. If it was to yield, it needed less a statute and more the public attention and drive a President could give toward its solution.

That, to repeat, was the single most important generalization applying to everything that could be done on the President's unaided executive authority. The Assistant Attorney General in charge of the Civil Rights Division would have to have public evidence of the President's interest and trust. The same would hold for the head of the Office of Education. At lower levels, a great deal of staffing would have to be done within existing appropriations. Very often, therefore, the borrowing of personnel from within the government would be necessary, and if that was to work rapidly and result in the assignment of first-rate people, it would also have to receive the President's attention from time to time. Personnel would be needed not only for the litigating, technical assistance, and conciliation programs but for the others as well, since nondiscrimination policies could not just be decreed; they would have to be worked out to suit conditions, and they would have to be policed. Neither the mere appearance of discrimination nor of nondiscrimination would necessarily be true to the reality of things. It would often be necessary to investigate and to grant hearings. Finally, funds would have to be found within existing appropriations, and that also would require a form of personally conducted presidential arbitrage.

But the returns could be high. The suggestions touched on here are far from being all that an imaginative rummager might have found in the back-closet of presidential powers.

Review:
The
Kennedy Record
at Mid-term

3

THE PRECEDING SECTION of this chapter canvassed the possibilities for action on civil rights that seemed open to President Kennedy at the beginning of his administration. In view of these possibilities, how did the performance measure up? A good point in time on which to fix for an assessment of the record is November 20, 1962, when Kennedy signed an executive order barring future discrimination in federally supported housing.[1] Asked why he had waited till midway in his term of office to take this promised action, the late President replied: "Well, I said I would issue it at the time that I thought it was in the public interest, and now is the time." Now was the time also, although nobody quite knew it then, when the opening phase of the Kennedy performance was drawing to a close. There would soon be an end of the beginning. Within a very few months events in Birmingham, Alabama, would permanently and radically alter conditions and launch John Kennedy on a second, quite new if foreshortened career as a champion of civil rights. There would be another record.

A portion of the first record, it may be said with no attempt at irony, was made in the presidential campaign of 1960. In the course of this campaign, Kennedy and Nixon established a firm national consensus, and finally fixed the broad and pervasive principle of the *School Segregation Cases* of 1954 as not only the judicial but also the political policy of the federal government. The campaign established a new mood of executive engagement in the civil rights struggle, and signaled an executive commitment to the morality of equal protection of the laws as a rule of independent, creative political action, rather than merely as an obligation to uphold the courts. As a direct consequence, some notable peaceful strides were made in school desegregation, and would continue to be made. The crisis at Ole Miss, although it was tragic, was rather an insignificant exception, as in their own context were the Montgomery Freedom Ride riots of the spring of 1961, which were followed by great progress in the peaceful integration of transportation facilities. The point is that after the campaign of 1960, forward movement in desegregation was—and was known to be—as ineluctable as the income tax or the social security system. This had not been the case before.

The Presidency, said Kennedy in 1960, quoting F.D.R., is "a place of moral leadership." So is a presidential campaign, at least for the eventual winner, and Kennedy seized the opportunity in his campaign. Beyond this, he made one specific pledge—the famous "stroke of the pen" about housing—which he redeemed. But he promised also, more generally, vigorous executive action on all fronts. The performance must be judged against the expectations so raised, which came to seem natural, although they would have appeared strange and visionary during the previous decade.

A first and quite obvious generalization is that the performance through 1962 was wholly executive. The Administration broke no lances in Congress. As to this one need perhaps say no more than that President Kennedy was a realist, and that he had troubles enough in what was to all intents and purposes a three-party legislature, with a species of Free Democrats (à la West Germany's) holding the balance of power. A second and more interesting generalization, qualified by the housing order, is that the performance was heavily a litigating one. With this aspect of the performance I propose now to deal in some detail, before returning to the housing order and to other acts of commission and omission.

Transportation. Perhaps the most spectacular achievement was the apparently effective and almost universal desegregation of interstate transportation, including terminal facilities. It isn't very fruitful to debate whether the Administration's action was a consequence of the freedom rides in the spring of 1961 and of sit-ins before and after or was an independent initiative. The fact is that in a well-conceived and flawlessly executed move the Justice Department obtained from the Interstate Commerce Commission a self-enforcing order integrating not only interstate buses but also the terminals they use. The order evidently worked, although in some localities custom tended after a while to reassert itself, with the aid of unofficial white pressure. Where local officials tried to interfere, the department followed up by obtaining injunctions against them in the federal courts. Segregation on interstate trains had long since been abandoned, and it seems never to have been in effect on planes. But many terminals and airports remained segregated. Pursuing an altogether commendable and lawyerlike policy that it is worthwhile having a try at negotiation before filing suit, the Justice Department obtained the agreement of the chief Southern railroads, eighteen in number, to integrate their terminals; and this was done in hundreds of places. Again, where official state interference was attempted, court action followed. As to airports, the problem was somewhat different, being both easier, because federal funds often helped to build the facilities, and harder, because these are often—especially in their restaurants —more of a multi-purpose local institution. Both the Civil Aeronautics Board and the Federal Aviation Agency exerted pressure, and the Justice Department negotiated and in a few instances litigated. Results here were perhaps a little slower in coming—and it is again possible that in some places the actual practice soon reverted to earlier custom—but the point was reached in the fall of 1962 where Attorney General Kennedy could report that "virtually every airport" as well as bus and railroad station in the South had been desegregated.

Voting. From Reconstruction to 1964, Congress legislated twice and only twice on racial discrimination. It passed the Civil Rights Acts of 1957 and 1960. These closely connected statutes prescribed procedures for enforcing the Negro's right to vote, which is most explicitly guaranteed by the Fifteenth Amendment, and charged the Attorney General of the United States with the duty to prosecute the necessary lawsuits. The Eisenhower administration, though it sponsored both bills, implemented them with about the vigor and imagination displayed by William McKinley in enforcing the Sherman Antitrust Act of 1890. The Kennedy administration put life and purpose into these Civil Rights Acts.

The Eisenhower administration filed six voting suits. It settled one and tried two. The other three had been filed too late to come to trial before Eisenhower left office. The Civil Rights Division in the Department of Justice, authorized by the 1957 act, was tardily organized and staffed by a handful of lawyers. Under Kennedy's Assistant Attorney General in charge of the division, Burke Marshall, a distinguished Washington lawyer, the legal staff was increased many times. By the end of 1962, it was nearing fifty and still growing. Collection, storage, and retrieval of evidence of discrimination— a massive task involving examination and classification of thousands of records of the registration of whites and the failure to register comparable Negroes—was systematized so that some of it could be performed by trained clerks. The FBI was heavily enlisted in gathering testimonial evidence, and its effectiveness was notable, owing, no doubt, to the fact that its agents had the confidence of the local whites. (Ironically—or sadly—enough, the FBI was less successful in interviewing Southern Negroes.) The number of suits that were brought stood at thirty-two after less than two years. When a suit was successfully concluded, the department collected compliance reports, and the FBI checked them.

This was and remains a magnificent effort—a tribute to Attorney General Kennedy who supported it and whose ultimate responsibility it was, and to Marshall and his First Assistant, John Doar, now himself the Assistant Attorney General, who directed and animated it. And it was bearing some fruit. The fact that Senator Lister Hill squeaked through to re-election in Alabama in 1962 by an incredibly narrow margin was generally taken to be a signal to Southern politicians that they had better abandon all support of the Administration and concentrate on trying to be more reactionary than their new Republican opponents. But Hill carried two counties in which the Justice Department had recently succeeded in registering substantial numbers of Negroes, while losing neighboring counties in which Negro registration was still negligible. Justice Department officials believed that, although there might be some panic to the right among Southerners in Congress, the more perceptive among them would realize that their future lay in an opening to the moderate left. For the reactionary position was being conclusively pre-empted by a new breed of Southern Republicans, while there would soon be many more counties like Bullock and Macon in Alabama, where the number of Negro voters was beginning to be counted in the thousands.

Yet other observers, admiring the moving of mountains, feared the production, in the end, of mice. It was not merely that litigation, no matter how formidably conducted, is a slow and piecemeal process. Nor was it merely that the law, legislative and judicial, was inadequate. To be sure, a statute making a sixth-grade education conclusive proof of literacy, such as the Administration had proposed but hardly pressed, would expedite litigation. But it could not avoid it. And it would not get at the root problem, which is that you can perhaps make sure a qualified Negro will be registered, but you can't qualify him, or make him want to register, or, once registered, to vote.

In some degree the trouble is affirmative acts of intimidation and discouragement—violence and the threat of it, economic reprisals, and the perverted use of state legal processes in frivolous, harassing prosecutions. The violence and the prosecutions are directed as often as not at members of such organizations as the Student Non-Violent Coordinating Committee, which conducts schools in registration procedures, and at leaders of the Negro community. In two instances as of the end of 1962, in Mississippi and in Georgia, the Department of Justice went to court for injunctions against intimidation by sheriffs and other officers, and against groundless prosecutions for vagrancy and breach of the peace, aimed at stopping registration drives. Workers of the Student Non-Violent Coordinating Committee and like organizations complained, however (and they still do), that the department was laggard in this aspect of its litigating activity. But such suits are nearly as difficult to prepare and frame as the suits that open registration books to begin with, and they are much harder to win. Perhaps the answer was that a concerted attempt to protect registration drives would have to await completion of the effort to make registration possible, though this was a hard answer for dedicated workers on the scene to swallow.

Intimidation and reprisals, in any event, may be the relatively minor obstacle. The heart of the matter may be apathy, born of poverty, ignorance, and consequent passive alienation. The right to vote, Attorney General Kennedy said, is basic, "and from it all other rights flow." This was the hope that informed the Justice Department's enormous effort, and this was, in part, the justification for slighting other possible initiatives open to executive power, which were, indeed, relatively slighted. But it may be—there is evidence in the North to support this hypothesis—that those who are deprived of other rights tend not to exercise the right from which the others flow, even when they are free to do so. It may be, in other words, that the cart was placed somewhat before the horse. No one of sound mind and worthy intentions would have wished to see the marvelous operation that was mounted in the Justice Department stopped short of full success in making the franchise at least available, whether or not availed of. But perhaps this operation should have been regarded less sanguinely. Perhaps it ought to have been seen more clearly that its success depended ultimately on simultaneous and equally important efforts in other directions.

Education and employment. One of the most dramatic results of the registration drive came in Macon County, Alabama, where registration shot up from a handful to some 2,800. Macon County is the home of Tuskegee Institute. Other relatively high figures were also brought about in areas, mostly urban, where Negroes have reasonable employment and education. How were more such areas to be created, especially in the depressed 100-county Black Belt? Economic and technical aid was needed, of course—some sort of Point IV or *Alianza para Progreso;* and it could not be allowed to bog down in seeking to abolish segregation, but would have to pursue its own prior objectives. Yet such aid would at least have to be administered so as not to perpetuate the existing social system, and it would have to aim first at elevating the poorest of the poor. Officials of the government's Distressed Area Redevelopment Program were said to have these ends in view. They were said to be aware of the special needs of the Black Belt, and to be consulting with Negro leaders and with the Justice Department's Civil Rights Division. Out of such consultations grew a program in Lafayette County, Tennessee, a sharecropping area where the Justice Department had to sue to prevent potent economic pressure against Negro registration. The Cabinet committee studying a project for a domestic Peace Corps was significantly headed by the Attorney General, and it could be expected to have in mind the connection between

economic development and political and social rights. But these
were comparative bywaters of government activity. Programs of
a different order of magnitude were needed, as was a major school-
aid bill, which the Kennedy administration was unable to put
through.

There were a number of other existing programs, which were
perhaps peripheral, though not in the aggregate, and which were
not all being exploited with vigor and imagination. A committee,
continued from the Eisenhower administration and headed by then
Vice-President Johnson, was attempting to persuade government
contractors, including the large defense contractors, to hire Negroes.
This was certainly a step in the direction of ensuring, in a phrase of a
California court, that some democracy stuck to funds disbursed by
the federal government. Yet other opportunities had too long been
—and some were still being—missed. Thus the Department of
Health, Education and Welfare conducts a program of vocational
and technical education into which, of course, go federal funds. The
following paragraphs appeared in a reply, dated April 19, 1962,
by the department's Office of Education to an inquiry from Mr.
Sanford Jay Rosen, then of the Yale Law School, concerning measures, if any, to foster integrated training for Negroes:

Vocational programs under the Federal-State cooperative program
are administered by the State board for vocational education in each
State. Training is available for both Negroes and whites *according to the*
State and local patterns of school organization.

The problem of the Negro insofar as vocational training is concerned
has been primarily due to the fact that *in many Negro schools the train-*
ing has been limited to a few trades in which there were employment
opportunities. With Negroes being denied employment in certain occupations it would have been an obvious waste of school money and dis-
appointing to the Negro to take training and yet not be able to get a job
for which he had been trained. With the job opportunities increasing as
a result of non-discrimination clauses in defense and other Federal Government contracts and other factors schools are now offering vocational
courses in a wider range of occupations for Negroes. [Italics supplied.]

The tone of such a letter spoke for itself—and not in the accents of
the campaign of 1960. No doubt, lack of Negro skills had impeded the
efforts of Vice-President Johnson's committee, for whose fruition
the Office of Education appeared to be waiting. The policy of HEW

in this matter was said to be undergoing change for the better. But there was no indication that making jobs available to Negroes was a concern of the U.S. Employment Service, which supports state employment services, some of which, in turn, surely were laboring hard to perpetuate existing job discrimination. Of course, these are problems that will not yield easily. And the exertion of federal money-pressure is necessarily a subtle and gradual process. But there was some evidence here of a failure of coordinated purpose. Unity of purpose over the full range of federal programs was—and remains—essential, for the plight of the Negro in our society is a complex social, economic, and political problem, and no single, isolated line of effort can attain truly significant results.

A degree of failure of coordinated purpose was further apparent with respect to the government's commitment to spur the desegregation, "with all deliberate speed," of public schools. As early as 1959, the Civil Rights Commission had reported that many school districts attempting to evolve desegregation plans suffered from having "no established source to which to turn for information and advice."[2] The gathering and active dissemination of such information was a function that could clearly be undertaken by HEW's Office of Education, which is empowered by its organic statute to "promote the cause of education throughout the country."[3] The phrase "throughout the country" could well be emphasized with salutary effect, for the office could do a great deal not only in teaching the lesson of the growing number of successful experiences in the South but also in helping to work out techniques for dealing with *de facto* segregated situations in the North, some of which were then just beginning to come into litigation. Given good faith, or a court order, or both, desegregation is, after all, a skill, a professional task. The federal professionals should be in it up to their necks. Moreover, the development of an accessible body of knowledge on the subject and of proved techniques would also help and speed the process of litigation itself, for judges will readily draw on the views of experts. The shelves are groaning with "how to . . ." books, and the federal government floods the country with them on everything from animal husbandry up and down. Only the educators were not educating.

The Office of Education could also, as its statute commands, "promote the cause of education" by engaging generally and systematically in conciliation and negotiation, with a view to easing and

speeding the process of school integration. HEW did in fact cooperate on an *ad hoc* basis with Assistant Attorney General Marshall
to bring pressure to bear in the so-called impacted areas surrounding
defense installations, where local school systems are heavily supported by federal funds (to help them absorb the children of federal
personnel), and where in too many places they nevertheless remained segregated. The federal government had available the alternative of building its own schools on the military reservations. It
was obviously more desirable, however, to support and integrate the
local schools. To this end, all else failing, litigation was necessary,
and the Justice Department in the fall of 1962 filed the first such
suit in Prince George County, Virginia, the site of Fort Lee. There
was some legal question whether the Attorney General had, as the
phrase goes, standing to bring such a suit. It might be that private
persons would have to act as plaintiffs. This doubt accounted in part
for the government's relative tardiness in bringing the first action.
In the judgment of many lawyers, however, the government's legal
position was sound and its chances excellent.[4]

It should be added here that in the instances—from Montgomery
through New Orleans and St. Helena Parish and Prince Edward
County, Virginia, to Oxford—where the process of desegregation
boiled up into crisis, the government intervened, vigorously and
imaginatively, not only with force but with litigating help in court.
It did so, for the most part, as a friend of the court, in suits initially
commenced by private parties. This was an activity that was begun
on a small scale by the Eisenhower administration, but was much
expanded under President Kennedy, and included appearances in
major arguments in the Supreme Court. There is respectable opinion
that the government was and still is overdoing this; pushing its
friendship for the courts, as it were, to oppressive lengths. But in
each crisis the President might have to discharge his obligation to
take care that the laws be faithfully executed. Surely it is not un-
reasonable for his representatives to go in and assist—by expressing
an opinion binding on no one—in the effort to prevent a crisis or to
resolve it peaceably. Actually, quite often, the government's friendship was extended to the courts at the latter's invitation.

Federal grants-in-aid. It is a commonplace, illustrated by several
of the government activities mentioned earlier, that the welfare

state is here, and that it is substantially financed by federal money. There could be little doubt that the President had the power—perhaps the obligation, but in any event subject to his political discretion—to take care that federal moneys were expended in programs that conformed to the Constitution, as the Supreme Court had construed it and as he himself understood it. Before as after the Civil Rights Act of 1964, his ultimate sanction—more expeditious than litigation, but not necessarily exclusive of the latter—was to withhold funds from programs that did not so conform. This is the power that was available with respect to government contractors, vocational training programs, the employment service, and impacted schools. And it is the power that was finally exercised in the Kennedy housing order. Of course, it is a power that could be effective prospectively only. If a little democracy was to stick to federal moneys expended in the past, the adhesion would have to be established by litigation. Prospectively, therefore, the housing order applied to housing built with federal money or with federally guaranteed loans. The order was well conceived, but much remained to be learned about it in the execution. It did not apply to private loans that are not guaranteed by the federal government, although made by banks that benefit from federal insurance of their funds; and it was going to be administered so as not to cover individually owned homes outside developments. These restrictions were wise initially, for it is in such circumstances that discrimination is most difficult to detect, and enforcement might have been more sham than genuine. It was reasonable, therefore, to concentrate federal energies first on what could be more easily achieved. In this fashion the more difficult problems would be rendered soluble. All measures in the civil rights field depend on each other for the effectiveness of each, but each also, within its own segment of the total problem, is habit-forming and has the sure tendency to snowball.

There were, however, a number of grant-in-aid programs—in addition to the few already mentioned—as to which neither the power exemplified by the housing order nor the threat of it had been employed. A highly selective list included the Hill-Burton Hospital Construction Act of 1946, the Library Services Act of 1956, and a rather remarkable variety of statutes providing aid to universities. The Hill-Burton Act carried a separate-but-equal clause which was as plainly unconstitutional as the state statutes segregating the schools of Mississippi. The clause had no legal effect on the President's powers. In May, 1962, the Justice Department intervened in a lawsuit in North Carolina to support, with ultimate success, the demand of Negro plaintiffs that two Greensboro hospitals, built in part with Hill-Burton funds, be enjoined from segregating or excluding Negro patients.[5] But in announcing his action, Attorney General Kennedy took pains to forswear any use of the executive power to cut off future funds to hospitals that insisted on discriminating. Library and—with one discrete exception—university funds also continued to go to institutions that segregated or excluded Negroes.

Justice Department officials argued that it is no simple matter to exert pressure through grants-in-aid, and that the federal government must be wary of cutting off its funds to spite its face. There is a hard-core area in the South, they maintained, where funds would be resolutely refused if the integration string were tied to them. To withhold funds there—where they are often most needed—would be counterproductive; it would hurt the Negro community ultimately, and sometimes hit it hardest immediately. And if funds continued to go to these areas, despite discrimination, how could the federal government threaten to withhold them in the upper South or on the border in order to force desegregation? That would be to put a premium on hard-core resistance. But there were those, not excluding the staff of the Civil Rights Commission, who thought—in the words President Kennedy used when deprecating alarms that his housing order would stop much new construction—that these "fears have been exaggerated." Moreover, would not another presidential dictum, also delivered with reference to the housing order, be applicable: "In any case, it is sound public constitutional policy and we've done it"? It might be done again, many observers urged, in different contexts, as carefully and with as much restraint as in the housing order. Only the visionaries objected to a wise gradualism. But it was not visionary to wish to make a start.

Federal appointments. One of the Kennedy administration's proudests boasts—and justly so—was that it had gone out of its way to employ Negroes in the government in other than the sadly customary menial positions. Negroes were also appointed to high office, including judicial office. All this was as it should be and, since things had scarcely been as they should in the past, was admirable. But it was perhaps more than offset by certain other judicial appointments in the Fifth Judicial Circuit, which covers much of the Southern area where the racial problem was then and is now at its most acute. Lawyers representing private parties in racial cases in the South complained bitterly that a number of new Kennedy appointees, especially among the district judges, were totally out of sympathy with the Supreme Court cases on equal protection and that they showed it in their opinions and orders. This was a matter of the first importance, for district judges have life tenure, of course, they ordinarily sit alone, and they have much discretionary power which is not easily subject to review by the Court of Appeals, let alone the Supreme Court.

One device available to district judges, which may often defeat the purpose of a litigation and is almost totally beyond control, is simple delay. District Judge J. Robert Elliott, for example, a Kennedy appointee in Georgia, employed this device substantially to the disadvantage of a Negro protest movement in Albany, Georgia, despite an intervention by the Department of Justice on the side of the Negroes. Other Kennedy appointees exhibited a distinct tendency to exercise all available discretion against Negro plaintiffs or the federal government, to the point even of publishing rather transparently willful opinions. An example was *Anderson v. Martin*.[6] This was a suit attacking the constitutionality of a 1960 Louisiana statute which required the listing on the ballot of the race of all candidates in both primary and general elections. District Judges E. Gordon West of Baton Rouge and Frank B. Ellis of New Orleans, both Kennedy appointees, held, in the face of persuasive if not strictly binding precedent to the contrary from another Court of Appeals, that the statute was perfectly constitutional, because it merely informed the electorate, and because it was applicable, after all, to every candidate—white, colored, or Mongolian. This is the spirit of *Plessy v. Ferguson*, not of *Brown v. Board of Education*. Said Circuit Judge John Minor Wisdom, an Eisenhower appointee, dissenting: "In the eyes of the Constitution, a man is a man. He is not a white man. He is not an Indian. He is not a Negro. If private persons identify a candidate for public office as a Negro, they have a right to do so. But it is no part of the business of the State to put a racial stamp on the ballot."

The *Anderson* case was appealed to the Supreme Court, which reversed in short order.[7] But the attitude displayed by Judges West and Ellis remained disturbing. Was it a fair charge against the Kennedy administration that it appointed men to judicial office who rather plainly disagreed with current law on racial matters and who apparently stood ready to do what they could to give effect to their own contrary views? After all, these judges were acting within the limits of a power that is lawfully theirs, however much one might be convinced that they were acting wrongly and even abusing their discretion. Kennedy appointees went to no greater lengths than one or two others who were on the bench by appointment of prior Presidents. Moreover, judicial philosophies are notoriously unfathomable in advance.

But judgment, though fallible, is possible. There were instances— Judge Elliott was one of them, and so was Judge William Harold Cox of Mississippi—where an extraprofessional record of actions and associations made prediction more than possible. Justice Department officials maintained that, of course, President Kennedy would not have appointed a man who he had reason to believe would fail to do his duty; which one could cheerfully grant, whatever it might mean. And they said further that senators from the state concerned have a virtual veto over appointments, and that the choice was therefore not among various possible appointments but between a semi-permanent vacancy and the one man who could be confirmed. Vacancies are serious, no doubt. However, the Chief Justice of the United States has ample and frequently exercised power to assign judges from other districts, including retired judges, to districts where there is a vacancy. It was such an assigned judge from one of the Dakotas who was sitting in Little Rock at the time of the trouble there. This was surely a usable counterpressure to the senatorial veto. And the South is not devoid of men who will do their judicial duty in an ampler sense than merely by not committing impeachable acts. President Eisenhower found a goodly number of them, as did even President Truman, whose judicial appointments are not his greatest claim to enduring renown. And so, to be sure, did President Kennedy—with, however, what appeared to be some rather glaring exceptions.

Such were the salient features of the record at mid-term.

More
on the
Kennedy
Judges

4

Judge Clarence W. Allgood. At a crucial point during the demonstrations in Birmingham, Alabama, late in May, 1963, when the mass marching had stopped and the violence of the whites seemed under control, a segregationist group on the Birmingham Board of Education expelled or suspended over a thousand Negro children from the public schools for participating in mass marches earlier in the month. Dr. Martin Luther King, urged by his more militant adherents to resume marching, responded by opting first for the processes of law, and two days later he was rewarded with the back of the hand of District Judge Clarence W. Allgood, one of the earliest of President Kennedy's appointees to the federal bench in the South.

An undistinguished Birmingham lawyer whose experience ran heavily to service as a referee in bankruptcy ("That's about all there is," said a knowledgeable Southern source in Washington when asked for further information about the judge's career), Judge Allgood, as Claude Sitton reported in the *New York Times,* is "considered a segregationist by Birmingham Negroes," who it should be remembered possess the discrimination to distinguish on this score between "Bull" Connor and their present mayor, Albert Boutwell. Judge Allgood dismissed the suit for reinstatement of the Negro pupils out of hand, on the pleadings and without taking evidence, even though the school board's position was self-contradictory in several respects. The judge paused only long enough to give his gratuitous views on "experts in the field" (meaning Dr. King) who "exploit" the Negro children and cause them to run "loose and wild in all directions," and on "the patience and good judgment of the people of Birmingham and the police."

It so happened that there was an applicable precedent on public school expulsions in Judge Allgood's jurisdiction. In March, 1960, the Alabama Board of Education expelled some students from the Alabama State College, a Negro school, for having taken part in sit-ins in Montgomery the previous month. The Court of Appeals for the Fifth Circuit, Judge Rives of Montgomery writing, held the expulsion invalid because the students had not been granted a hearing on the charges against them. (The case, for easy reference, is *Dixon v. Alabama State Board of Education.*[1]) There was no hearing in the Birmingham case either. It is not too much to say that a judge without prejudgment would have followed this precedent, or at least explored the facts before him with a view to determining its applicability.*

No doubt President Kennedy would not have appointed Allgood had he not believed that Allgood would, as a judge, do his constitutional duty. But that is much too porous a test. It is not good enough to appoint an Allgood because he is not all bad, is rated "qualified" by the American Bar Association, and has been identified with civic good works. There is a great deal of discretion open to a judge within the limits of his constitutional duty. It would have been well within the limits of Judge Allgood's duty to find the Birmingham situation distinguishable on its facts, and thus to hold the *Dixon* case precedent inapplicable. It was certainly well within Judge Allgood's power to decline to take the broader ground taken by Judge Tuttle of the Court of Appeals in ordering the Birmingham pupils readmitted. It is precisely because judges have discretion,

---

* Judge Allgood's action was promptly cured by Chief Judge Tuttle of the U.S. Court of Appeals, who issued a temporary order reinstating the expelled and suspended pupils. Subsequently, a full panel of the Court of Appeals reversed Judge Allgood's decision. Woods v. Wright, 334 F.2d 369 (5th Cir. 1964).

because, as everyone should know by now, they make rather than find much of their law, that the appointing power must worry not only about whether prospective judges will do their duty but about how they are likely to see their duty. Senatorial pressure is no excuse. The matter is too important; it reaches too far into the future.

Judge E. Gordon West. The following passage is from the opinion of Judge E. Gordon West, a Kennedy appointee to the United States District Court for the Eastern District of Louisiana, in the case of *Davis v. East Baton Rouge Parish School Board,* decided on March 1, 1963:

> I could not, in good conscience, pass upon this matter today without first making it clear, for the record, that I personally regard the 1954 holding of the United States Supreme Court in the now famous Brown case as one of the truly regrettable decisions of all time. Its substitution of so-called "sociological principles" for sound legal reasoning was almost unbelievable. As far as I can determine, its only real accomplishment to date has been to bring discontent and chaos to many previously peaceful communities, without bringing any real attendant benefits to anyone.
>
> And even more regrettable to me is the fact that almost without exception the trouble that has directly resulted from this decision in other communities has been brought about not by the citizens and residents of the community involved, but by the agitation of outsiders, from far distant states, who, after having created turmoil and strife in one locality, are ready to move on to meddle in the affairs of others elsewhere.[2]

The *Davis* case had originally been filed in February, 1956. Now Judge West was acting under a binding mandate from the Court of Appeals, dating from 1961. He ordered the school board to present a desegregation plan to him no later than July, 1963. But first he made the statement quoted above. Then he added that he had "no choice, however distasteful it might be," but to follow the mandate. Then he complimented "the local Negro leaders" for not having pressed for more speed during the two years since the mandate had been issued. And finally, "therefore, reluctantly" he was "constrained" to act.

This is what the rare case may look like in which duty leaves a man of Judge West's persuasion no recourse but to uphold Negro claims. Or it may look like *McCain v. Davis,*[3] decided on May 15, 1963, in which a three-judge federal district court in New Orleans struck down a Louisiana statute enforcing segregation in hotels. The thing to wonder at in this case, of course, is not the result but the fact that such a litigation was not initiated and brought to this result much earlier. Judge West was one of the three judges who acted in *McCain v. Davis*. He did not disagree with his colleagues in holding the Louisiana statute unconstitutional. Rather he fastened on an innocuous expression in the majority's opinion justifying the unusual procedure of convening a three- instead of the normal single-judge court (a procedure with which also he did not disagree) and used this as a pretext to deliver himself of an advisory opinion to the hotel owners of Louisiana, as follows:

Just as I believe that the federal government may not legally force the owner or operator of a private business to integrate [no such federal law existed as of then, nor was remotely before the court in this case], so do I believe that the state or local government may not compel the owner or operator of a private business to segregate [there is no record of Judge West's opposition, before his federal appointment, to Louisiana's many segregation laws]. Such continued and extended interference by state and federal government into the operations of purely private business will surely spell doom to our long cherished system of free enterprise. . . . Where, such as in the case of hotels, the business is not a state or federally franchised, monopolistic enterprise, the right of freedom to choose those with whom the owner or operator wishes to do business is just as fundamental as any of the so-called civil rights of which we lately hear so much. . . . In my opinion, the only right involved is the right of the hotel owner to conduct his business without undue governmental interference, rather than the right of the Negro to be admitted to the hotels in question. . . . After the discriminatory law in question is held unconstitutional, and therefore no longer effective, the same private persons may continue, with complete immunity, to voluntarily discriminate to their hearts' content in the conduct of their private affairs.

Perhaps Louisiana hotel owners needed no invitation to continue discriminating. But in another sense they certainly needed no such invitation from a federal judge. Judge West handed a weapon to those among them who wished to resist the pressure of national opinion. He also—by his wholly gratuitous remarks—strengthened the hand of opponents of the Administration's Civil Rights Bill, then in Congress. He had, of course, no business doing any of this. Judge

West purposefully and quite improperly used his office to further the segregationist predilections he has elsewhere openly declared.

A case in which duty leaves Judge West no choice may also look like this: In the summer of 1964 Judge West had to be directly ordered by his superiors on the Court of Appeals for the Fifth Circuit to issue a decree in a school desegregation case. The Negro plaintiffs were forced to institute a mandamus proceeding against Judge West, which is about as rare a thing as is known to the law, and which can succeed only if the appellate court is convinced that the judge has been guilty of what in any other officer of government would be called, bluntly and simply, dereliction of duty. Against Judge West, it succeeded.[4] But at what cost! The case involved the school system of St. Helena Parish, Louisiana. Suit was begun over eleven years ago. By February, 1962, all possible issues of any substance had been litigated, and the Supreme Court had denied a second appeal. At this time, Judge West was asked to issue a decree. He did not even set the case down for a hearing. Plaintiffs went back to Judge West a year later. Now he set the case down for a hearing, but he never held one. A year later the plaintiffs were back again, and Judge West did hold a hearing, in March, 1964. But then he neither did anything nor expressed any intention to do anything, not even after the petition for mandamus had been filed. Pretty clearly, if the schools of this parish were going to be desegregated, Judge West was not going to be the one to do it, no matter what the Supreme Court might say.

Judge William Harold Cox. The Civil Rights Act of 1960 provides that the Attorney General may address a demand in writing for the production of federal voting records "to the person having custody, possession, or control" of them, so that they may be inspected for evidence of discrimination against Negro voters. If the demand is not voluntarily met, the appropriate federal district court is to issue an order for the production of the records.

In the case of *Kennedy v. Owen*, decided on July 3, 1963,[5] the Attorney General had addressed his demand in writing to the proper persons "having custody, possession, or control" in several Mississippi counties. He had addressed his demand to them by name, and they had received it. But in his letter to them he had called them circuit clerks, which they are. He had omitted to address them also by the title of registrar, which is also part of their official designation. They refused to comply, and Judge William Harold Cox, a Kennedy appointee to the Federal District Court for the Southern District of Mississippi, upheld them with respect to records in their possession as registrars rather than as circuit clerks, meaning probably that he upheld them altogether, for it is very likely up to them to decide which records are in their possession under which hat. This is farcical. It is straight out of *Jarndyce v. Jarndyce,* or out of Kafka. It is also willful. Judge Cox got himself summarily reversed by the Court of Appeals for the Fifth Circuit. But time was lost. And, although there can be no further delay on this score, there is no law on the books that is not open to this kind of tactic.

THE NEGRO
PROTEST MOVEMENT
AND THE
CIVIL RIGHTS
ACTS OF 1964 AND 1965

III

Civil Rights
and
Civil
Disobedience

5

THE REVOLUTION in the American law of race relations dates from May 17, 1954, when the first decision in *Brown v. Board of Education,* the *School Segregation Cases,* was handed down. This revolution of law culminated ten years later in the Civil Rights Act of 1964, and now starts all over again. There is another revolution in American race relations, which the law in some measure sparked and which has had its impact on the law, but which is distinct and separate and is affecting society beyond the confines of the legal order. This is the revolution in the streets. It, too, came to a point of culmination with the Civil Rights Act of 1964, and for it also this climax was not the end. The Negro protest movement continues.

There are, of course, demonstrations and demonstrations. They differ in purpose, manner, and effect. Some are within the law; most are in one or another degree without. Most—whether legal, like the march on Washington in the summer of 1963, which had the permission and protection of the competent authorities, or illegal, like climbing to the top of the Florida exhibit at the New York World's Fair, or lying down in General Motors showrooms in San

Francisco—are attempts to change the legal and social order through the application of pressure from without, circumventing deliberate, established procedures. Whether government should tolerate direct action of this sort and how much of it should be tolerated are troubling and important issues. To label a demonstration legal or illegal is not to resolve these issues. Additional judgments are called for before we permit ourselves to commend, or condemn and suppress. Does the individual have a moral duty in all circumstances to obey all laws and to abide the law's own procedures for advancing beyond itself? This is a question that not all philosophers answer simply or in the same way. Moreover, we are not a unitary state. We have laws within laws, and laws above laws. In our federal structure, one system of laws, valid and authoritative within itself, may be called into question by appeal to another, superior system, and this has consequences for the duty to obey. Finally, one should bear in mind the tradition of protest and extralegal action that has grown up in American history alongside of the tradition of legality—from the Boston Tea Party, through opposition to the Fugitive Slave Law, to the struggles of labor to achieve industrial democracy.

The most striking characteristics of the Negro protest movement are its generality and its variety. It has been everywhere, and almost everywhere it has been different in ends and methods. So it must be assessed at retail. The first and major distinction that must be taken is regional. In the South, where the movement started, prospects, aims, and problems are not the same as in the North.

In February, 1960, a group of Negro students sat in at lunch counters in Greensboro, North Carolina, not only quietly and peaceably but immovably, until, having been refused service, they were arrested. What they did, and what many others did following their example throughout the South, was illegal under local laws valid at the time; it disturbed the peace of the community, and it not infrequently led to violence. But the local law is not, in our federal system, always the last word. And so the local law, while enforceable for the time being, may need to be tested by those willing to bet on its ultimate invalidity. This was what the sit-ins did. The violence they sometimes led to, which was almost always the fault of others, is one of the risks our society assumes in setting up a tension between two systems of law, state and federal; for it is a natural exercise in law reform to exploit this tension. In a unitary system the sit-ins, disobeying the positive law, might have been seen as appealing to a higher law and might have gained moral approval in this fashion; but, in any view, they would have had to be considered a revolutionary act, at war with the legal order. In our federal system, however, the appeal to a higher law is not a call for revolutionary change to be imposed on the legal order by forces operating from outside, but an appeal—almost in the technical legal sense—to higher lawmaking institutions, which the system provides. In such a system some flouting of the local law, aimed at provoking action by the higher sovereignty, is virtually invited.

The sit-ins did not win their bet in the federal courts. The Supreme Court never declared a constitutional right to equal service in places of public accommodation. But the sit-ins did gain their end in Congress, which created a statutory right in Title II of the Civil Right Act of 1964, and the Supreme Court subsequently held— not without some straining, perhaps—that passage of this statute wiped out trespass convictions in sit-in cases which did not involve violence and which were still pending on appeal, even though these convictions might have been valid when imposed.[1] In many communities, of course, the sit-ins had achieved voluntary concessions and the quashing of prosecutions. And yet, triumphant as they have been, the sit-ins do not now pass into history as classic little case studies of the kind of direct action that is tolerable and even to be expected in our system, and often happily successful in forming new and beneficial law. That it is overly sanguine to expect an end of sit-ins is a lesson taught by a somewhat different sort of demonstration, which took place a year after the first of the sit-ins, in the spring of 1961.

Against the advice of Attorney General Kennedy, groups of young people ran some integrated buses into the deep South. These were the Freedom Rides, and they led to riots in Alabama that finally caused President Kennedy to send in a force of federal marshals. The Freedom Rides tested not the state but the federal law. It needed no new federal law, even as of 1961, to establish Everyman's unqualified right, without restraint of local segregation practices, to travel freely in interstate commerce. The Freedom Riders attempted to verify the obedience of the other system of sovereignty, the state, to the superior federal law, which, they found, was simply not being observed in Alabama. There will be places where the public accommodations title of the Civil Rights Act of 1964 will similarly not be observed. It may not always be altogether prudent to test the act in such places, because of the possibility of violence in tense situations, as Attorney General Kennedy rather thought it was imprudent at the given time to test the federal right of free movement in Alabama. But, although there will be problems of enforcement, and the wisdom of provoking a pitched enforcement crisis may sometimes be dubious, anyone has an unquestionable legal right to exercise his federal rights, and to claim the protection of federal authority and federal force, if necessary, in doing so. Maintaining a public order that is consistent with observance of federal law where local authorities are prepared to impose order only in violation of the federal law is a function of the President of the United States.

The Freedom Rides, then, can in no sense of the term be thought of as acts of civil disobedience. And the sit-ins, if they can be called instances of civil disobedience at all, are peculiar ones, which our system of dual sovereignty rather subsumes. At another extreme are the riots that took place in the Negro slums of many Northern cities during the summer of 1964. Various proposals, heard during the same summer, for stall-ins, or for indiscriminate pulling of emergency cords on subways, or for wasting water, may be classed with the riots as unacceptable acts of terrorism. The responsible Negro protest movement has manifested itself in an area well this side of the extremes of violence and terrorism. But it has also gone well beyond lawful tests of established law, and beyond even the attenuated form of civil disobedience which consists in breaking a local law in order to get a supervening lawmaking authority to change it. The movement has come into the streets, not in violation of a law it deems unjust and wishes to have changed, but often in violation of laws irrelevant to its ends; not in any sort of appeal to higher legal authority, but simply to bear witness to its own purposes and to show its force—peaceable force, but force; not to demand the intervention of a higher authority, but to bend local institutions to its will; not to activate legal processes of change, but to impress on the legal and social order the necessity for change, and if possible to impose change, all in ways altogether external to the legal and even the political process.

The movement has marched near the precipice of revolution. *Liberator*, a militant Negro monthly which does not follow Dr. Martin Luther King (rather, to judge by its title, William Lloyd Garrison), set forth in its issue of December, 1963, what it viewed as the dilemma of Dr. King's leadership. It quoted him as having made the following remark just before he addressed a mass meeting on the eve of the Montgomery, Alabama, bus boycott in December, 1955: "How could I make a speech that would be militant enough to keep my people aroused to positive action and yet moderate enough to keep this fervor within controllable and Christian bounds?" There is a great deal of room for maneuver in the area between Freedom Rides and sit-ins and the riots of the summer of 1964. But the bounds of legality are soon passed. They were passed by the mass marching in Birmingham in April and May, 1963, for example, and may in some circumstances be passed even by continuous mass marches of voting applicants to the registrar's office, as in Selma, Alabama, in the spring of 1965. Of course, as President Johnson has remarked several times, there is a federal constitutional right to assemble and to petition for a redress of grievances, and in many instances the action of the police in forbidding a march or assembly is itself illegal. But it is sometimes questionable even then whether the legal way to test the legality of the police action is to persist against police orders. And the First Amendment creates no blanket right —for Negro demonstrators, for the American Legion, or for the Philadelphia Mummers—to march at will, any time, any place, in whatever numbers. This is not to say—not ever—that brutal police action against peaceful demonstrators is justified. Nor does it mean that convictions of demonstrators will necessarily always be upheld by the Supreme Court. It is to say, however, that there is legitimate, if not unlimited, power in local authorities to regulate and even at times to forbid demonstrations in the interest of public convenience and order.[2]

But to recognize the illegality of some demonstrations is by no means to have arrived at a sufficient judgment about them. The ordered processes of litigation and legislation have never been the only legitimate ones in our system for the solution of social and economic problems. Another traditional—if extralegal and sometimes illegal—process is the peaceful trial of strength between contending forces; the trial of numerical, economic, and moral strength, which agitates public opinion until from it rises, as Brandeis once said in reference to the struggle of industrial combatants, a generally acceptable concept of mutual "duty to the community."[3] This is a costly process, and the Negroes of Birmingham, Selma, and other places have willingly paid its price. The tradition in which they have acted is that of the early labor movement (though the Negroes have abjured the inadmissible violence that sometimes marred that movement); indeed, it is the tradition of the more stylized trials of strength, called strikes, that the law itself allows for in our labor-management relations to this day. These are extralegal processes of law formation, and it is nonsense to apply legal judgments to them. Such a movement is justified because it is right, because behind the force of numbers is moral force, because the law it seeks to establish is right, not because it derives a right from established law. The Birmingham and Selma police were wrong procedurally, to be sure; horribly wrong to use dogs on children, and high-pressure hoses. But beyond that they were wrong because the social and economic system of their cities and state, against which the Negroes were contending, was morally wrong even when it was not illegal.

In cases such as the sustained marching in Birmingham, then, it is no use, on the one hand, making believe that what is happening is necessarily covered by the First Amendment; and, on the other hand, no technical judgment of the legality of a demonstration should determine whether the President steps in with federal force to maintain a just peace when, as can well happen, demonstrations and counterdemonstrations get out of hand and are met with brutal and one-sided repression by local authorities. Of course, the first thing to do, as the Kennedy administration did in Birmingham even before a Community Relations Service had been set up by the Civil Rights Act of 1964, is to mediate, so that the parties may be brought to negotiation and settlement. From such settlements law may eventually be enabled to speak with assurance. The precipitate presence of federal troops, or even the early threat of troops, would generally be regrettable and, whatever the immediate effect, ultimately counterproductive. For, to cite another Brandeisian maxim, responsibility is the great breeder of men. Men of sense and decency in Birmingham, for example, were negotiating with Dr. King and his lieutenants even as the police were fighting the marchers. Thus, at long last, these men were facing the realities and moralities of their situation, and they were doing so out of a sense of responsibility, into which they had been rudely jarred. President Kennedy did well not to deprive them of it by taking over too soon. Deprived or, if you will, relieved of their responsibility, they might have thrown up their hands or, if they had continued negotiating, they would have considered whatever agreement was reached not theirs, but in effect the President's. Eventually, the consequences would have been evident and baneful.

At some point it may become necessary, however, to establish and maintain a federal peace. Presidential authority to this end is ample. There may well be inherent constitutional power, and there is certainly plentiful statutory power. A President need not wait until after tragedy has struck, nor is he required to credit the good faith of local authorities. And, while the question is not one of legal or constitutional duty, but of political and moral judgment, it remains clear, as it was to President Kennedy in May, 1963, and, if a bit tardily, to his successor two years later, that the President should in the end use federal force to protect such protests as those staged in Birmingham and Selma. It is the proper office of the President, naturally, as of governors and mayors, to condemn violence and to warn against it. But how one regards action that, although illegal, is not itself violent or aimed at violence, but merely carries the risk of it, and how one goes about the necessary task of controlling and suppressing violence when it occurs are different matters. A society that has oppressed a portion of its people the way the Negro has been oppressed, especially in the South, is after all fortunate if all it gets in return is mass marching. It is not an adequate answer to the ancient grievance of the Negro to provide him with slow, deliberate legal means for its redress and ask him to be satisfied, because ultimately these means will work and ultimately his reliance, as ours, is in the rule of law. The Negro is heir to a deep legacy of cynicism about the law. It was bestowed on him by the whites, and it has found expression in demonstrations of all sorts. It behooves the white society to understand this, and to be willing to subject itself to some inconvenience and risk while we attempt to make proof to the Negro of the law's efficacy and good faith.

The patience and understanding of the white majority have been tried even more sorely, perhaps, in the North than in the South. In the nature of things, if somewhat paradoxically, the level of frustration is higher on both sides in the North and is likely to continue on the rise. A certain order of minimal objectives which the Negro is contending for in the South has been attained in most of the North. The franchise is available and public accommodations are open. In many states there are even laws and ordinances against employment and housing discrimination, and there is no legal school segregation. Again, there are surely few places in the North where it is necessary to demonstrate in order to get a city to put some Negroes on its police force. The North may not have all the laws it needs, nor is it adequately administering all the laws it has. By and large, nevertheless, grievances in the North are difficult, and in the short run often impossible, to redress. They go, by and large, not to deficiencies in the legal order or to blatant discriminations that can be stopped with immediately visible results but to deeply entrenched features of the society, which can be reorganized only over time. As these grievances are formulated in immediate demands, they often cannot—literally *cannot*—be met.

Early in the spring of 1964 the Brooklyn chapter of CORE planned a stall-in on the opening day of the New York World's Fair. (The chapter was disowned by the national organization, and the stall-in failed to materialize.) These are the demands which the stall-in was to force the city to accept:

Employment: Close down all construction sites immediately until the work force in that industry is fully integrated.

Slum Housing: Begin an immediate "rent strike" throughout the ghetto areas.

Schools: Produce immediately a plan with a timetable for total desegregation of schools.

Police Brutality: Create a public review board, selected by civil liberties, civil rights, and church groups, to investigate complaints of police brutality.

Now, the city could not close down all construction, and obviously should not if it could. Nor could the city conduct a rent strike, even if it were true that a rent strike would magically transform slums into garden apartments. A plan with a timetable for total "desegregation" would be a sham. And finally, although a public review board in the police department is far from an impossibility, there are things reasonably to be said against it, and in any event it is questionable whether such a board ought to consist of the representatives of churches and the like.

These were, all in all, impossible demands. The grievances that underlie them are just, but with the best of faith and greatest of skill and imagination it will take time and more time to do something about them that actually affects the daily lives of masses of people. The upshot is frustration. The responsible leadership knows this, of course, and applies pressure, for the most part, only when some intermediate, attainable objective is denied it or when it senses that interest in pursuing a long-range remedy is slackening. But the established leadership does not control the newer militants who have staged some of the school boycotts and other demonstrations in the North. The aggressive, scattered, self-starting new leadership that has caused and will cause the brouhaha in the North is young. Often it is composed of very recent arrivals from the deep South. The most encouraging thing about the new militants is that most of them do not seem to hold Black Nationalist views. They operate—this was typically true of the expelled Brooklyn chapter of CORE that planned the stall-in—within the main tradition of the civil rights movement from the inception of the NAACP some fifty years ago onward, in cooperation with whites. The most disturbing thing about them, white and Negro, is not the disrespect they show their elders, which is natural to the young and does the average elder more good than harm, but their affinity to nihilism. But then this is an attitude which we all encourage in them when we lightly condemn their activities as lacking in intelligent purpose or as misdirected at unattainable purposes.

The only intelligent purpose of a demonstration is not necessarily to cause someone to institute some specific, immediate reform, or even to sustain the white society's zeal for long-range improvements in Negro conditions. The Negro masses have been socially and politically dormant for decades, and it is desirable from every point of view that they be organized and led. Demonstrations alert them, and train and sort out their leaders. They are as often aimed at increasing the Negro's awareness of his condition as at calling the white society's attention to it. They may be intended to give the Negro community coherence and confidence and pride in itself and in its capacity to take concerted action, and they may, perhaps most simply, serve to let off the steam of frustration. Despite the cost, and provided there is no violence, is that not in the public interest? The frustration is there, and will continue to be there as we make progress and as expectations naturally rise. Would it be wise to deny it relatively tolerable outlets?

The demonstrations in the spring of 1964, on the opening day of the New York World's Fair, were widely condemned because, it was said, they lacked all rational purpose. But it makes no radical difference that there was nothing in particular wrong with the New York World's Fair and that there was nothing very specific being demanded of the white community with respect to the Fair. The Fair was a fitting target, being an ordinary commercial enterprise, but the most lavish and spectacular one around, a symbol of affluence, smugness, and advertising fervor. Of course it is disagreeable for young men and women—easily as many white as colored—to drown out a speech by the President of the United States, as they did at the United States Pavilion on opening day at the Fair, and also extremely stupid, considering the record of this President. But Adlai Stevenson once had eggs thrown at him by the young gentlemen of Yale University during one of his presidential campaigns. James Farmer, the head of CORE, also demonstrated at the Fair and did so in dignified and responsible manner, although he illegally lay down in front of an entrance and got himself arrested. He wanted to emphasize, Mr. Farmer said, "the contrast between the glittering gold of fantasy and the real world of brutality, bigotry and poverty." A well-taken point. We are entitled, no doubt, to suppress violence and other forms of terrorism with all available resources. But we are not entitled to demand that all demonstrations have an immediately attainable purpose or that they always spare the general public inconvenience and risk.

In the turbulent spring of 1963, when the demonstrations in Birmingham broke upon the nation's consciousness, there was a great deal of hand-wringing and garment-rending among people of good will, and a great deal of scurrying to shelter under the principle of law and order. In our most legalistic of societies, most people do not really understand the sources, the nature, the possibilities, and the limits of law—domestically any more than internationally. We did absolutely nothing for decades, and when the Supreme Court acted in 1954 we thought we had a law and that we could pretty well continue to do nothing. Judge-made law reached its limit of effectiveness as early as 1957, if not before, and it took us a few years longer to understand what kind of political action is needed to make judicial law effective when it is challenged. In 1964 we got another law, of a different and stronger kind, but the possibilities of this law for the achievement of speedy and pervasive results are also not without limit, and we should not righteously condemn all who would still presume to act outside it.

Law is a process. It is the process of establishing norms that will not need to be frequently enforced. It is necessarily gradual and slow. It aims at stability and values order. It can actually bear down on men and their behavior only episodically. Such is law, at any rate, made by judges or by legislatures, and applied by courts. Law has an ampler sense, to be sure. There is lawful executive and administrative action that can master and channel swift events, and itself produce rapid change in some circumstances. But all law, and the law of legislatures and judges in particular, can prove insufficient, as the rising expectations of the American Negro have found it to be. This is what should be borne in on us by the demonstrations. It is a hopeful fact. It presages real, major beneficial changes, proceeding from private as well as public initiatives and working in all sectors of society. We may be about to fall off the square edges of the conventional legal universe, but that is no cause for lament.

No doubt the years of unthinking emphasis on law and order and nothing else in the face of Southern resistance to the Supreme

Court's desegregation decisions have led many people to a halting and embarrassed attitude toward the Negro movement of protest and agitation. At the time of the Birmingham demonstrations, James Reston argued in the *New York Times* that the federal government cannot consistently take its stand against segregationist quasi insurrections in Mississippi and Alabama and then "support demonstrations that break the law." But Mr. Reston's dilemma—are we or are we not for law?—is a false one, deriving from too constrained a view of Southern massive resistance. The South opposed and disobeyed the Supreme Court's law because its leaders thought it bad. Until 1960 all we did was to enforce the law when the contest became pitched, and that was proper enough, since maintenance of the integrity and general utility of the process of judicial decision making requires—it is an irreducible requirement—that force be applied to coerce obedience to specific decrees of the courts. For the rest, however, we contented ourselves with condemning all resistance as somehow illegitimate. But it wasn't illegitimate, except as it grew violent. It was wrong because the law in question was right, and it took us a long time to see and say that, and even now the emphasis is more on abstract law and order than on the morality of the law that is being defended and enforced. But we cannot, by total reliance on law, escape the duty to judge right and wrong. There is a difference between the segregationist mob—even if it had acted peaceably—on the campus of the University of Mississippi in October, 1962, and Dr. King's mob in the streets of Birmingham. It is the moral difference in the ends that the two mobs sought to attain.

Even violence is not to be condemned for all time and in all circumstances merely because it is illegal and terribly costly. There are good laws and there are occasionally bad laws, and it conforms to the highest traditions of a free society to offer resistance to bad laws, and to disobey them. High-minded people disobeyed the Fugitive Slave Act in the 1850's, and Garrison said that the Constitution was "a covenant with death and an agreement with Hell," and he burned it. And, indeed, a system that thought itself constitutionally required to maintain slavery *was* morally wrong and ought in the end to have been opposed by revolutionary means, as in the end it was. Law, it is said, is the only thing that stands between us and anarchy. But not if it is bad, and not if we close off extralegal avenues of reform.

Undoubtedly, anarchy is not only the possible end of a rigid system of legality that tolerates no extralegal movement of reform; it is also the ultimate destination of a course of continuous and always freely permitted civil disobedience. For civil disobedience is habit-forming, and the habit it forms is, as such, destructive. It is essential that there be a general custom—which we may like to call a duty—to obey the law. While strict and uncompromising legality will not do, neither will a free-for-all of disobedience, proceeding from individual moral judgments. There must be a balance and, indeed, an imbalance on the side of legality. But this balance cannot itself be stated in terms of a legal rule. The rule of law is a valid, a necessary aspiration. It is even, certainly in this country, a valid general description of conditions. But the Rule of Law cannot be reduced to a rule of law. There can be no rule of universal application that prescribes a duty to obey and its limits, if any— once and for all, and without allowance for deviations based on particular moral judgments. A balance must rather be struck from time to time by the political process, which is capable in each instance of registering the common moral judgment.

Every demonstration, every act of civil disobedience, is a problem to be solved by executive officers, mayors, governors, and the President, who must decide whether to permit a demonstration, to suppress it, to make arrests, to prosecute. The legal judgment that may follow such political decisions will most often be plain. "Whether persons or groups should engage in non-violent disobedience to laws with which they disagree," Mr. Justice White has said, "perhaps defies any categorical answer for the guidance of every individual in every circumstance. But whether a court should give it [nonviolent disobedience] wholesale sanction is a wholly different question which calls for only one answer."[4] Justice White may have been right or wrong in the particular circumstances in which he was speaking, but he was surely describing what will ordinarily be the simple duty of judges. How much civil disobedience should be allowed and how much it should be made to cost the demonstrators—these are essentially political questions to be decided by political officers; and it is for courts to follow their lead. Whether the political judgment was right or wrong is, in turn, a judgment that will be rendered by events and by history.

In July, 1894, Eugene V. Debs led the famous and, incidentally, illegal Pullman strike, centered in Illinois. The governor of Illinois at the time, the great John Peter Altgeld, was sympathetic to the strikers and maintained more or less of a hands-off policy. President Cleveland then broke the strike with federal troops. In 1936-37, the United Automobile Workers conducted sit-down strikes in General Motors plants in Michigan, which in their way are the models for the later NAACP lie-downs in General Motors show-rooms in San Francisco. The governor of Michigan was Frank Murphy, later a justice of the Supreme Court of the United States, and he refused to have the National Guard dislodge the strikers despite the plain illegality of their action and continued to refuse even after an injunction had ordered them out. President Franklin Roosevelt did not act. Such are the political decisions that are called for. History has regarded Altgeld and Murphy and Roosevelt more kindly on this score than Cleveland. It has been more impressed—as to the Pullman episode—with the attitude of Mark Hanna, of all people, who got less mad than Cleveland, and saw beyond the simplicities of law and order. "Oh, hell," said Hanna. "Go live in Pullman [the company town] and find out how much Pullman gets selling water and gas ten per cent higher to those poor fools."

We are a big, rich, and stable, if tense and heterogeneous, society and we have sustained and can sustain a great deal of agitation and inconvenience in a just cause. In some measure it is because such safety valves are open that we are stable. The condition of the Negro, cruelly neglected for so long, cannot be remedied all at once. Until it is, we deserve no peace. Rather than get unduly exercised at demonstrations, we might reflect that industrial peace was fifty years or more in coming—and we do not fully have it yet. It makes a difference, of course, whether the cause in whose name we are disturbed and inconvenienced and in whose name the civic ordinances that guard our tranquillity are disobeyed is a just cause; it makes all the difference. Otherwise, the Pullman strike of 1894 is not to be distinguished from the mob violence that interfered with the Freedom Ride buses in Alabama in 1961. Otherwise, James

Farmer's demonstrators at the World's Fair and Dr. King's marchers in Birmingham in 1963 and Selma in 1965, although, to be sure, they offered no violence, are not clearly distinguished from some of the mobs convened by Governors Wallace of Alabama and Barnett of Mississippi. But the cause of the Negro protest movement —the underlying cause, seen in the large—is just, and that is a decisive judgment we are required to make. The law—and particularly ordinances pertaining to traffic and to minor trespasses— does not relieve us of the responsibility to make this judgment, any more than antiquated common law rules of property relieved an earlier generation from the necessity of deciding whether the cause for which unruly organizations of laboring men fought was just.

The
Civil
Rights
Act of 1964

6

AT A NEWS CONFERENCE IN 1962, John F. Kennedy coined the phrase "sound public constitutional policy," a hybrid of constitutional law and public policy. Constitutional law is the work-product of the Supreme Court. Public policy—hopefully sound—is what the political institutions, Congress and the President jointly, and often the President on his own, evolve and put into effect. Kennedy's phrase characterized with precision the civil rights commitment he took in the campaign of 1960 and the civil rights program he pursued in the first two and a half years of his brief administration. The broad principle of the *School Segregation Cases* of 1954, Kennedy had promised, would thenceforth be not merely the judicial policy of the federal government but also the political policy of its executive branch.

Kennedy redeemed his pledge substantially, making the best civil rights record of any national administration since Reconstruction. But such a statement, although entirely accurate, says more than it means. It means that the Kennedy administration exerted executive power, although often too hesitatingly, along many lines and achieved some concrete results. The Administration was also trying to improve general economic conditions, and it was well aware of the bearing of these efforts on the civil rights problem. But the long-range philosophy that informed the first two and a half years of the Kennedy administration could fairly be stated as follows: The Negro must be put in possession of political power in the South. This means the vote, which ought to be achievable through the concerted efforts of the Department of Justice within a decade. Then the log jam will be broken, not only in Congress but in the state governments, and there can then be major moves on all fronts, by the executive as well as by the legislatures; for, as every political realist knows, different attitudes in Congress would not only make it possible for the President to obtain legislation, but would free him to act in areas in which he was now inhibited, even though theoretically he had sufficient independent power.

In the first two and a half years President Kennedy demanded little of Congress, and nothing very insistently. He asked and was not granted perfecting amendments to the Civil Rights Acts of 1957 and 1960, dealing with the right to vote. It was February 28, 1963, before he sent his first full-scale civil rights message to Congress. He reported on his past independent initiatives and promised further ones. He asked again for improvement in the statutes guaranteeing the right to vote, and he added a modest request for authority to extend technical and financial assistance to school districts in the process of desegregation. That was about all.

Then, two months later, came Birmingham. In April and May, 1963, the Negroes of Birmingham, men, women, and children, under the leadership of the Rev. Dr. Martin Luther King, marched relentlessly up and down the city's streets, withstanding the assaults of Birmingham police, state troopers, and white mobs, through tear gas, fire hoses, police dogs, rocks, dynamite, and bullets. Their demands were precise and minimal: a few Negroes on the police force, the opening of lunch counters, and a few jobs downtown. President Kennedy sent Assistant Attorney General Burke Marshall to help negotiate peace between Dr. King's marchers and the white power structure, as it is tiresomely but not inaccurately called. He also moved federal troops into position to intervene. An agreement of sorts was reached, and by June, although a fatal bombing of a

Negro church was yet to come, the turbulence in Birmingham subsided.

Birmingham was not the first instance of violently resisted Negro demonstrations, nor even of mass marching through the center of a city. Direct action had been undertaken many times before. Albany, Georgia, preceded Birmingham, as did the Freedom Rides of the spring of 1961. Sit-ins had started early in 1960. And before that there had been the successful bus boycott in Montgomery, Alabama, in 1955-56. But the marching in Birmingham, although it was not first and not even unique, became one of those events which seem to turn the course of history; or if that sounds insufficiently deterministic, then one of those events for which the course of history seems to wait before turning. Perhaps it was that Birmingham—with the notorious Bull Connor in charge (now no longer) —had become something of a symbol of Southern racism. Perhaps it was that police reaction in Birmingham was more brutal than elsewhere and that for this reason the marching there seized the attention of more people over the country and affected more consciences. Perhaps the murder from ambush, at about the same time, of Medgar Evers, the NAACP's man in Jackson, Mississippi, heightened the effect. And perhaps the consequences of Birmingham are explained by Aldous Huxley's remark that experience is not what happens to us but what we do with what happens to us. Birmingham, it may be, was a turning point not because it caused President Kennedy to register a sharp change in his policy on civil rights but because that was what President Kennedy was willing and able to do with Birmingham. In the long term, very probably, broad new federal legislation was inevitable, but for the moment John Kennedy surely had a choice. He could have stood on a platform of law and order, deploring not only violence but all attempts, which are ever fraught with violence, to change the legal order by extralegal or illegal means. And he could have coupled this attitude with a promise to pursue more vigorously the executive program on which he was already launched.

No doubt the President, in common with others in Washington, anxiously faced the prospect of further demonstrations and of real bloodshed. He did not harbor the neat illusion, however, that any statute could produce social change rapidly and radically enough to take the steam out of the Negro protest movement. The notion that he could bring the demonstrators from the street into the court-room attracted him momentarily, but he soon saw through it. There would be more demonstrations in any event, or they would peter out in any event. If anything, presidential calls to order might help stop them. The option to stand pat on law and order and executive action was fully available. Yet this was not the choice Kennedy made. Instead, less than three months after his February message, he called off his old bets and went to the country and to Congress with eloquence and passion, setting radical new objectives. And so it was through John F. Kennedy that the Negro, without waiting for the vote, operating outside the law and also outside the cus-tomary political channels, touched the levers of political power. The result, thirteen months later, was the Civil Rights Act of 1964, a fundamentally new departure in federal legislation.

An omnibus civil rights bill, drafted in the Department of Justice, was sent up by President Kennedy on June 19, 1963. It led off with the President's proposals of February to strengthen the voting pro-visions of the Civil Rights Acts of 1957 and 1960, and it included also the proposals concerning assistance to desegregating school districts. Then came the new matter. The bill prohibited discrim-ination in public accommodations, meaning privately owned facil-ities catering to the general public. It authorized the Attorney Gen-eral to bring suit to desegregate public schools. And it authorized the President to exact promises of nondiscrimination from recipients of federal financial assistance "in connection with any program or activity by way of grant, contract, loan, insurance, guaranty, or otherwise." The bill contained no general fair employment pro-vision, but it enlarged the jurisdiction of a presidential commission, which has existed by executive authority since the Eisenhower administration, and which tries to ensure that the government's contractors, and its defense contractors in particular, institute and pursue nondiscriminatory employment policies. Finally, with lucid awareness of the limited possibilities of enforcement through litiga-tion, the bill established a Community Relations Service, whose function it would be, "in confidence and without publicity," by negotiation, persuasion, and other dark arts known also to labor mediators, to induce voluntary compliance with the public accommodations title of the bill, and to attempt to settle other racial disputes as well. The Service put on an institutional footing the function discharged in Birmingham by Assistant Attorney General Marshall. It was inspired by the sort of mediation board that played an important role in the development of early labor relations policy and by the present Federal Mediation Service, which is still far from obsolescent.

For the next few months, through the fall of 1963, tripartite negotiations took place, involving the Kennedy administration, the Republican leadership of the House, and a bipartisan group of liberal House members. In the wings was the Leadership Conference on Civil Rights, a coalition of over seventy organizations interested in obtaining the broadest possible statute. At this stage an excellent fair employment title, superseding but not displacing the presidential commission which deals with the government's contractors, was added to the bill. But there were also at this stage two significant subtractions from the Administration's draft. A section was dropped from the voting rights title, under which federal courts would have been required, themselves or through federal registrars, to see to the speedy qualification of Negro voters in areas of lowest Negro registration. And the Community Relations Service was killed. Perhaps— there is no other ready explanation—the Community Relations Service fell victim, at this point, to the most advanced liberals, who wanted, as the headlines called it, the "toughest" possible bill, providing for enforcement, not namby-pamby mediation. To be sure, there was enforcement power in the bill as it stood, but the idea may have been to afford the Admnistration no alternative to the use of that power. This is a highly illusory kind of "toughness."

On the floor of the House, where it was passed handsomely on February 10, 1964, the bill suffered some further wounds, thin and quickly administered, but not altogether shallow. The provision, which had been rewritten and improved in committee, authorizing the President to see to it that there is no discrimination in federally financed programs, was amended to apply only to programs receiving federal assistance "by way of grant, loan, or contract *other than a contract of insurance or guaranty.*" This is and was intended to be an exemption for housing built or purchased on mortgages guaranteed by the Federal Housing Administration or the Veterans Administration. Such housing was covered by the executive order on Equal Opportunity in Housing, issued by President Kennedy on November 20, 1962, in the exercise of his independent executive power. The order applied to housing "provided in whole or in part with the aid of loans [mortgages] . . . hereafter insured [or] guaranteed . . . by the Federal Government," and it reached the practices of lending institutions "with respect to residential property . . . insofar as such practices relate to loans hereafter insured or guaranteed by the Federal Government." The purpose of the order was not to coerce an individual homeowner to sell to a Negro. The order was aimed at developers of real estate, and it was meant to exert pressure on banks to make mortgage loans to Negroes who have found a willing seller on the same terms as to whites, which is far from the prevalent practice. The great problem with the exemption in the House amendment is not so much that Congress has chosen to leave FHA and VA mortgages unaffected by this statute, but that the amendment may well abrogate the executive order to the extent that it does cover such mortgages. The managers of the bill disclaimed any intention to do this, and similar disclaimers were later entered in the Senate, but the result may nevertheless follow as a matter of law. For it is quite clear that Congress did not wish to deal with discrimination in FHA and VA housing. As a general legal proposition, the President may have and may enforce an independent policy of his own in matters such as this so long as Congress has not legislated a contrary policy. He may fill a policy vacuum, or complement a Congressional policy, but he may not displace a Congressional policy, not even a negative one. And so a portion of the executive order on housing was thrown into doubt, to say the least, although the Administration, relying on the Congressional disclaimers, continues to regard it as effective.

A number of further changes made on the floor of the House must be noted. The provisions dealing with education were amended so as to render them almost wholly inapplicable to the Northern problem of racial imbalance. The House extended the fair employment title to prohibit discrimination based on sex as well as race, religion, and national origin. This amendment, although conceivably a worthy one on its own merits, is concerned with a different and quite separate problem, which should have been dealt with separately. The House also saw fit to safeguard an employer's right to refuse to hire an atheist, a pretty clearly unconstitutional proviso, which was later struck in the Senate. Again, the employment title was changed in the House to exclude assorted Communists and subversives of whatever race, religion or sex from the benefits of the bill—another provision of doubtful constitutionality, which remains in the act. But the bill was also repaired in one important respect on the floor of the House. The Community Relations Service, eliminated in committee, was put back, although in somewhat crippled shape. It was finally restored to full health by the Senate.

The main event in the progress of the bill to triumphant passage in the Senate, under cloture on June 19, 1964, was a series of amendments evolved chiefly by Senator Everett M. Dirksen of Illinois, the minority leader. Aside from tinkering with the bill here and there, and sometimes improving it, the Dirksen amendments were directed at the enforcement provisions of both the public accommodations and equal employment titles. As these provisions came to the Senate, both private parties and the government, through the Attorney General and a federal Equal Employment Opportunities Commission, were authorized to bring enforcement suits. For these simplicities the Dirksen amendments substituted a labyrinth of procedures, intended to emphasize private as against government litigating initiative, and to give state authorities, where relevant ones exist, a first crack at settling or litigating any complaint.

The only significant change made in the Senate that was not a part of Mr. Dirksen's package was a provision granting jury trials to defendants charged with criminal contempt of court. The upshot of litigation under the statute will be a judicial decree ordering somebody to do something or desist from doing it—serve Negroes at a lunch counter and stop refusing them service, employ a given applicant for a job and stop excluding others because of their race, and the like. Such orders are made effective by the power of the federal courts to hold violators in contempt. This is a twofold power. A court may put a person in jail or subject him to a fine until he obeys, and this is called civil contempt because it does not purport to punish but merely to exact obedience. A court may also, after the fact, punish a person for the crime of having disobeyed a decree in the past, and this is called criminal contempt. The amendment in question, proposed by Senator Morton of Kentucky, does not affect the power of federal courts to enforce their orders by civil contempt proceedings. Nor does it affect voting cases, which are governed by a compromise embodied in the Civil Rights Act of 1957. It affects only—as to all titles of the act save the title dealing with the right to vote—a judge's power, on his own, without a jury, to punish for criminal contempt. Undoubtedly, for the foreseeable future it will be difficult to make a charge of criminal contempt stick before a Southern jury in a civil rights case. But the civil contempt power is an ample one. Moreover, in the judgment of many lawyers it is wrong on principle to dispense with juries in this sort of criminal case, which is not easily distinguishable from the common run of criminal cases, in which, in turn, trial by jury is a defendant's constitutional right.

The act that emerged, from these origins and along this legislative path, is a statutory booklet some 18,000 words long. It is divided into eleven titles or chapters. Title I, on voting, which is in the form of amendments to the Civil Rights Acts of 1957 and 1960, applies only to federal, not state, elections. It is now largely superseded by the Voting Rights Act of 1965, but is worth brief examination nevertheless, as it may continue to have some application outside the hardcore South. It orders state registrars to use the same standards in qualifying Negro voters as in qualifying whites, and forbids them to disqualify an individual for trivial errors in an application to register, which are not material to his fitness as a voter. Thus the title seeks to counteract the widespread practice in some states of disqualifying Negroes for failure, in effect, to dot their i's and cross their t's—e.g., failure to state age not only in years and months but in exact number of days. Under this provision it will no longer be necessary to go through an elaborate process of proof that the practice is discriminatory. The title then deals in some detail with literacy tests. It provides that they may not be administered to any applicant for registration unless they are administered to all applicants, and that they may be given only in writing, a certified copy of the test being furnished to the individual upon request. But the Attorney General may, in effect, exempt from the application of these requirements states which, he is satisfied, administer their literacy tests without discrimination; so that practices in the North are likely to remain largely unaffected. There follows a provision that anyone with a sixth-grade education, obtained in any school in which instruction is carried on predominantly in English, is presumed to be sufficiently literate to vote in federal elections, and a state must prove him to be illiterate if it wishes to disqualify him, which is to say, it must show to the satisfaction of the federal courts that its standards of literacy, as applied to such an individual, are not discriminatory. A presumption only is established on the basis of a sixth-grade education, however, and while it may help procedurally, it is unlikely to change the substance of what in each case the government must still prove to make out discrimination. Finally, this and other titles—by enabling the Attorney General to get voting and other cases heard by three-judge courts, rather than by single federal judges—give him the means to circumvent delays and obstructionist tactics to which he has been subjected by a few segregationist federal judges in the South. It is unfortunate that such a cumbersome procedure should have had to be imposed on a busy and overburdened federal judiciary, and the necessity for it emphasizes the importance of care in the selection of federal judges in the South.

Title II is the public accommodations title. It defines a public accommodation as any inn, hotel, motel, or other establishment providing lodging to transient guests, excepting only what came to be known in Washington as Mrs. Murphy's boardinghouse, meaning an establishment which offers no more than five rooms for rent and in which the owner also lives; any restaurant or other place that sells food for consumption on the premises, including lunch counters in retail stores; any gasoline station; any place of entertainment, including theaters and sports arenas; and any other establishment which is physically located within the premises of one of the places just listed, and which holds itself out as serving the patrons of such a place, this being the provision under which some bars and barbershops, for example, may be included. A public accommodation, so defined, is subject to this title if "its operations affect commerce, or if discrimination or segregation by it is supported by state action."

Commerce is said to be automatically affected by all the establishments in the hotel category. Establishments in the restaurant

category and gasoline stations affect commerce if they serve interstate travelers or if a substantial portion of the food or gasoline or
other products they sell has moved across state lines. Places of entertainment affect commerce if the thing or performers they exhibit
have moved across state lines. Discrimination or segregation is supported by state action, and thus prohibited whether or not the
establishment affects commerce, if it is required by a state, formally
by statute or informally by official action or pressure. But all these
definitions are expressly made inapplicable to a bona fide private
club or other establishment not open to the public, except as a club
or the like may open some of its facilities to the general public, in
which event the title is applicable to those facilities. In establishments covered, the act declares all persons to be entitled to full
and equal enjoyment of everything that an establishment offers,
without discrimination or segregation on account of race, religion,
or national origin. It is unlawful also for any third party to attempt
to prevent an establishment from extending the privileges secured
by this title to an individual or to attempt to prevent an individual
from claiming his privileges.

Persons aggrieved by a violation of this title may obtain from a
federal court a decree directing that the violation cease. And there is
a valuable provision authorizing the courts to appoint an attorney
for a complainant in a suit under this title and to allow him a reasonable attorney's fee as part of the costs awarded to him if he wins.
However, if the violation occurred in a state which prohibits discrimination in public accommodations under its own law, complaint
must first be made to the state authorities, and there can be no
suit in the federal court until the state authorities have had thirty
days to deal with the complaint. Subsequently, the federal court
may stay its own proceedings until the termination of any local
proceedings that may have been undertaken. But ultimately, if he is
unsatisfied with what the state has been able to do, the complainant
retains his essential federal right to redress. In a state which has no
public accommodations law of its own, the federal court in which
suit has been brought may refer the matter to the Community Relations Service for a total of no more than 120 days, if the court
believes that a reasonable possibility exists of securing voluntary
compliance. The Service may investigate and hold private hearings.
Suits by the Attorney General on behalf of the government are

possible only when he "has reasonable cause to believe that any person or group of persons is engaged in a pattern or practice of resistance."

Title III authorizes the Attorney General to bring suit to desegregate public facilities, other than public schools or colleges, which are owned or operated by or on behalf of any state—such as parks, golf courses, municipal auditoriums, and the like. Judicial decisions have long since made clear the law as to such facilities, which turns on a constitutional right to equal access as part of the general right to equal treatment at the hands of all units of government. The point of this title is merely that the Attorney General is now enabled to bring suit, rather than private parties only.

Title IV is the education title. It requires the Commissioner of Education, who heads the hundred-year-old Office of Education in the Department of Health, Education and Welfare, to make a survey and report, within two years, on the availability of equal educational opportunities to individuals of all races and religions in public institutions at all levels throughout the country, North and South. As of the summer of 1965, this project had not yet got off the ground. The further provisions of this title, applicable almost exclusively in the South, have been described in detail in Chapter I.

Title V extends for four years the life of the Civil Rights Commission, an investigative body established by the act of 1957, which may be expected to continue and enlarge its extremely valuable work in building a library of the relevant and hard-to-come-by facts of education, employment, housing, and the like. Too much of what we think we know about race relations is still drawn from statute books and reports of appellate cases, and too little from real life. The Commission has also been able to dramatize conditions by holding public hearings.

Title VI embodies the requirement that there be no discrimination in federally assisted programs (other than those assisted by way of contracts of insurance or guaranty) and empowers the President ultimately to withhold funds as a penalty for noncompliance. The title carries certain procedural safeguards, as it ought.

Title VII is headed "Equal Employment Opportunity." It applies to any individual or corporate or other legal entity regularly employing 25 or more persons, to employment agencies, including the

United States Employment Service and the system of state and local employment services which receive federal assistance, and to labor unions. Employers and labor unions are covered only if they affect interstate commerce. Unlike the public accommodations provisions, this title does not spell out the meaning of the technical phrase "affect commerce," for its own purposes, but adopts the well-established and entirely relevant definition that has been evolved under the federal labor law, and that covers a very great deal, indeed. The title makes it unlawful for any employer to fail to hire or to discharge, or otherwise to discriminate, in compensation or other terms of employment, against any individual because of his color, religion, sex, or national origin. Similar prohibitions apply to employment agencies and to labor unions. The latter are also forbidden to cause an employer to discriminate, and apprenticeship and other training programs must be open to all without discrimination. Exemptions are provided for the case where religion, sex, or national origin may be a legitimate occupational qualification. With a view to demands sometimes voiced by Negro organizations in the North, the title specifically forswears any requirement of preferential treatment for the purpose of curing an imbalance in the racial composition of a given body of employees or apprentices.

Complaints of a violation of this title may be made either by a person aggrieved or by a member of the Federal Equal Employment Opportunity Commission, which the statute establishes. The initial federal addressee of such complaints is the Commission. The Commission is to investigate, and without undue publicity make every attempt to secure compliance with the law. Its visitatorial powers are considerable. It is authorized to examine witnesses under oath and require the production of documentary evidence, and it may seek the aid of federal courts when it runs up against a recalcitrant witness. It may require employers, labor unions, and employment agencies to keep relevant records and to make periodic reports, and it may cause them to post conspicuous notices on their premises informing all concerned of their rights and privileges under this title. In a state which has a fair employment practices law of its own, the local authorities are given a period of up to 120 days to deal with any complaint, and before that period is up the federal Commission may not intervene. Elsewhere, federal jurisdiction attaches immediately. In either case, if the federal Commission, having investigated and tried persuasion, fails to achieve compliance, an aggrieved individual may bring suit in a federal court, which is again empowered to appoint a lawyer for him and to award him a lawyer's fee if he wins. The court may not only order the defendant to stop discriminating on pain of contempt of court but may also give special remedies, such as an order of reinstatement of an employee with back pay. The Commission itself has no litigating authority, except that it may initiate civil contempt proceedings when a decree handed down in a private suit has been disobeyed. But as under the public accommodations title, the Attorney General is authorized to sue to enforce this title when he finds that there is "a pattern or practice of resistance," and it may be that he will in practice act as the Commission's litigating arm.

Those portions of this title which establish the Commission and give it its investigatory powers went into effect, like the rest of the act, when the President signed it. But the substantive provisions of this title, the provisions defining and prohibiting discriminatory practices, did not go into effect until a year later. There was that much of a period of grace and adjustment. Moreover, these provisions became effective in July, 1965, only for employers of 100 or more. Another year must pass before they are applicable to employers of 75 or more, and they will be fully applicable to all employers covered after yet another year, that is, in 1967. Unfortunately, President Johnson took nearly a year to make the necessary appointments to the Commission. Since it was intended that the Commission would spend the year before the title became otherwise effective doing essential preparatory work, the President's delay virtually doubled the initial period of grace.

Of the remaining four titles one (X) sets up the Community Relations Service; another orders a special census of voters, with a view to the highly remote and, on its merits, highly dubious possibility of applying Section 2 of the Fourteenth Amendment, which would cut down the representation in the federal House of states that deny the vote to some of their citizens. For the rest, there are some technical provisions, the most important of which, mentioned earlier, deals with jury trials.

Without question, this Civil Rights Act is a momentous statute, comparable in importance to such organic measures as the Interstate

Commerce Act of 1887 and the reforms of the first Wilson administration and the first two administrations of Franklin Roosevelt. Over time, the significance of such a statute rises quite above this or that inadequacy in its provisions. The point is that it commits the federal government, and particularly Congress, which can do things neither the President nor the judiciary, despite their prior commitments, could do alone, to a set of national goals that reach beyond minimal constitutional requirements. The commitment is not likely to be revoked and the goals are not likely to be reduced. An organic enactment like this trails further administrative, judicial and legislative law in its wake. There will be interpretations and amendments, all striving to make it, like the federal Union itself, "more perfect." And they will be achieved, despite occasional setbacks, more easily than the initial step. Such a statute affects the expectations and aspirations of our people, and the sense of duty and function of the institutions of government. For everyone concerned, it changes the universe of discourse.

But that looks far ahead. More immediately, how will the statute be translated into everyday life, North and South? The address of the statute is largely to the South. In its education and employment titles, and in some measure even in the federal assistance title, the statute explicitly excludes application to problems that are typically Northern. To be sure, conditions in the North do not, by and large, allow of expeditious cures. It is not to be supposed that great or even significant advances could be achieved in the North through federal legislation. Yet it is regrettable that the act on its face looks in many places like a regional measure. It is thus laid open to the charge, vigorously made by Senator Russell of Georgia and others, which is deadly because it carries a grain of general truth, that Northerners are mostly interested in dealing with the racial difficulties of others, but not with their own. Even so, the act will not be entirely without effect in the North. It will have some supportive effect on extralegal pressure applied by the Negroes themselves. The public accommodations and employment titles will activate similar laws that have lain in some disuse in many states. And these titles will be widely obeyed in the North, even by people who in the past chose to shut their eyes to the state statutes.

In the South results should be forthcoming, in some areas at least, within a reasonably short time under Title VI, which deals with federally financed programs, of which there are a great many, including disaster relief, hospital construction, urban renewal and other housing, agricultural assistance, libraries, vocational training, aid to education, and more. Regulations were issued under this title within six months after signature of the act, and they can cut deep into American life. They are likely to do more, for example, than any other part of the statute to speed up school desegregation. They require pledges of nondiscrimination from recipients of federal funds, and establish procedures for policing these pledges. Enforcement can ultimately be accomplished not merely through a relatively self-defeating cutoff of funds, but also through judicial decrees following suit by the Attorney General. But this title is an instrument of direct and continuous federal pressure, and its effect will be felt if enough resources and executive energy are put into its administration, quite aside from enforcement proceedings.

The public accommodations and employment titles, affecting as they do the actions not only of officials but of many thousands of private persons and institutions, must, like all such pervasive regulatory measures, gain general acceptance, however grudging, in order to be effective. It will take, said Senator Goldwater, a police state to enforce this law, and he was almost right; it *would* take. Absolute enforcement of any statute that is resisted consistently and on principle by substantial numbers of people would require a police state. But we do not expect absolute enforcement in such circumstances. We are a free society and an open one, and we do not pay the price of absolute enforcement. By means of occasional enforcement, *pour encourager les autres,* and by other means of inducement and persuasion, we undertake rather to reduce the number of those who resist. That is what is in prospect in the South for the public accommodations and equal employment titles, and that is why the Equal Employment Opportunity Commission and the Community Relations Service, which are inducing rather than enforcing agencies, are so important. Of course, inducement, persuasion, and meditation would not be very effective if the law did not declare in mandatory fashion some standard of behavior to which the mediators can urge people to measure up. And persuasion is not unnaturally hampered if an adamant refusal to be moved by it is known to be an alternative that never costs anything.

Yet, while enforcement is a sword that is sometimes wielded, its chief uses are Damoclean.

In the first few years, however, litigation will play a most important role, out of proportion to its eventual significance in rendering the public accommodations and equal employment titles effective. The constitutionality of the public accommodations title was immediately challenged, and it was promptly affirmed by the Supreme Court on December 14, 1964, in two cases involving a motel in Atlanta and a relatively small restaurant in Birmingham. Further constitutional attacks on this title and on the employment and financial assistance titles may be expected, even though the outcome of such litigation is almost entirely free from doubt. The public accommodations and employment provisions rest on the power of Congress to regulate interstate commerce, a concept broadly defined in many contexts in the past, some of which, such as wages-and-hour and child-labor legislation, the Pure Food and Drug Act, labor legislation in general, and the Mann Act, are quite analogous. Congress is authorized to regulate the movement of goods and persons across state lines and it may concern itself with events that precede or succeed that movement and have a bearing on it. And for purposes of ease of administration, Congress may go beyond even these loose limits. Events preceding or following the interstate movement need not in themselves have a primary commercial or economic significance. The evil of child labor or of prostitution, for example, is not primarily economic. The established constitutional content of the Commerce Clause is a definition—very broad indeed—of the circumstances in which Congress may act, not of the ends it may seek. Nor is there any doubt of the power of the federal government to set conditions on the disbursement of federal funds; indeed, under decided cases, there is considerable doubt whether the federal government may constitutionally allow its funds to be used in discriminatory fashion.

Beyond the constitutional issue there will be, as with all new statutes, issues of its meaning and application about which doubt is legitimately possible on the face of the act, and which only litigation can authoritatively resolve. Such questions, becoming increasingly marginal, will continue to arise throughout the life of the statute. A number of initial ones can be foreseen. There are sure to crop up in the South things like "intrastate hotels" accepting no interstate travelers, "intrastate theaters" offering only local entertainment, and all varieties of private clubs. Their bona fides will be subject to litigation, as will the question, assuming bona fides, whether the statute was intended to cover them. In one instance —in the case of restaurants—the statute speaks of a "substantial" connection with interstate commerce. It remains for litigation to determine just exactly what that means, and the concept of a substantial connection may conceivably be read into other portions of the statute as well. Again, the Attorney General's authority to sue is limited to cases where he finds a practice or pattern of resistance, under both public accommodations and employment titles. What does this phrase mean? What is its geographic coverage? Are statistics a sufficient proof of a pattern of resistance? Must the Attorney General name as parties all persons involved in such a pattern or will the decree he obtains bind the world, and how much of the world?

Much will depend in the South on the amount of pressure exerted by Negro communities, and on the effectiveness of the Community Relations Service and the Equal Employment Opportunity Commission. The kind of public support the President gives these agencies will be extremely important. But in any event, the goals are set and they are set high. They will be attained, sooner or later. This statute was the point of no return.

The
Limits of
Effective
Legal Action

7

INITIAL COMPLIANCE WITH TITLE II, the public accommodations title, of the Civil Rights Act of 1964, which was the only provision imposing an immediate duty on the general public, has been rather better than expected. A survey of 53 cities of over 50,000 population in the 19 states that have no public accommodations laws, which was conducted by the Community Relations Service within weeks after enactment of the statute, showed that as early as then, over two thirds of the relevant facilities, including hotels, motels, restaurants, theaters, sports facilities, parks, and libraries, had been desegregated. There was some variation, to be sure. The two-thirds figure applied to motels in only 46 cities, for example, and to sports facilities in only 48. And some of the desegregation represented by these figures had taken place before the statute was enacted. Nevertheless, what one Justice Department official called major compliance—conspicuous places in substantial cities—was a fact shortly after Title II became law.

These heartening statistics must not delude us into thinking that the public accommodations title (let alone the rest of the act) is now effective and that the problem is solved. It is an all too common delusion with us that the way to dispose of a social problem finally is to pass a law and then forget it, and we are naturally prone to seize on facts that seem to confirm what we wish to believe. But the evidence so far is not conclusive. There is some basis for feeling sanguine, no doubt. And yet a good initial response is not infrequently achieved by laws whose implementation later gives rise to many difficulties. It seemed for a while, after enactment of the Eighteenth Amendment, that prohibition would prove effective. So the Wickersham Commission reported ruefully a decade later. And for the first two years or so there was a good deal of voluntary compliance with the Supreme Court's school desegregation decision of 1954. In both instances, of course, there was plenty of trouble later.

Voluntary compliance may loom large at first because there are always people who have been waiting—out of timidity or inertia—for the law to nudge them into doing what they have really considered the right and profitable thing to do all along. The forces of resistance, on the other hand, need time to cohere and to encourage themselves. It is noteworthy in this connection that some good missionary work by the Department of Justice and others in 1963-1964 succeeded in obtaining considerable desegregation even before there was a law to comply with. Mostly it was chain organizations and establishments in metropolitan areas that agreed to desegregate. This has, by and large, continued to be the pattern. Compliance is far from universal in hard-core areas. And we cannot be sure that all the desegregation in the cities was genuine, rather than a token show to be followed by subterfuges of various kinds. Again, conspicuous initial compliance does not mean much if the Negro community does not fairly continuously use the facilities involved, either because of inertia or because of economic and other pressures skillfully and quietly exerted to discourage genuine integration. Finally, there is the problem of the large number of "private clubs" that are newly rising all over the South.

These caveats are not meant to suggest that the public accommodations title and other portions of the Civil Rights Act are likely to fail, or that they can work, as Mr. Goldwater said in the Senate, only if we institute a police state. The point is that the act is likely—it is virtually bound to—fail if we take the fatuous assumption that it is bound to succeed. Laws are not always effective simply because they are there and because violators are subject to suit. To think so is to forget what the late Roscoe Pound almost fifty years ago called "the limits of effective legal action," to forget that only in a certain kind of social and political situation is law self-executing through its own institutions, and that there are times when extralegal resources must be brought to the aid of the law in order to make it attain its end. Enactment and enforcement of law are sometimes only episodes, even if the single most important and influential ones, in a long and varied process by which society, working through a number of institutions, manages to realize a given purpose.

The limits of law are the limits of enforcement, and the limits of enforcement are the conditions of a free society; perhaps, indeed, the limits of government altogether. If substantial portions of the statute book had to be enforced by direct action—whether through civil or criminal litigation—against large numbers of people, we would have a very different and infinitely more disagreeable society than we do. To be sure, there is always a residuum of the antisocial, whose numbers the enforcement process, most often the criminal process, strives to reduce, although never with absolute success. And there may be laws, such as narcotics statutes, which some people may be simply incapable of obeying. Still, laws about killing and stealing, about the payment of taxes, about contracts, about torts, about labor relations, and even about traffic are effectively, if never absolutely, in force. And yet we have a free society, not a police state. We invest relatively limited resources in the effort to enforce law, and we sacrifice relatively little of other values in the process. The well-known secret of this operation is that most people, most of the time, need only to be made aware of the law in order to obey it. Much of litigation is the consequence of differences of opinion about what the law is or ought to be, not of failure to obey what is clearly the law.

In a simple system, when, as Pound pointed out,

men demand little of law and enforcement of law is but enforcement of the ethical minimum necessary for the orderly conduct of society, enforcement of law involves few difficulties. All but the inevitable antisocial residuum can understand the simple program and obvious purposes of such a legal system. . . . On the other hand, when men demand much of law, when they seek to devolve upon it the whole burden of social control, when they seek to make it do the work of the home and of the church, enforcement of law comes to involve many difficulties. . . . The purposes of the legal order are [then] not all upon the surface and it may be that many whose nature is by no means anti-social are out of accord with some or even with many of these purposes.

It is then, Pound added, that "we begin to hear complaint that laws are not enforced and the forgotten problem of the limitations upon effective legal action once more becomes acute."[1]

When people in the millions or even hundreds of thousands are opposed, intensely, consistently, and on principle, to a law bearing directly on their conduct of ordinary affairs, effective enforcement is possible, if at all, only through military occupation. Effective enforcement in the face of determined and widespread opposition is possible, this is to say, only if the private conduct that is to be regulated is subject to more or less continuous official scrutiny and to more or less continuous coercion. It makes no difference, with regard to the enforcement problem, that the opposition is nationally in a minority. As Walter Lippmann remarked in 1926, writing about prohibition, "when the object is to regulate personal habit and social custom, the majority which matters is the majority of the community concerned."[2]

People in the sort of numbers we are talking about will, of course, control some state governments and many other local authorities, and these in turn may decline to cooperate in the enforcement of locally unpopular federal law. But the chief source of the difficulty is not that the federal government lacks the basic police power and is helpless without the cooperation of the states. The heart of the matter is that no normal police and prosecuting activity can be effective in such circumstances. Nothing short of the pervasive presence of armed men will do.

As a temporary measure, in case of a breakdown of elementary public order, this has proved necessary in the past, may again be necessary on future occasions, and is well within the authority and capability of the federal government. But as a regular and more or less permanent device, it is something from which we recoil, deeming it destructive of the values of a free society, and in the end, quite possibly, counterproductive even in terms of its immediate aim. The true alternatives, therefore, are reducing the opposition by a process of inducement and persuasion, or abandoning the law. Abandonment of the law is not incompatible with occasional enforcement in pitched circumstances. And abandonment does not have to be formal, at least not immediately; the law may stay on the books for a while, it may even be observed in some parts of the country, but if it is substantially abandoned in practice, that in the end is what really matters. Noncompliance is contagious, and the statute book will conform to the practice.

Most laws, very nearly all laws, it need hardly be repeated, are readily accorded general acquiescence, and are easily effective. But that the alternatives otherwise are as I have stated them, that there are times when law does not gain general consent merely by virtue of having been authoritatively pronounced, and that lacking such consent it cannot be effective—this is demonstrated by antigambling statutes, which coexist with widespread gambling, and by laws regulating common sexual practices, which lie largely in disuse. Further, dramatic proof of the proposition may be drawn from two notorious experiences in American history.

The Fugitive Slave Act of 1850 was enacted as part of that year's broad compromise on the slavery problem, engineered by Henry Clay and seconded by Webster in the famous 7th of March speech. The act had firm support in the Constitution. But it was repugnant to much of the North. Emerson, no wild abolitionist, called it "this filthy enactment," and wrote in his journal: "I will not obey it, by God!" Others, like Theodore Parker of Boston, agitated against it publicly and fiercely. William R. Day, then a boy in Ravenna, Ohio, later a justice of the Supreme Court of the United States, remembered to the end of his days the heated meetings and resolutions against the act, and retained a sense of the limits of federal law. Many Northern states passed "personal liberty laws," as they were called, which were inconsistent with the act and were really thinly veiled attempts to nullify it. Efforts to enforce the Fugitive Slave Act were often resisted by mobs, were in any event not significant, and soon pretty well ceased. The end result was a hardening and broadening of Northern antislavery sentiment.

Nearly three quarters of a century later prohibition was imposed on the country by constitutional amendment. The amendment was proposed by the necessary two-thirds vote of the Congress, and ratified by the legislatures of ten more states than necessary, forty-six in all. There was some thought that the amendment might, paradoxically, itself be unconstitutional, and the matter was carried to the Supreme Court by distinguished counsel, but the Court held otherwise.[3] In some states prohibition was effective, and almost everywhere it abolished the old-fashioned saloon. But in many areas, and signally throughout the urban United States, enforcement soon became a shambles. Large numbers of people discovered, if they had ever thought about it before, that they did not really want prohibition. The Volstead Act was, of course, openly disdained. Perfectly respectable and substantial people advised violation of it, and public officials condoned violation, to say the least. By the middle of the decade, when repeal did not yet seem a realistic possibility, leaders of opinion talked of nullification in one form or another. "Conscience and public opinion," wrote Arthur T. Hadley, president emeritus of Yale, in 1925, "enforce the laws; the police suppress the exceptions." In this instance, conscience and public opinion opposed the law, and the exceptions were the rule. Hence no enforcement was possible; the law was no law.[4] And it wasn't. When, under President Hoover, an effort was made to achieve more widespread and efficient enforcement, the only result was that sufficient steam was finally generated for actual repeal.

What do these ominous lessons from history teach about prospects for realization of the aims of the Civil Rights Act of 1964? It is first to be remarked that the Fugitive Slave Act *was* an immoral law, and that the Eighteenth Amendment attempted to regulate conduct that is morally neutral, and as to which one's neighbor or a majority of one's countrymen ought, of right, have no power to impose their views. The Civil Rights Act of 1964 is a very different affair.

Now, such judgments are not to be escaped. They are decisive, and if by any chance the Civil Rights Act cannot validly be distinguished in this fashion from the Fugitive Slave Law and the Prohibition Amendment, then it may meet their fate. That is the blunt truth, and we may as well be aware of it. If, on the other hand, as so many believe, the Civil Rights Act is a just law, embodying minimal moral requirements that a national majority may properly attempt to impose on everyone, then what the earlier experiences teach is that the country now faces a task of persuasion and inducement, a task of political and social leadership and education.

Pronouncement of the law is the first step, and in itself an important persuasive and educational action. It must be followed not merely by a concerted campaign to convince everyone of the morality and justice of the law but also by an effort to bring home to the minority the intensity with which by far the greater number of their fellow citizens hold to the law. This will appeal to the minority's interest, which goes beyond the immediate issue, in conforming to the wishes of a national majority, with which, we may assume, they desire to continue in mutual profit to form part of a single body politic. The crucial point is that there is in prospect a contest of wills. We must not think that it was resolved in Congress and is now behind us. The preponderant majority and the resistant minority remain, in the phrase that was so popular in the Kennedy administration at the time of the Cuban missile crisis, eyeball to eyeball, and if the majority relaxes, in a failure of patience or in discontinuity of purpose, as it did after Reconstruction, or if it thinks it can devolve its responsibility on some enforcement officials in Washington and forget about it, as it largely did during Reconstruction, the law is from that moment moribund.

A normal rate of enforcement is part of the process of persuasion and inducement. Litigation, even if its other consequences are not overly onerous, is at the least expensive, and the possibility of it will deter in some measure, for although not nearly everyone can be sued, no one knows who may be. But other means of pressure and inducement must also be employed, by the government and by private groups and interests favoring the law. The inducement of compliance with this law must be a consideration at every one of the countless points at which the activities of the federal government —both the civil and military establishments—touch on the private sector and constitute an actual or potential source of benefits. Private entities—not only the Negro organizations but all who would like to see this statute rendered fully effective—have an obligation to exert economic, social, and moral pressure and to set an unwavering example. If it is understood that the triumphant passage of this civil rights statute launched a great reforming enterprise, to be carried on by the society as a whole and not merely by the enforcing arm of the federal government, then there is every probability of success.

The
Voting
Rights
Act of 1965

8

For the period of the 1964 presidential campaign the established Negro leadership urged a moratorium on demonstrations, and, perhaps somewhat surprisingly, its advice was generally followed. (No one should classify the riots that took place in Harlem, Philadelphia, and other Northern centers in the summer of 1964 as demonstrations.) It was January, 1965, before organized demonstrations, under responsible leadership, were resumed, and the first of them, running into the spring, took place in Selma (Dallas County), Alabama. The stated reason why Negroes led by Dr. Martin Luther King engaged in mass marching in Selma was that litigation seeking to force registration of Negro voters there, which the Justice Department had instituted four years earlier, produced next to no appreciable results.[1]

It should not be imagined, and Dr. King cannot believe, that everything would be different or that anything would be very different in Selma if the Justice Department's lawsuit had borne more fruit. "At least in the short run," former Assistant Attorney General Burke Marshall has conceded, "it cannot be argued that securing the right to vote leads to other federal rights. It is not that easy."[2] Political power has to be used to be effective, and that will take a great and expensive private effort—against considerable apathy and cynicism, reinforced by white pressure and economic blackmail—to see that those who can register do so, and that they vote. Even so, political power will not by itself change the shape of society, at least not quickly. But the vote *is* something, of course. And as a mark of full membership in the society it is a great deal.

Voting litigation has achieved substantial results elsewhere in Alabama, for example, in Macon County (Tuskegee). Here U.S. District Judge Frank M. Johnson ordered the registration of specified Negro applicants. Judge Johnson also did more. The Court of Appeals for the Fifth Circuit, which affirmed his actions, described his decree as follows:

The decree requires that registration applications be received [in Tuskegee] on at least two days a month and that the hundreds of Negroes then on the appearance list be processed at the rate of at least six simultaneously. The decree then provides that the Registrars must hold regular voter application days monthly processing, in regular and expeditious order, white and colored applicants in accordance with the appearance list to be maintained without racial discrimination. The Registrars may use racially nondiscriminatory writing tests of not to exceed 50 consecutive words from the Constitution. Registration applicants are to be notified within twenty days of the acceptance or rejection of the application and, where rejected, the exact reason therefor. An elaborate continuous policing machinery is established. This is done by requiring a monthly report to the Court of the dates and places of holding voter registration, the name, race and date of every application received, the action taken by the Registrars, and the date the certificate of registration was mailed or notification of rejection sent. A copy of every notification of rejection is to accompany this monthly report. The decree also prescribes that voting records should be open to examination by agents of the United States. It then requires a monthly report by the United States Attorney covering much of the data called for in the report from the state.

It is therefore evident that the district court thought it incumbent that the Federal Court, in many and varied ways, engage in a most detailed supervision of the day-to-day operation of voter registration.[3]

Thus were results achieved by Judge Johnson in Tuskegee and in one or two other places in Alabama. But where federal judges—e.g.,

W. Harold Cox of Mississippi,[4] and at least in one instance, Daniel Holcombe Thomas in Dallas County itself[5]—actively obstructed the government's lawsuits, or where, because they were busy or uninterested, they merely did not see fit to invest their energies after the fashion of Judge Johnson, the result was the snail's pace of Selma.

The Civil Rights Act of 1960 offered an alternative to the busy federal judge who hesitated to enter upon the all-absorbing kind of labor in voting cases that Judge Johnson undertook in Macon County and elsewhere. At the request of the Attorney General, the judge could make a finding that discrimination against prospective Negro voters was not isolated or scattered, but was "pursuant to a pattern or practice," and he could then appoint one or more federal "voting referees" and empower them in effect to qualify and register Negro applicants. These referees were to test the qualifications of Negro applicants, not in accordance with a strict reading of the state law, but by criteria no more stringent than the state registrar had in fact been using to qualify white voters. This was extremely important, for the state law generally prescribes very tough standards, which are in practice applied to disqualify those few Negroes who actually reach the registrar's desk, but are ignored for white voters. Each applicant for registration coming before a federal referee had first to prove, however, that he had tried and failed to obtain registration from the appropriate state official. Given the forbidding and sometimes violent atmosphere of the typical Black Belt county registrar's office and the many inconclusive delaying tactics available, this presented a serious obstacle to the federal registration of large numbers of Negroes. Nevertheless, federal referees could have achieved results, and in any event, things never got far enough for the obstacle just described to operate.

With one insignificant exception,[6] federal judges did not use the referee provision of the 1960 act. Some, of course, would not dream of using it. Others, with the best of will, must have felt that they were asked to take too great a responsibility. The statute never said that they *shall* appoint referees, only that they *may*. It was expecting quite a bit of district judges, with their local connections and their essentially local dependence, on their own responsibility to take what must be regarded as a radical, even a revolutionary, measure in the context of the traditional federal-state relationship, when Congress gave them discretion not to take it.

That the 1960 act placed an almost unsupportable burden on the district judges was foreseen by many at the time of its passage, and it was consequently proposed that the appointment of federal voting registrars be made an executive rather than a judicial function. Experience under the 1960 act made it quite clear that this was the only real solution. Anything else could be substantially frustrated not only by recalcitrant federal judges but also by communities with the will to confront the average federal judge with last-ditch resistance.

The Kennedy administration was moving in the necessary direction in June, 1963. The original Kennedy draft of what finally became the Civil Rights Act of 1964 included a provision empowering the Attorney General to ask federal judges, in effect, to qualify and register Negro voters in areas in which fewer than 15 per cent of Negroes of voting age were registered. When the Attorney General made such a request, this proposal left the federal judge with no discretion. There were no findings left for him to make. He had either to act or to fail to perform a plainly stated statutory duty. If he was too busy to act himself, he was firmly invited to appoint federal referees to assume the burden for him. Unfortunately, this provision was dropped early in the course of consideration of the act in the House.

In February, 1965, after the first few weeks of marching in Selma, the Johnson administration let it be known that it was preparing a new voting bill. It was widely assumed that the provision that was dropped from the 1964 act would be the starting point now, although, to be sure, this provision did not itself go far enough, since it failed to make the appointment of referees a political rather than a judicial responsibility. Then events took charge. On Sunday, March 7, Selma exploded. A proposed march of 50 miles on the highway from Selma to Montgomery (an exercise very dubiously, if at all, within the protection of the First Amendment, yet one carried out later in the month under the proper and more effective protection of federal troops) was stopped by order of Governor George Wallace of Alabama. Having stopped the march, Alabama state police and a mounted posse, assembled by Sheriff James G. Clark, Jr., of Dallas County, brutally attacked the crowd of Negroes and "outside agitators," including many white sympathizers who had come to Selma from around the country. Clubs and whips were freely used, and there were many injuries. Afterward a white Unitarian clergyman from Boston was beaten to death on the streets of Selma. It was a shocking episode, perhaps worse than anything that had happened in Birmingham two years earlier.

Although he declined to send in a federal force at this time, President Johnson a week later, on March 15, 1965, responded with a memorable address to the nation, delivered before a joint session of Congress. Like John F. Kennedy two years earlier, in the spring of Birmingham, President Johnson embraced the Negro protest movement. And like Kennedy before him, the President spoke with passion and genuine eloquence.

Having asked for a new voting rights bill, of which more presently, Johnson said:

> But even if we pass this bill, the battle will not be over. What happened in Selma is part of a far larger movement which reaches into every section and state of America. It is the effort of American Negroes to secure for themselves the full blessings of American life.
>
> Their cause must be our cause too. It is not just Negroes, but all of us, who must overcome the crippling legacy of bigotry and injustice.

And then the President added, in the very words that have been flung in the faces of the Sheriff Jim Clarks of the South: "We shall overcome." It signifies a very great deal in American life, and for the fulfillment of the promise of American life, that the President of the United States spoke this famous chant to a receptive joint session of the Congress. Johnson did not fail—as a Chief Executive cannot fail—to deplore any recourse to violence and to call for respect for law. We seek peace, he said, order, and unity. But, again like President Kennedy before him, he was not afraid to say also: "We will not accept the peace of stifled rights, the order imposed by fear, the unity that stifles protest. For peace cannot be purchased at the cost of liberty."

A few weeks later the bipartisan bill that became the Voting Rights Act of 1965 was sent up. It is a tough measure, make no mistake, the toughest since Reconstruction, and quite a different article from the Civil Rights Act of 1964. That statute proclaimed broad norms, concerning complex and ramified social problems and affecting the daily activities of millions of people, and it necessarily demanded no more than that the country live up to those norms, by and large, over time. No more could very well be expected. This voting statute deals with a narrow problem that has been solved in some places and reduced to clearly understood and manageable proportions elsewhere by intensive investigation and litigation over the past six or seven years. Its objective is no longer openly controversial in respectable quarters, as the objectives of the Civil Rights Act of 1964 still are. Not even Governor Wallace openly opposes the principle that qualified Negroes should vote and that Negroes should be qualified by the same standards as whites, although he and others argue on principle against desegregated schools and public facilities, for example.

The President's bill, therefore, could afford to be all muscle, and it was. It not only became the toughest statute since Reconstruction, it is a Reconstruction measure, for its coverage is frankly regional. But then voting is the one aspect of all the many aspects of the racial problem in the United States that is strictly regional. The right to vote may be impaired in one or another undesirable manner elswhere as well, but where else is it systematically denied on account of race? The Fifteenth Amendment forbids any state to deny the right to vote to anyone "on account of race, color, or previous condition of servitude," and that is all it does. The Voting Rights Act aims to enforce the Fifteenth Amendment, and that is why it is a regional measure. The South ought not to be singled out in respect of racial problems that it shares with other parts of the country. But voting is not one of these.

As passed in the Senate, the act would apply to those states and counties where, as of November, 1964, prospective voters were required to pass various tests (for example, literacy), where fewer than 50 per cent of individuals of voting age were registered or voted in November, 1964—a figure well below the average in the rest of the country—and where more than 20 per cent of persons of voting age are "nonwhite," according to the 1960 census. In addition, and regardless of tests, voter turnout, or nonwhite percentages, the act would apply also wherever a special survey, to be made at the request of the Attorney General, may show that fewer than 25 per cent of Negroes of voting age are registered. The area affected consists of Alabama, Georgia, Louisiana, Mississippi, and South Carolina, which administer tests and have more than 20 per cent nonwhites of voting age, and where the vote was under 50 per cent in November, 1964;* thirty-four counties in North Carolina, a state that has tests and 20 per cent nonwhites, and where the vote fell under 50 per cent in these 34 counties, although it was 51.8 per cent state-wide; a number of counties in Virginia, which has a literacy test and where the state-wide vote was 41 per cent, but where only some counties have over 20 per cent Negroes of voting age, the state-wide percentage being just under 20; and possibly some counties in Texas or Florida, for example, where it may be determined that fewer than 25 per cent of Negroes of voting age are registered, although the state-wide figure is certainly higher and although no tests are administered.

In the area affected, the right to vote may not be denied for failure to pass a reading or writing test, or one of the many kinds of tests requiring an applicant to show that he can correctly interpret, say, a provision of the state constitution, or that he knows and understands the federal and state constitutions and like documents. Nor may an applicant be disqualified for failure to prove "good moral character," or because he has not been vouched for by other registered voters. Only such qualifications as age, citizenship, residence, and perhaps soundness of mind and lack of criminal record remain unquestionably valid. But statistics alone do not lead to invocation of the statute and of these prohibitions. The statistics must coincide with past discrimination of continuing effect. Once the Attorney General and the Census Bureau have certified that the statute covers a given state or county, it is open to that state or county to come before a federal court and prove that it has not been discriminating or that "the effects" of its discrimination, if any, "have been effectively corrected" by its own action, so that, as Senator Mansfield said in debate, "persons of voting age desirous of voting were actually voting after having been registered without discrimination." To be sure, this is no easy escape hatch, since a state or county that has discriminated in the past is likely to be required, again as Senator Mansfield said, "actually to conduct registration or reregistration without tests over a period of time without any racial discrimination."[7] But if it has not discriminated or if it meets this requirement, it becomes as free of the provisions of this act as Maine or California.

* It was 36 per cent in Alabama (22.4 in Dallas County), 43.2 in Georgia, 47.3 in Louisiana (15.2 in West Feliciana County), 32.9 in Mississippi (13.3 in Tunica County), and 38 in South Carolina.

Where the statute applies, the Attorney General is empowered to have the Civil Service Commission appoint examiners who are authorized to register voters. Applicants need not have tried to register previously. However, it is not to be supposed that the Attorney General will send examiners to a county where Negroes have freely registered, even though such a county—and there are a few—may be located in a state that is covered as a whole. And indeed the statute forbids sending examiners to a county that can prove in court that it has registered over 50 per cent of its Negroes and that they continue to register and vote freely. Yet this escape clause, unlike the more rigorous one mentioned earlier, enables a county to avoid only the presence of federal examiners. More proof, showing that the effects of prior discrimination have been corrected, is required before the provisions outlawing tests can be escaped.

The elimination of tests, and particularly of literacy tests, has raised some constitutional doubts. For the basic constitutional position is that the state, not the federal government, sets qualifications for voting. The Constitution gives Congress some control—it is not clear how much—over this function as far as the election of federal officers is concerned. Hence it was thought by many that Congress could abolish by statute the poll tax in federal elections, although in the end even this was accomplished by constitutional amendment, just recently enacted. As to local elections, only the Fifteenth and Nineteenth Amendments are express statements of federal power, and they are restricted, respectively, to conferring the franchise on women and to forbidding discrimination because of race. Any other federal power over state elections must be found in the Fourteenth Amendment, which forbids actions that are arbitrary or capricious or that conflict with fundamental principles of fairness, liberty, and self-government, as the Supreme Court reads those principles in the American tradition. The Constitution also guarantees to "every State in this Union a Republican Form of Government," but this clause is generally regarded as the ultimate federal weapon, to be invoked only in the case of a radical abandonment by a state of democratic institutions.

The theory on which the act outlaws literacy tests and other devices is that they have in fact been used to discriminate against Negroes, and that they are, moreover, the natural breeding grounds of discrimination, since they are vague and subjective and confer broad discretion on the officials who administer them. Congress is entitled to draw a lesson from well-documented experience, to distrust local officials in certain areas, and to forbid them to impose any sort of literacy requirement until it is satisfied that past discrimination has been cured and that future discrimination is no longer likely. Congress is entitled also to outlaw existing tests, by whomever administered, for they are the classic instruments of discrimination. But what is the justification, once a federal examiner is on the scene, for outlawing and disregarding not merely existing tests but also the requirement of literacy as such, which has been held to be valid under the Fourteenth Amendment and, everything else being equal, also under the Fifteenth?[8] The answer may be that since Congress has the power to, and did, outlaw the requirement of literacy in places where it does not expect federal examiners to be assigned, it would be anomalous for that requirement to continue in force in places in which examiners are installed. Examiners are withheld, after all, from counties that behave themselves, and are sent to the hard-core ones. Those that are behaving should not be penalized by being required to register illiterates, when the policy of their state is not to do so and when others who have sinned more gravely need not do so. A county might come to prefer the presence of examiners rather than make its own efforts to cure discrimination, and that would certainly be a counterproductive result.

Apart from any constitutional inhibition, which the act quite probably thus avoids, and despite the fact that any literacy requirement will surely disqualify many Negroes in the South, and will do so, with painful injustice, because of the state's past neglect of its duty to educate Negroes as well as whites—apart from and despite all this, one may still doubt the wisdom of enfranchising illiterates in the South or anywhere. And the act need not be construed so as necessarily to enfranchise illiterates or result in anomaly unless it does. The act makes clear that an examiner may register as voters only those persons who "have the qualifications prescribed by State law not inconsistent with the Constitution and laws of the United States." The Attorney General and the Civil Service Commission are charged with telling the examiner what those qualifications are. They can, and in my judgment should, instruct the examiner that literacy is a qualification where in fact it has been. They should, however, also instruct him that (1) he may not apply any existing state literacy test, but should devise and administer a simple reading or signature test of his own, and that (2) he may not impose a literacy requirement at all where in fact (as is often true in hard-core areas) the local registrar has in the past not applied one to whites who are still on the voter rolls. Whatever test is devised for use by examiners should be permitted also—and can be permitted under the statutory definition of outlawed tests and devices—in areas that are covered by the act, but to which no examiners have been sent. So administered, the statute would not abolish the literacy qualification for voting where it has existed—existed not just on paper but in the actual implementation of the state voting law. The statute would abolish only literacy *tests* (not the qualification as such) that have been used to discriminate, and its effect would be the same, as it should be, whether or not examiners were on the scene.

Qualifications other than literacy imposed by such states as Alabama, Louisiana, Mississippi—interpretation and understanding tests, good moral character, vouchers—are different and must be regarded as outlawed altogether in any form. There can be no doubt that federal examiners should be instructed to ignore these qualifications entirely. And that is because, unlike literacy, these additional qualifications can be proved, in the process by which they were enacted—many of them quite recently—and in their consistent administration, to have had absolutely no purpose other than to discriminate against Negroes. They are simply not a bona fide exercise of the power of the states to set voter qualifications. Thus, while this statute was being drafted, the Supreme Court declared unconstitutional a Louisiana "interpretation" test (an applicant must "be able to understand" and "give a reasonable interpretation" of sections of the state or federal constitution as read to him by the registrar[9]), and indicated its readiness to strike down a similar Mississippi test, as well as a "good moral character" requirement.[10] Moreover, in the Louisiana case, the Court forbade application of a new "citizenship" test, unless all whites now registered should be purged from the rolls and required to reregister under it. And in December, 1964, in a case from Walthall County, Mississippi, the Court of Appeals for the Fifth Circuit found that whites were regularly "permitted to register without complying with the current and increasingly difficult provisions of the voters' registration statutes enacted by the state of Mississippi on a time schedule that coincided with the indications that more Negroes would make the effort to register." The Court therefore ordered that Negroes also be registered without regard to these "increasingly difficult provisions," subject only to a simple demonstration of literacy.[11] There was no constitutional difficulty in issuing this decree, and there will be none when federal examiners are instructed under the 1965 act to do what the Court of Appeals and the Supreme Court have done. If a state wishes to challenge the registration of one or more applicants (presumably on the ground that state qualifications have not been observed), it may do so before an examiner, and then in federal court. The facts of discrimination will then be placed on the record, as in the Walthall County case and in the Louisiana case decided by the Supreme Court, and that will conclude the matter. In the meantime, the challenged Negro voter may vote.

The essence of the 1965 act, and the source of its great promise, is that it makes an end run around the judicial process, and confronts recalcitrant Southern officials with the real locus of continuously effective federal power, which is the executive rather than the judiciary. Even under the best of conditions, the judicial process is sluggish and prone to delay and complications, and the best of conditions are far from prevailing with respect to voting cases in federal courts in the South. This act takes the federal district courts in the South out of the serious voter-registration business. Not even the initial test of the constitutionality of the statute as a whole can come up in a federal district court in the South. That test will have to be made in the federal courts of the District of Columbia. It is in the District of Columbia courts also that a state or county will have to try to take itself out of the provisions of the statute by proving that it has been guilty of no discrimination against Negro voters. Challenges to the action of an examiner in registering a Negro will go to federal courts in the South, but not to district courts, rather to courts of appeal, where the incidence and influence of segregationist judges is much lower. And—what is of the greatest importance—the burden of coming forward to litigate will rest on the state or county, not on a Negro applicant or on the Attorney General, and registration and voting will not have to await the outcome of the litigation but will proceed, following the examiner's initial action, while the judicial process winds its way to a conclusion. Moreover, the facts on which the judicial judgment will ultimately rest will be those found by an examiner—expeditiously, fairly, even perhaps sympathetically to the Negro applicant—not by such easily self-blinded federal judges as, say, Cox of Mississippi or Thomas of Alabama. The findings and decision of the examiner—called a hearing officer for purposes of passing on a challenge to a registration—will be conclusive on the court, as in the case of decisions of other administrative agencies, "unless clearly erroneous." These provisions spell action.

But there is one provision, slipped into the act on the floor of the Senate, that spells trouble. The act requires that persons illiterate in English be permitted to vote if they can show that they have completed the sixth grade in a school in Puerto Rico or elsewhere in the United States in which the language of instruction is not English. Sponsored by Senators Robert F. Kennedy and Jacob K. Javits of New York, this was an amendment intended to nullify the New York law making literacy in the English language a qualification for voting. It is thought that thousands of Spanish-speaking Puerto Ricans have been thus disqualified, and the amendment would enfranchise them. This may or may not be a desirable reform. Despite the existence of a foreign-language press, the stream of political information and argument in this country, and in New York, too, runs overwhelmingly in English. If a literacy requirement is reasonable, therefore, it is at least as reasonable that it be a requirement of literacy in English. On the other hand, it is surely reasonable to place greater stress than does New York on the ideal of universal suffrage, to have greater confidence in the foreign-language press, and perhaps also to be less impressed with the value of supposed direct personal communication between candidate and voter, especially by means of the printed word. But it is precisely this balance of reasonableness that puts the Kennedy-Javits provision in the gravest sort of constitutional doubt. For it derives no support from the Fifteenth Amendment, since the racial issue is not involved, but rests on the Fourteenth, if anywhere. Yet if Congress can use the Fourteenth Amendment any time it wishes to substitute a reasonable policy of its own for another equally reasonable policy preferred by a state, then there is nothing left of the state's power to prescribe such reasonable qualifications for voting as it sees fit.

This view of the constitutional position did not prevail in the Sen-

ate against Robert Kennedy's Puerto Rican amendment, but it gained
a narrow majority against a proposal by his brother Edward of
Massachusetts to outlaw the poll tax in the four states (Alabama,
Mississippi, Virginia, and Texas) that still levy it in state elections.
There would be no difficulty with the Edward Kennedy proposal if
evidence were at hand to show that the poll tax has been and is
systematically used to discriminate against Negroes. But there is
little such evidence. After all, when literacy and other tests, as well
as many forms of extralegal pressure, have been so successful in
keeping Negroes from registering, it is hardly to be expected that
the poll tax should have had any important effect. Yet although the
poll tax is small (especially since the act forgives taxes past due,
which would fall particularly on Negroes kept from voting in the
past), it does discriminate against the poor, and most Southern
Negroes are poor. But the white poor are hit also, always have been,
and were intended to be when the poll tax was first enacted as an
anti-Populist *and* anti-Negro measure. And so the argument must
proceed to the Fourteenth Amendment. Now, the sales tax also discriminates against the poor, and so does the cost of a driver's license
or a parking ticket. The Fourteenth Amendment does offer some protection to the poor, particularly as it renders matters somewhat
more equal for them when they find themselves in the clutches of
the criminal process, yet sales and license taxes remain pretty safely
constitutional. If a state were to impose one of those stiff eighteenth-
century property qualifications for voting, the Supreme Court ought
surely to strike it down as incompatible with more modern notions of
representative government. But the poll tax will amount to a dollar
or two. It is more of a nuisance than a real impediment to voting,
and if it is an impediment, then it is not a more serious one than the
literacy requirement or even just an annual registration requirement.

But is the poll tax, as the Fourteenth Amendment requires, reasonable? Literacy, age, residence, sanity, good moral character, absence
of a criminal record—all these are, everything else being equal,
rational considerations in the selection of a suitable electorate. But
what in the world does possession of two dollars have to do with
fitness to vote? Well, there are things to be said. The poll tax, it will
be argued, though small, gives pause. It ensures that the act of voting
is deliberate, that the citizen participates in the process of government

not casually but with a certain will. And if this point and other ones are no more than faintly plausible, the answer is that no more than faint plausibility should be required to save an exercise of an otherwise plenary state power from being held arbitrary and capricious.

In *Breedlove v. Suttles*,[12] decided in 1937, the Supreme Court sustained the poll tax against a Fourteenth Amendment attack. This does not mean that the issue is settled forever—the Supreme Court may unsettle it in a case coming from Virginia that is before it now—and it does not mean that the sense of Congress, which is that poll taxes are bad, will be entirely without influence. But an assertion by Congress that the poll tax has been used to discriminate against Negroes remains no more than an assertion if the facts do not support it. And the exigencies of the racial problem ought not to result in encroachments on the state power to set voting qualifications when those exigencies are not pressing or even present. Happily, aside from the Puerto Rican amendment, the Voting Rights Act as passed in the Senate will at last do all that is necessary, but will also do no more than is necessary, to eliminate racial discrimination in voting. This was the scheme of the Fifteenth Amendment also.

THE
WARREN
COURT:
DEFENSES
AND CRITIQUES

IV

Chief Justice
Warren
and the
Presidency

9

After President Eisenhower's heart attack of 1955 there was a season when it was assumed that he would not run for a second term. During that season, which extended into early 1956, speculation was rife that Chief Justice Warren, but recently retired from active politics (he was governor of California when he came to the Court in 1953), would be the Republican presidential nominee. And this despite the fact that, at his earliest decent opportunity, the Chief Justice had declared that he felt happy and useful where he was and did not intend to re-enter politics.

Although there was no evidence of general public alarm, it is fair to say that a slight shudder of apprehension disturbed the body politic at mention in this fashion of the name of the Chief Justice of the United States. For the possible entry into, which is itself a form of actual presence in, the political arena of a member of the Supreme Court necessarily raises issues of the function of the Court and the nature of the judicial process. With, in Melville's famous phrase, a shock of recognition, we see both the incompatibility of that process with politics and its inextricable involvement in politics.

The incompatibility comes about, paradoxically, because of the involvement.

De Tocqueville early remarked that "scarcely any question arises in the United States which does not become, sooner or later, a subject of judicial debate." For this reason the Supreme Court of the United States, more than any other court in the world, requires of its members the talent and the training for statecraft. "The considerations which determine decision [in the Supreme Court] are more often an understanding of practical situations, an appraisal of practical needs and a choice between competing policies than they are . . . a knowledge of legal lore." So wrote a great teacher of constitutional law, the late Thomas Reed Powell.

There follow two consequences, which are in a sense at war with each other. One is that quite naturally, given the requirements of the Court's work, its members are often men of political stature and availability or at least men whose talents would incline them toward political office. Though only lawyers have been appointed, we do not customarily choose our Supreme Court justices from a professional pool of leaders of the bar, nor do we employ a regular system of promotion of lower court judges to the Supreme Court. The second consequence is that with respect to no other court is it so important that politicians or potential politicians translated to the bench remove themselves from—rise above, we like to think—political life. The Supreme Court, not an elective body, time and again decides questions which our elective institutions dealt with only the other day. This would be intolerable were the Court not free of the infirmities we put up with in the legislative and executive branches. There would then be no justification for the Court's electoral irresponsibility. We persist in regarding politics tolerantly as something of a game. But we think of the Supreme Court as entirely serious business. We want from it "a sober second thought" on the merits, not a replaying of the game. And it strains our belief in the strength of man's character to trust a Supreme Court justice who is actively interested in partisan political considerations to disregard them in rendering judgments to which they can be related with such singular ease.

So it is that in appointing successful politicians, fitted to perform the Court's task of statesmanship, we insist that they become former ones. This is a lot to ask, and it is taking chances. History records predominantly the success of the system, but also instances in which the gamble has failed, and justices have succumbed, with unfortunate consequences for the Court, to the pull of the life that once they had led or of the aspiration that once they had harbored.

For about a generation, commencing before the Civil War and ending some time after the contested election of 1876, the Court went through what is perhaps the period of its lowest prestige and effectiveness. There were, no doubt, a number of causes for this, some of the Court's own making, some not. But it is more than coincidence that this period embraced the tenures of four justices who entertained open presidential aspirations and engaged in vigorous political activity. The most notoriously politically minded of these was John McLean, whose biography, by Francis P. Weisenburger, is fittingly titled *Life of John McLean: A Politician on the United States Supreme Court*. McLean had been in the Cabinet of Monroe and J. Q. Adams, and came to the Court in 1830 by appointment of Andrew Jackson. He was a presidential candidate in 1836, in 1848, and in 1852, failing of nomination each time. In the Republican convention of 1856 he hit a high of 196 votes. Throughout his career he consistently aired his views on current political questions, including questions which were on their way up to the Court. He was frequently and strongly attacked for his behavior, and made no great mark as a judge.

Three of Lincoln's appointees followed, though not as flagrantly, in McLean's footsteps. Salmon Portland Chase, the sixth chief justice, had been senator and governor, and a candidate at the Republican conventions of 1856 and 1860. Until 1864 he had been Lincoln's Secretary of the Treasury, and had finally resigned for reasons not entirely unconnected with an abortive candidacy to succeed Lincoln in that year. After Chief Justice Taney's death in 1864, Lincoln, although he had previously indicated that he had Chase's appointment in mind, hesitated for several months before sending his name to the Senate, because he feared that Chase would be unable to abandon his ambition to be President. Lincoln was quite right. In 1868 Chase sought the presidential nomination on both tickets, though he made a stronger attempt in the Democratic convention. He was unsuccessful, despite his own efforts and those of his celebrated daughter, the beautiful, beguiling, and influential Kate Chase Sprague. According to one of Chase's biographers, this political activity did not fail to shake public confidence in the disinterestedness of the Chief Justice's decisions.

In 1872, after ten years on the bench, David Davis, Lincoln's friend, mentor, and 1860 convention floor manager, accepted, without resigning, a presidential nomination from a minor party, with a view to enhancing his candidacy at the Liberal Republican convention of that year. His effort came to nothing. Five years later Davis left the Court to take a seat in the Senate. Like McLean, he had been criticized for his political activity.

Stephen J. Field, the last of Lincoln's appointees to pursue the Presidency, was considerably the strongest judge of the three; indeed, he is a massive figure in the history of the Court. Field had had a political and judicial career in the rough-and-tumble of frontier California before his appointment in 1863, but had not been a national political figure. At the Democratic convention of 1868, he was placed in nomination, although this was a move apparently made without any encouragement from the Justice. Following the contested election of 1876, however, Field, while he publicly maintained a relatively correct attitude, began to work hard for the Democratic nomination in 1880. His biographer intimates the suspicion that Field's opinions of the period, among them a dissent from the Court's holding that the Fourteenth Amendment decreed equality in jury service for Negroes, might have been politically motivated.

Other incidents might be mentioned. Inaugurating the McLean tradition, Justice Smith Thompson in 1828 made an unsuccessful race for the governorship of New York against Martin Van Buren. Earlier yet, but in quite a different fashion, John Jay, first in the line in which Chief Justice Warren is fourteenth, was a candidate for the same governor's chair. He lost in 1792, and won three years later, resigning from the Court. Neither time did Jay campaign. But the single remaining important episode, a relatively recent one, contrasts significantly with the experience of the Civil War period described above. It was unprecedented when it occurred, and is likely to remain unique.

Charles Evans Hughes, then governor of New York, was appointed a justice in 1910 by President Taft. In 1912 the Republican party was hopelessly split between Taft and Theodore Roosevelt, and Hughes was approached concerning the nomination. He emphatically and publicly refused to permit his name to be used, writing the chairman of the Republican convention that he would decline the nomination if tendered. In 1916 the Republican schism was equally serious. Only Hughes could come close to commanding the allegiance of both the Progressives and the Old Guard. Hughes again wrote a public letter declining to be a candidate and asking that his name not be presented. Nevertheless, there was a considerable public boom for him and much private activity in his behalf. At no time did Hughes take the slightest part in any of this. He was nominated—truly drafted—and promptly resigned from the Court. No issue was made of his judicial behavior during the campaign. Holmes wrote him: "Your first thought was of duty." Hughes subsequently served as Secretary of State, and later yet returned to the Court as chief justice.

The Court has endured despite the McLeans. But its experience with the McLeans demonstrates that the recurrence of justices with manifest political aspirations would in time destroy an institution whose strength derives from consent based on confidence. On the other hand, the Hughes episode surely proves that it is possible for a man of unimpeachable integrity to satisfy the demands of political duty without first impairing his usefulness to the Court and the Court's usefulness to the nation. The line to hold is that of scrupulous abstention from political activity before resignation to make a political race. In these circumstances, that is, following a genuine draft, there is little harm in the resignation. The danger lies in suspicions, arising before resignation, that a justice is permitting the discharge of his functions to be influenced by the desire to, or by the likelihood that he will, make a political race.

The situation is for all the world like that which prevails in an academic community when romance threatens between a member of the faculty and a student. There is not much harm in their being married. Anxiety centers on the courtship. It is awkward, unseemly, and may give occasion for dire suspicions. The more so if there is no marriage. Such a union must simply happen—suddenly. But marriages like that between Justice Hughes and the Republican party in 1916 are rarer than those made in heaven.

History did not repeat itself forty years later. For this we may be grateful indeed. Attitudes toward the Court in 1916 were altogether peaceable. The Court in 1916 was relatively removed from the center of the political struggle. This was not the case in 1956. Speculation about the Chief Justice's possible candidacy was happily short-lived, and the Chief Justice himself was so obviously remote from it that no one could well mistake his position. But had the speculation continued, and even had the Chief Justice been drafted, much additional fuel would have been innocently but effectively provided to those—especially in the South—who were mounting a concerted and remarkably unrestrained attack against the Court and all its works.

The
Law
Clerks

10

THE AMERICAN PEOPLE have always had a consuming and not very sympathetic curiosity about confidential advisers to their high officers of government. The real or supposed influence of such advisers —from Amos Kendall and the other members of President Jackson's "kitchen cabinet," to Wilson's Colonel House and to Harry Hopkins and Harry Vaughan and Sherman Adams—has been an indestructible political issue. And naturally so. For the issue evokes our people's sound distrust of anonymous or otherwise apparently irresponsible power.

Given the agitation about the Supreme Court, and the condition of sputtering rage that grips the Court's more excitable critics, it was to be expected that the Justices of the Court would not long be spared the fate of many another public man: that is, a flanking attack intended to strike at them through their entourage. For, while it is most often legitimate and frequently necessary in a democratic society to inquire into the role and authority of an official's private advisers, it is unfortunately also too easy and too readily profitable to do so. Hence, whether or not legitimate, it is standard technique; a first resort when passions rise, particularly against a formidable foe. And so the Justices' private secretaries—law clerks, as they are called—have recently come in for some ill-tempered and ill-intentioned scrutiny.

The law clerks have been characterized as a "second team," as "ghost writers," and, more insinuatingly, as wielders of "unorthodox influence." The charge has also been made that the influence they exert comes from the "political left."[1]

The short answer is this: first, the law clerks are in no respect any kind of kitchen cabinet, though they are not to be dismissed as just messenger boys either; second, their political views and emotional preferences, while they enliven the lunch hour, make no perceptible difference to anything; and third, as a group the clerks will no more fit any single political label than will any other eighteen young Americans who are not picked on a political basis. These assertions can be substantiated by a look at what is known of the clerks and their function.

To begin with, who are they and how do they get there? Their positions are created by statute. There are two to each Associate Justice, three for the Chief Justice, and incidentally, one each for judges of the lower federal courts. The Justices, except for Justice Douglas, who has been making do with one, normally take their full complement. The clerks are recent law school graduates, usually young men in their mid-twenties. Their records at their respective schools are always among the best. That is ordinarily the principal factor in their selection. And their careers are almost certain to have included service on their school's law review. These reviews are a singular species of scholarly publication, being student-edited and largely student-written. I shall say more presently about them and about their role in the profession.

A law clerk is normally appointed by his justice on the strength of the recommendation of a law school dean or other professor. Of course, there will generally have been a personal interview, and the Justice may well have laid down some specifications, such as that his clerks come from the region of his own origin. Tenure is one year, sometimes two, very infrequently longer. Over the long run, the great national law schools, such as Harvard, Yale, Columbia, Pennsylvania, Chicago, tend to be most heavily represented. But the lesser schools are by no means excluded. The group of clerks in office during one recent year picked at random included graduates of the law schools of the University of California, New York University, U.C.L.A., and Notre Dame, Southern Methodist and Washington Universities.

This is how clerks are made. What they are made to do is not quite so simply described. For one thing, there are variations from office to office, and from time to time in the same office, and from case to case with the same clerk. For another, there can be no up-to-date particulars, for such particulars involve live issues and live judges, and the judicial process requires a degree of privacy incomparably stricter than is fitting in the legislative or executive process. Yet some general matters have become common knowledge, based in large part on historical information that has emerged following the longish period of incubation imposed by the requirements of judicial privacy. There is, one might add, also some information that has been let out before the period of incubation has run. Naturally, this information is half-incubated, or as some might say, half-baked.

Law clerks, then, generally assist their respective justices in searching the lawbooks and other sources for materials relevant to the decision of cases before the Court. The task of legal research has become enormous for everyone in the profession. The day of the single, unassisted practitioner is over, and so is the day of the unassisted judge. The clerks often present the fruits of their searches to their justices together with their recommendations. They go over drafts of opinions and may suggest changes. They tend to see a lot of their justices, and talk a great deal with them. And the talk is mostly about law and cases. They listen a good deal also, being the only properly available sounding board aside from other justices.

The process of selection described above is sufficient, I should think, to explode the assertion that the political views of the "left" tend to predominate among the clerks. Only on the hysterical assumption that our universities are staffed by Machiavellian radicals and that our brightest young men are incapable of thinking for themselves can such an assertion be maintained. But the indication, also given above, of the tasks performed by the clerks cannot be said to prove anything one way or another about their influence on the disposition of cases that come before the Court. And of course the parties to such cases and their counsel might well be disturbed to think that influence of this sort is exerted. Yet we can surely start with the presumption, as far as specific results are concerned, that it is likely to be beyond the power of these inexperienced young men, as it would be beyond the power of wiser and older heads, to turn the minds of the generally strong, experienced, and able lawyers and statesmen who sit on the Supreme Court.

Nothing that is known about the present Court and nothing in the historical record—nothing that is not either unfounded rumor or remote hearsay—speaks against this presumption. But what history does reveal and what reflection can confirm and generalize is that law clerks are nevertheless more than just youthful runners of research errands. The larger function they perform is to be understood in light of a suggestive remark of Jeremy Bentham's. "The law," said Bentham, "is not made by judge alone, but by judge and company." We take our judicial law, that is, not merely from nine men, but from a profession—with all that that implies in intellectual discipline and in standards rooted in tradition.

The role that the profession plays—by subjecting the Court's work to informed criticism and appraisal and by producing disinterested scholarship—can be plainly, sometimes spectacularly, traced in the development of all branches of our law. It is to be traced, however—*pace* litigants and counsel—to the process; and the process of lawmaking is not arrested and it is not characterized by the decision of any single case. It lives by testing and enlarging general ideas, and it is forever rethinking last year's case and projecting future, as yet unformed, cases. It is to be observed not so much in the specific disposition of a case—though that is important, to be sure—as in the opinion that explains and justifies and generalizes the result.

In the early days, it is fair to say, the nexus between the Court and the profession—the company in which a justice made law—was chiefly an intimate, well-informed, specialized, largely resident Supreme Court bar. Such a bar is no more. Today, fewer and fewer lawyers, aside from the handful—albeit the very distinguished handful—in the Office of the Solicitor General of the United States, appear regularly before the Supreme Court and regularly scrutinize its work. Most lawyers who come there now pay the Court only episodic attention. I don't mean that the practicing bar as a whole has lost touch with the work of the Court; certainly not the organized bar. But there has been a change. The place of an intimate Supreme Court bar has been taken by the academic branch of the profession, which has itself become established and accepted only since the turn of the century, in the wake of the very changes that have caused the disappearance of the Supreme Court bar as a discrete group.

But, of course, the law teachers of the country are spread over the fifty states. What they lack in continual attendance at the Court they make up through the law reviews and through the Justices' law clerks—two institutions which, by what can hardly be deemed mere historical accident, have also come to maturity only since the turn of the century.

The role of the law reviews is readily apparent. It is there that those who make it their business to analyze and appraise the work of the Court do their analyzing and appraising. And it is there that under their guidance—perhaps auspices is a better word; on most law reviews the reins are exceedingly loose—students publish research of the most painstaking sort. Concerning the role of the law clerks it is necessary to start with a disclaimer. Of course, no law teacher whose student is about to commence a term as law clerk to a justice gives him instructions to convey certain ideas. To believe that this could happen is to take a naïvely depreciating view of everyone concerned, not least of all the clerk. And yet the clerks, arriving every year, *are* a conduit from the law schools to the Court. They bring with them, and they convey with varying degrees of explicitness, the intellectual atmosphere from which they are newly come. They complement the law reviews on the Justice's desk with the additional, rather more inchoate ideas and arguments and puzzlements that fill the classrooms and corridors of any university worthy of the name. And that is performing no trivial function. The marble temple in which the Justices have their being and exercise their great powers can be a very isolated place. In such a place, who can doubt the value of a bright young fellow, fresh from the interplay of ideas that marked his law school and law review career, and now poised at the Justice's elbow, always willing and able to do intellectual combat?

Of the more precise nature of the law clerk's function (as well as of its limitations), the record of history provides some illustrations. Perhaps one example will be of interest. In the course of the Court's consideration of a case decided in 1922, Justice Louis D. Brandeis prepared a memorandum for his colleagues urging them to overrule an early doctrine under which many state license and other taxes had been struck down as violating the Commerce Clause of the Constitution. The doctrine had been much criticized by the profession, notably by Professor Thomas Reed Powell of Harvard, whose articles Brandeis had read, as his notes show. Brandeis prepared a first draft of a memorandum himself, and showed it to his law clerk, William G. Rice, a Harvard law graduate, now professor of law at the University of Wisconsin. Rice joined issue vigorously and radically; not on the result in this case—that wasn't in question —but on what new doctrine, what new generalization was to grow out of it. The new test, Rice thought, should simply be whether the state tax discriminated against interstate commerce. Anything else, Rice wrote the Justice, would be "a very primitive conception." Well, "a very primitive conception" is what emerged in the end, but there is a draft in Brandeis' hand in which he tried out Rice's idea—which, in turn, was not altogether new, had other advocates, and has since gained fresh adherents, including some justices.[2]

Evidence of such interplay between clerk and justice, which cannot but be fruitful, is repeated again and again in the Brandeis judicial papers. Sometimes an idea or a striking phrase or sentence offered by the clerk would find its way into an opinion. What is more important, the way to the Justice's mind was always open.

In this fashion the law schools and the law reviews, and through them the law clerks—the law clerks, and through them the law schools and the law reviews—make their limited yet important contribution. We should, I suggest, draw much assurance from that contribution, for it serves to enhance the intellectual integrity of the judicial process and is in its modest way one of the influences that keep judicial law rationally responsive to the needs of the day. Only those who cannot conceive of intellectual disinterestedness, those who, having despaired of our system of higher education, have totally despaired also of the nation's future—only those have cause to be uneasy that there are law clerks at Court.

The relationship between the Court and its professional company is not a one-way street. It should be apparent that the institution of clerking has also the attributes of any craft's apprentice system. Great judges project their influence into the future—in ways that are beyond the printed word—through their law clerks. Whether this will be true of the present generation of clerks we cannot know. But in the past the relationship again has been with the universities more than with any other of the walks of a lawyer's professional life. Over half of Justice Brandeis' twenty-one law clerks became teachers of law, and they are all marked men. One, David Riesman, has strayed, but not from the universities. Five of Justice Stone's clerks are outstanding law teachers, as are a number of Justice Holmes's. And Dean Acheson, who clerked for Brandeis, is not without academic connections, having served for over a generation as a Fellow of the Yale Corporation. Of course, many clerks become important practitioners or judges. Thus Brandeis' first clerk, Senior Judge Calvert Magruder of the federal Court of Appeals in Boston, is one of the two or three ablest judges in the country. And one former clerk (to the late Chief Justice Vinson) is now Justice Byron R. White, the first law clerk to return home in this splendid fashion. All this, though it merely evokes the golden past, deserves mention just the same as exemplifying the finest traditions of an apprentice system, which might be thought not to need additional excuses for existing. These, however, it has.

Curbing
the
Union

11

This engagingly ominous title, suggested to me by Professor Karl W. Deutsch of the Political Science Department at Yale, is a fair comment on three states' rights constitutional amendments put forward in December, 1962, by the Council of State Governments. Two of these proposed amendments were approved by thirteen state legislatures, a fact that subsequently brought considerable notoriety to all three. It is not too much to say, indeed, that the amendments caused widespread alarm. They are interesting, however, not so much because of any danger they still represent to the existing constitutional structure (although there is about them something of the menace of the unexploded bomb) but because they bespeak a certain discontent, a certain mood and certain grievances that stir a substantial and perfectly respectable body of opinion.

Briefly (I shall give the full text presently[1]) the first of the proposed amendments would alter the Amending Clause itself. It would enable two thirds of the state legislatures to initiate a constitutional amendment without action by Congress, or by a national convention, or, indeed, in any national forum whatever. The second would overrule *Baker v. Carr*, the famous legislative apportionment case of 1962, and the decisions that followed it. The third would create a Court of the Union, consisting of the chief justices of the fifty states, as a more supreme Supreme Court, empowered to overrule the decisions of the present Supreme Court in certain circumstances.

Discussion must begin by placing these proposals in context. The Supreme Court, possessing, in the famous Hamiltonian phrase, neither the sword nor the purse, but relying only on its place in the hearts of its countrymen and on their law-abiding habits, is engaged in a continuous colloquy with the nation. Over time, the Court proposes and the nation disposes. This relationship breaks up roughly into recurring cycles. The Court proposes major ideas—they are relatively few in number—and a period of vigorous debate follows, during which the Court's proposed principles are far from stable. Eventually, and for a time, consensus is arrived at, which may or may not coincide in this or that degree with the principles initially broached by the Court. There follows a period during which the Court consolidates the position on the basis of the consensus, and this is normally a period of relatively placid acceptance of the Court's work. Then, before long, the Court tackles some other subject, or an old one once more, and the cycle begins again. Of course, I oversimplify. This is a model. Real life is not so neat. Yet, schematically, this is how things operate, and since 1954, when the *School Segregation Cases* were first decided, we have been in a cycle of debate and turmoil. If there is anything unusual about this particular cycle, it is only that the Court has not waited as long as may have been usual in the past to consolidate its gains from its first enterprise—the segregation decision—before floating one or two other major principles.

It is characteristic of the debating portion of the cycle that constitutional amendments are proposed by the bushel. Like various legislative proposals aimed at reforming the Court or overruling its work—"curbing the Court," in a phrase popularized by former Justice James F. Byrnes in the spring of 1956[2]—proposed amendments serve as convenient summations, rallying cries, or slogans, and they constitute quite an accustomed feature of the debate. They have been with us during the decade since the decision in the *School Segregation Cases*, as the most casual survey of the Congressional Record will readily reveal. They have always been with us. I am about to touch on a recently suggested amendment which would empower Congress to override any constitutional decision by a two-thirds vote. Senator LaFollette made the same proposal in the course of his third-party presidential campaign in 1924. In those years also, Felix Frankfurter favored repealing the Due Process Clauses of the Fifth and Fourteenth Amendments.[3] And there is good reason to believe that so—privately—did Justice Brandeis.

I offer—chiefly for the edification of the collector of curios—a sampling of proposals for constitutional amendment culled from the Congressional Record from 1954 to date. It turns out, to begin with, that the first of the proposals put forward by the Council of State Governments, the one to amend the Amending Clause, is nothing new. It is, moreover, comparatively conservative. In 1955 a Joint Resolution was introduced in the House to amend the Constitution so as to provide that the legislatures of any twelve states could submit an amendment directly for ratification, without the intervention of any Congressional action.[4] Nor is the proposal to overrule *Baker v. Carr* new. Thirteen House Resolutions proposing constitutional amendments to overrule *Baker v. Carr* were introduced in the first year or so following decision of the case. In June, 1964, the Court extended the holding of *Baker v. Carr* in a series of new decisions, and a second rash of proposed amendments immediately broke out, including one—relatively moderate—that was endorsed by the Republican platform of 1964, and is sponsored by the Republican leadership in Congress.[5] Going further afield and listing draft amendments in a vague descending order of importance and generality of application, one finds: A series of proposals to restrict the Supreme Court's power to reverse its own precedents—which the Court, of course, did in the *School Segregation Cases;*[6] another series, similar to the LaFollette proposal already mentioned, seeking to empower Congress to overrule the Court's constitutional decisions;[7] a proposal —which might seem too outlandish to mention even in this context were it not that its author was the recently retired dean of the House, the powerful Carl Vinson of Georgia—in effect to reverse John Marshall's decision in *McCulloch v. Maryland* (1819) and to enforce a reading of the Constitution as granting to the federal government only those powers which are *expressly* mentioned, to the exclusion of any implied powers;[8] a proposal to reverse the gradual process by which portions of the first eight Amendments— the Bill of Rights—have been made applicable to the states, and to free the states of any further embarrassment from those Amendments;[9] an ample and continuing series of proposals to reverse not only the *School Segregation Cases* but all other racial decisions, and to leave the states entirely to their own devices in regulating the relations between the races;[10] and finally, an equally ample and continuing series of draft amendments that would make structural changes in the Court, such as requiring unanimity before a state statute could be declared unconstitutional, or changing the lifetime tenure of the justices to a term of years, or prescribing new qualifications for appointment, including one that would allow only sitting members of state Supreme Courts to be appointed to the federal Supreme Court.[11]

All these attempts to reform the Supreme Court and to correct its work are by way of attempted constitutional amendments. I have yet to offer even a sampling of proposed *legislation* aimed at the Court and at its recent controversial decisions. Legislative efforts are, of course, much more dangerous. It is not easily forgotten how close some of the notorious Jenner-Butler bills of 1957 and 1958 came to enactment. These bills would have removed from Supreme Court jurisdiction—and though they were of somewhat doubtful constitutionality, they would nevertheless in some degree have been successful in removing—all cases (a) affecting the conduct of Congressional committees, (b) relating to security dismissals of government employees, and (c) having to do with state antisubversive legislation.[12] Nor should the famous H.R. 3 be forgotten, which would have materially, if somewhat unpredictably, altered the Court's function in reconciling concurrent or conflicting federal and state statutes under the Supremacy Clause.[13] But there is also a large variety of other proposals that have never been heard of. There have been a number attacking the Court's jurisdiction in racial cases.[14] And there have been legislative attempts, quite possibly valid if enacted, to hamper the appointing power by imposing a set of qualifications for prospective justices, although the Constitution now mentions none.[15]

The point of this parade of horribles is that in such a period as this such horribles are always with us. There is, therefore, nothing particularly startling in themselves about the three proposals put forward by the Council of State Governments. They simply take their place in the parade. If there is anything notable about them, anything at all extraordinary, justifying the brouhaha they have provoked, it is not in their nature or timing, nor in their adoption by a baker's dozen of state legislatures, but in their sponsorship. Thirteen state legislatures—that is not really an alarming number, no more alarming than the number of voices that can be summoned against the Court in a Congressional debate. You can probably get a dozen legislatures to come out in favor of almost anything that they do not themselves have the power to do and that they do not really believe in their heart of hearts will ever be done. Nor do I, for one, find confirmation here of the wisdom of *Baker v. Carr.* The short, silent, and then arrested progress of these amendments through thirteen state legislatures seems to me to illustrate not so much that our legislatures are unrepresentative bodies as that they are secret places. The notable thing about these amendments is that they were sponsored by the Sixteenth General Assembly of the States, held under the auspices of the Council of State Governments.

The Council of State Governments is an admirable organization, dedicated to high and worthwhile purposes, of which regrettably little is known. Perhaps this unfortunate circumstance is owing to the kind of subject matter that is generally grist to the organization's mill. It is a subject matter worthy in the extreme, but not as a rule highly charged. The Council of State Governments may be a relatively secret place for much the same reason that a state legislature is. In December, 1958, for example, the Council's General Assembly of the States, which four years later was to propose the constitutional amendments I am discussing, passed resolutions recommending study of problems of atomic energy, water development, flood insurance, mental retardation, the aging, and highway safety. These matters were to be studied. The only subjects on which the Assembly chose to commit itself flatly were statehood for Hawaii, which it was for, and the use of virulent hog cholera virus for vaccination purposes, which it was against and recommended prohibiting. Meaning no disrespect either way, the Council of State Governments reminds one of nothing so much as the Council of Europe—not any of the institutions of the Common Market or the Coal and Steel Community, but the Council of Europe, with its little Parliament of Man—or perhaps one or another of the technical agencies affiliated with the UN. The Council of State Governments normally labors earnestly and thanklessly in distant vineyards, has some influence, and can show some beneficial results, but is utterly without power and suffers not a little from a sense of frustration.

The Council originated in private initiative, and with an attachment to the Department of Political Science at the University of Chicago in the 1930's. As now organized, it is supported and recognized by state legislatures, which create local councils, called Commissions of Interstate Cooperation and consisting typically of ten members of the legislature and five administrative officials. The central Council is essentially a research organization, governed by a Board of Delegates drawn from the state councils. Information is exchanged, there are publications of common interest, there is a staff and an executive director, and secretariat services are provided for such bodies as the Governor's Conference, the Conference of State Chief Justices, the National Association of State Attorneys General, the National Association of State Budget Officers, the National Legislative Conference, the National Association of State Purchasing Officials, the Parole and Probation Compact Administrators Association, the Association of Juvenile Compact Administrators, and the National Conference of Court Administrative Officers. Biennially there is a General Assembly of the States, a little parliament to which the local councils appoint delegates, who are mostly state legislators. The states vote as units in the Assembly, each having one vote. The Sixteenth General Assembly of the States, which met in December, 1962, and proposed the amendments we are discussing, was attended by more than 300 people comprising delegations from 47 states. In the past, so far as I can discover, the Council of State Governments and its General Assembly of the States seem to have irritated or alarmed no one but the far-right fringe, which they have now, no doubt, delighted. A writer in the *American Mercury* for January, 1960, accused the Council of engaging in a "uniform mail-order law movement," of proposing "half-baked experiments in weird [*sic!*] fields, such as urban renewal demolition and mental health legislation," and, in culmination, of being "part of a linkage that leads into Red Russia."[16]

That from such an innocuous and well-meaning source should

come proposals to stand the constitutional system on its head—this, I think, is what was startling and alarming. This was what separated these proposed amendments out of the common run to which in such a time as this we are fairly accustomed. Here, then, are the amendments.

The first would amend Article V of the Constitution, the Amending Clause, to read in its entirety as follows:

The Congress, whenever two-thirds of both Houses shall deem it necessary, or, on the application of the Legislatures of two-thirds of the several states, shall propose amendments to this Constitution, which shall be valid to all intents and purposes, as part of this Constitution, when ratified by the Legislatures of three-fourths of the several states. Whenever application from the Legislatures of two-thirds of the total number of states of the United States shall contain identical texts of an amendment to be proposed, the President of the Senate and the Speaker of the House of Representatives shall so certify, and the amendment as contained in the application shall be deemed to have been proposed, without further action by Congress. No state, without its consent, shall be deprived of its equal suffrage in the Senate.

Under Article V as it now stands, amendments can be proposed by a two-thirds vote of both Houses of Congress or by a "Convention for proposing Amendments," which is to be called by Congress on the application of the legislatures of two thirds of the states. The convention method, never heretofore employed, is, incidentally, the method by which the Council of State Governments proposes that its three amendments, including this one, be submitted for ratification. The Council's proposals are all directed to the state legislatures, which are to transmit them to Congress in the form of a request to call a convention for proposing amendments, which, in turn, would then submit them to ratification. That is all that the dozen or so state legislatures that have acted on these amendments have done—they have transmitted them to Congress which, when two thirds of the legislatures of the states have made exactly the same transmittals, is to call a convention, which in turn may or may not submit these amendments for ratification by three fourths of the states.

This unprecedented, although allowable, procedure itself raises some interesting questions.[17] The proposed amendment to Article V, at any rate, while hoping to get itself enacted by this procedure, would then abolish it, and substitute direct proposing power on the part of two thirds of the state legislatures. Thus a method would be made available for proposing amendments without the need for discussion in any national forum. And there is another change, this time in the ratification rather than in the proposal process. As Article V now stands, Congress has the option to submit amendments, no matter how proposed, for ratification by three fourths of the states either through their legislatures or in special conventions, called in each of the states as Congress may provide. It is proposed to abolish the ratifying conventions as an option, and that is something of a change, although they are an option that Congress has exercised but once. Such are the proposed changes in Article V. The provision that no state may without its consent be deprived of its equal vote in the Senate is old.

The flaw in the proposal is obvious. When we come to changing the law under which we live as a nation we ought to discuss it as a nation in a national forum. The sum of discussions in fifty legislatures is not a national discussion, it is not national consideration in a national forum such as Congress or a convention for proposing amendments. Eliminating the option of ratification by state conventions is also objectionable because it would remove an element of flexibility, which, although it may not in the past have been of much use, cannot by the same token be pointed to as the source of any evil. If the question is, shall we or shall we not retain an element of flexibility which cannot be shown to have ever hurt anyone, the sensible position, proceeding from simple general principles, is to favor retention.

The second of the proposed amendments is as follows:

Section 1. No provision of this Constitution, or any amendment thereto, shall restrict or limit any state in the apportionment of representation in its legislature.

Section 2. The Judicial power of the United States shall not extend to any suit in law or equity, or to any controversy, relating to apportionment of representation in a state legislature.

This is the attempt to overrule *Baker v. Carr* and the other apportionment decisions, but only in their application to state legislatures. It does not touch these decisions as they may apply—and some lower courts have already so applied them—to representative bodies in the political subdivisions of the states, such as city councils. I expect that this was an inadvertent omission, rather characteristic, incidentally, of the drafting of all three of these proposals. Nor does this amendment touch the application of *Baker v. Carr* to Congressional apportionment. This, I expect, was an intentional omission, for it indicates the single-minded, almost obsessive motivation behind the proposals. These are not the usual Court-hating or even Court-curbing proposals, nor were they put forward in a blind and indiscriminate rage against federal authority as a whole. The purpose is the enhancement of state authority, the resumption by the institutions of the states of a place in the center of affairs, the return to them of competence in matters of importance, and thus also more generally of dignity and influence. There is behind these amendments something not unlike the Gaullist hankering after the old exalted place in the sun, the old power and the glory, a hankering which carries with it a bit of haughty indifference toward the arrangements *others* may make for *themselves*. And so let Congress and the Supreme Court decide between themselves who shall decide how *Congress* is to be apportioned.

Now, the reaction to *Baker v. Carr,* and even to the cases that followed it, has been on the whole favorable. Still there are those—both professional observers and others—who are troubled. From the point of view of those, then, like myself, who have misgivings about the decision, what is wrong with the proposed amendment? If we think the decision was wrong, must it not follow that the amendment is right? The answer is no, for two reasons. First, to borrow a phrase of Paul A. Freund, the misgivings come at retail, the amendment at wholesale. I do not object, for example, to having the Court strike down an utterly obsolete apportionment, such as the sixty-year-old Tennessee apportionment that was involved in *Baker v. Carr* itself; I object only to having the Court lay down, as it did in the later cases, its own standards for valid apportionments. I do not object, in other words, to having the Court tell a legislature that it must act; I object only to having the Court tell it, in these circumstances, how it must act. Others may qualify their objections in other ways. The proposed amendment makes no such discriminations. Moreover, in a case such as the famous Tuskegee gerrymander case,[18] where it can be objectively demonstrated that the sole purpose of a so-called apportionment is to disadvantage or invidiously segregate voters of a given race, purely on the ground of race, I do not object to having the Court strike down the legislative action, no matter how recent, and many other people who have misgivings about *Baker v. Carr* would also distinguish between that case and the situation just described. Again, the proposed amendment does not. To change the figure, it is cheerfully ready to throw out the baby with the bath. That is most frequently the case with proposed constitutional amendments. They are not often closely tailored to a limited purpose about which a consensus may be said to exist. Constitution-writing seems to have become a lost art.

The second, and in itself equally conclusive argument, against overruling *Baker v. Carr* by constitutional amendment is that to do so is both unnecessary and pernicious. If there exists the sort of consensus against the decision which would be necessary to get an amendment enacted, the decision is doomed—wholly and totally doomed—without the need to amend the Constitution. It is, in that event, only a matter of time before the Court itself abandons the path on which it set its foot in *Baker v. Carr;* the apportionment problem occurs regularly with every census, and can be freshly attacked after 1970. And so amendment is unnecessary. It is pernicious, because the practice of hastening or confirming in this fashion the demise of unwanted judicial doctrines would lead to a pestilence of amendment that would destroy the value of our Constitution as a symbol and as a cohesive force in society. "We must never forget," was John Marshall's famous admonition, "that it is a *constitution* we are expounding." Nor can we ever forget that it is a *Constitution* we are proposing to amend, and that if, in another phrase of Marshall's, it should come to "partake of the prolixity of a legal code," it will seem false and alien to the people, who are expected to pour into it their sense of union and common purpose, regardless of the ways and byways, the trial and error of judicial construction. When something has gone wrong, it is useful that we should know it was the Court, and not our Constitution.

There have been 24 amendments in nearly two centuries. I put aside the first 12, the last of which became effective in 1804, as part of the process of the original framing, although the eleventh was necessary to correct an error of drafting that a Supreme Court

decision had uncovered. I put aside also the three Civil War amendments, which constituted the treaty of peace. Finally, I put aside
the Seventeenth, Nineteenth, Twentieth, Twenty-second, Twenty-
third and Twenty-fourth. Four of these dealt with organizational
matters covered by very precise original provisions and not conceivably changeable otherwise than by an amendment; one, the
Nineteenth, dealt with a broad principle—woman suffrage—fully
appropriate in every sense for constitutional statement; and one,
the Twenty-fourth, which outlawed the poll tax in federal elections,
was also, though not so unavoidably, a fitting constitutional statement. That leaves three, and the two prohibition amendments, the
Eighteenth and its repealer, can safely be passed in silence. The
Sixteenth, the income tax amendment, is thus the only modern one
comparable to the proposed *Baker v. Carr* amendment. It was
enacted to overrule the Supreme Court's decision in *Pollock v.
Farmer's Trust Company*.[19] But there can be little doubt that had
Congress acted by new legislation, reaffirming the income tax act
that the Court had declared unconstitutional, as Congress at the
very time when it proposed the amendment at least half intended
to do, the Court would have reversed itself. And there is no doubt
that had the word "income" never been written into the Constitution,
as under the circumstances I project it would not need to have been
written in, we would have been better off, for we would have been
spared some unedifying interpretive decisions made possible by the
new constitutional term "income." The Sixteenth Amendment is an
illustration of the paradox that language added to the Constitution
in order to overrule the Court will generally enlarge as much as
restrict the Court's function. This is equally illustrated by the Eleventh Amendment, and by the first sentence of the Fourteenth, which
was intended to overrule the *Dred Scott* case. Constitutional language is the fuel on which the Court's engine runs. New words in
the Constitution are a source of new power, even when their primary
meaning was to diminish existing power.

The third and last of the proposed amendments is the most
complex:

Section 1. Upon demand of the legislatures of five states, no two of which
shall share any common boundary, made within two years after the
rendition of any judgment of the Supreme Court relating to the rights

reserved to the states or to the people by this Constitution, such judgment shall be reviewed by a Court composed of the Chief Justices of the
highest courts of the several states to be known as the Court of the Union.
The sole issue before the Court of the Union shall be whether the power
or jurisdiction sought to be exercised on the part of the United States is
a power granted to it under this Constitution.

Section 2. Three-fourths of the justices of the Court of the Union shall
constitute a quorum, but it shall require concurrence of a majority of the
entire Court to reverse a decision of the Supreme Court. . . .

Section 3. On the first Monday of the third calendar month following the
ratification of this amendment, the chief justices . . . shall convene at
the national capital, at which time the Court of the Union shall be
organized. . . .

Section 4. Decisions of the Court of the Union upon matters within its
jurisdiction shall be final and shall not thereafter be overruled by any
court and may be changed only by an amendment of this Constitution.

Section 5. The Congress shall make provision for the housing of the
Court of the Union and the expenses of its operation.

It is hard to escape the feeling, as one reads this extraordinary
prose, that the provisions for seating the Court of the Union in the
national capital and for requiring Congress to house and pay for it
are subtle compromises of the principles of the framers of the
amendment. Nor is it possible to avoid feeling that the last-
mentioned provision adds some insult to the injury it inflicts on
federal supremacy. Beyond this, one can only say with Dean Fordham of the Pennsylvania University Law School, that "there is so
much wrong with this proposal that one hardly knows where to
begin in discussing it."[20] Such a court would be institutionally incapable of acting as a court. It would either surrender its authority
to committees (to be called panels, no doubt) or act like a legislature, seeing issues in the large, without application to immediate
facts, and pursuing political rather than judicial methods, including
logrolling and other forms of give-and-take. Or it would do both.
What is not unrelated and at least equally important, such a court
would be incapable of taking a national view. It would arrive in
Washington to render its nationally applicable decisions only occasionally, and it would see the issues before it from the vantage

point of the local experience and local dependence of each of its members. This is intended, of course, but it is disastrous. A composite of local vantage points is not a national point of view, and national issues deserve to be decided on considerations that have national relevance. And so ultimately, and quite aside from everything else, this proposal is objectionable on essentially the grounds that make the first of these draft amendments, the amending amendment, inadmissible.

We need not idly guess at the parochialism and lack of constitutional sophistication of a pride of state chief justices in convention assembled. A conference of state chief justices exists as a going concern, and in December of 1958 it adopted, 36 to 8, a report of its Committee on Federal-State Relationships as Affected by Judicial Decisions.[21] This is an illuminating if depressing document, to which I shall return briefly in my conclusion. It deplores the making of social and economic policy, as opposed to the strict application of legal rules, by the Supreme Court, and the threatening fact that we are becoming a government of men more than of laws—and is thus not a little simple-minded. It tends to deplore also the use of the federal spending power—the very use of it, as in the social security program and various grants-in-aid, not merely the manner of its use—and is thus somewhat fatuous. And it criticizes various applications of the Fourteenth Amendment to the states, chiefly in matters of free speech and of criminal procedure, quite indiscriminately and without giving evidence of any organizing principle about the proper function of the Supreme Court of the United States, other than a generalized desire to be let alone.

Whatever might be said about the draftsmanship of the other two proposed amendments, the draftsmanship of this one is, in its indefiniteness, atrocious beyond belief. What is meant by a right reserved to the states or to the people under the Constitution? If Congress says something is interstate rather than intrastate commerce and the Supreme Court agrees, does that relate to a right reserved to the states or to the people? Suppose the Court holds that a private home may not be searched without a warrant? Does that so relate? Everything does or nothing does. The Tenth Amendment, which speaks in somewhat similar, although by comparison infinitely more precise terms, has been held, naturally enough, to be tautological and nugatory. Then, again, what is meant by the question whether the power or jurisdiction sought to be exercised on the part of the United States is a power granted to it under this Constitution? Who must seek to exercise power on the part of the United States in order to come within this formulation? Will the jurisdiction of the Court of the Union attach only when Congress has acted, or does the Supreme Court itself, construing the Constitution directly without the benefit of federal legislation, seek to exercise power on the part of the United States? What happens when the Supreme Court declares an act of Congress unconstitutional? Who then is exercising power on behalf of the United States?

These are the proposed amendments. It should, in justice, be remarked that the amendments are not all recommended by the General Assembly of the States with equal force. The first passed that Assembly by a vote of 37 to 4, four states abstaining. The second gathered 26 votes against 10, with ten states abstaining. The third barely squeaked by, 21 to 20, five delegations abstaining. Of the state legislatures that have acted, thirteen each completed action approving the first two, and only five adhered to the third.[22]

But it is not enough—it is neither fair nor in the long run wise— simply to dismiss these amendments as utterly improbable and of course unacceptable. Nor is it enough simply to think of them as speeches, like the flood of amendments, to which I have referred, that gets introduced in Congress—lines spoken in the continual and accustomed dialogue between the Court and the country. We deal here with a symptom of something more pervasive and more fundamental than displeasure and debate over this or that decision, more pervasive and fundamental than the endurance of this or that Supreme Court decision as a constitutional principle. We ought to pause and look past the symptom. Having joined in condemning Theodore Roosevelt's endorsement of the popular recall of judges in 1912, Felix Frankfurter went on to pinpoint what should be heeded about proposals such as these. "The policy of a specific remedy may be crushingly exposed," he said, "but we cannot whistle down the wind a widespread, insistent, and well-vouched feeling of dissatisfaction."[23] That, as I have indicated, is what we are dealing with here. It was evident in the ill-advised report of the Conference of State Chief Justices. "We believe," the chief justices said, that strong state and local governments are essential to the effective functioning of the American system of federal government; that they should not be sacrificed needlessly to leveling, and sometimes deadening, uniformity; and that in the interest of active citizen participation in self-government—the foundation of our democracy—they should be sustained and strengthened.

Many people will agree wholeheartedly with this statement, and more should than will. Similarly, the committee that reported these proposed amendments to the Sixteenth General Assembly of the States, said:

It is the ultimate of political ingenuity to achieve a vigorous federal system in which dynamic states combine with a responsible central government for the good of the people. Your committee is dedicated to this objective.

Again, many people share dedication to this objective. It is clear that the objective is in danger of being lost sight of in many quarters in Washington, not excluding the chambers of some Supreme Court justices.

This is not the place to discuss acts of commission and omission that are necessary to strengthen state government in this country. Moreover, most of these acts are not within the competence of the Supreme Court of the United States, and most past and present sins in this respect are not chargeable to the Supreme Court but to the other branches of our government, the two other federal branches, and to the states themselves. But the record of the Supreme Court is also not without blemish. I would call attention chiefly to decisions by the Court under the Supremacy Clause, especially in the field of labor relations, but in other areas of federal regulation as well, some of which have unnecessarily hampered or struck down concurrent state programs that were not really in conflict with federal policy. And I would note that not everyone is required to be entirely happy with the recent extension of federal supervision over the administration of criminal justice, rendering uniform—and not necessarily always more humane or liberal—the law as to the admissibility in evidence in criminal trials of the products of police searches and seizures.[24]

There is nothing more to be deprecated, wrote Holmes in 1921, than the use of the Fourteenth Amendment to prevent the making of social experiments that an important part of the community desires, in the insulated chambers afforded by the several States, even though the experiments may seem futile or even noxious to me and to those whose judgment I most respect.[25]

And Brandeis, a decade later:

It is one of the happy incidents of the federal system that a single courageous State may, if its citizens choose, serve as a laboratory; and try novel social and economic experiments without risk to the rest of the country.[26]

The bright and hopeful idea of federalism carries the seed of change, of improvement, and of truly meaningful democracy. But you could not tell it by looking at our states today. We are, of course, a nation, and as a nation we carry responsibilities not only for defense and for general welfare but moral responsibilities. One cannot concede to the "insulated chambers" of the states experiments that are morally abhorrent to the nation, or the *fainéant* maintenance of islands of poverty and misery, rather than the "courageous" pursuit of a "novel" social or economic policy. Nor can we concede effective withdrawal from the pursuit of nationally adopted policies, any more than withdrawal from behind the nation's defense shield would be tolerated or is desired. But we might, nevertheless, heed the admonitions of Holmes and Brandeis. We might have a care that we do not exaggerate the requirements of uniformity inhering in national policy. And we might be more slow to regard our every value, or even every national consensus, as a moral imperative that can brook no deviation. The lines we are thus required to draw are extremely difficult and uncertain, and they may be disagreeable. But the system demands that they be drawn, even though we all tend to forget it when our particular ox happens to be badly gored. In their clumsy, improbable way, the three constitutional amendments put forward by the Council of State Governments mean to remind us.

New
Troops
on Old
Battlegrounds

12

Since October, 1962, there has been a new Supreme Court in Washington. For nearly a generation the Justices have been closely divided over questions of the powers of the political branches of government and the limitations on those powers. These questions have emphasized profoundly different conceptions of the role to be assigned to a written constitution and to the Justices as its spokesmen in a democratic society. In April, 1962, President Kennedy appointed Byron R. White to succeed retired Justice Charles E. Whittaker. Late that summer he appointed Arthur J. Goldberg to replace Justice Felix Frankfurter, who had suffered a stroke. Thus the Court had two new justices. What is more, it lost the weight and the voice of Justice Frankfurter. Neither its unities nor its divisions could now be the same.

Such a retirement as that of Justice Frankfurter does more than merely change a vote; it alters the entire judicial landscape. To use another figure, it is the magnetic field in which the Justices operate that is altered. Actions, reactions, relations—all must rearrange themselves once a creative influence that has radiated powerfully for over twenty years removes itself. We know and should know very little of the stresses and pulls, the attractions and reactions that the present Justices produce and act under in their collegial deliberations. But the history of the institution teaches that its great figures dominate the development of American constitutional law; that they exercise their dominion not singly or absolutely, to be sure, but as often from a dissenting as from a majority position, for this is a matter not of votes and results but of interaction, of intellectual confrontations and the definition and choice of issues; and that they do so for whole eras at a time. Such an era closed with the retirement of Justice Frankfurter. There *is* a new Court. It will be some time before it quite finds itself, but for the first time, in two citizenship cases[1] decided on February 18, 1963, it manifested a new self in a significant context.

The issue in these cases was left over from one of those resounding philosophical clashes of the fifties. May the government, on various grounds, deprive native-born Americans of their citizenship? No, never, said Justices Black and Douglas; there is no such power in the federal government. Yes, as an exercise of a power to regulate the tenure of citizenship and in aid of such national functions as war and foreign relations, said Justice Frankfurter. Citizenship may be taken away, the Court held, Chief Justice Warren, Justice Black, and others dissenting, for voting in a foreign political election. It may not be taken away, the Court held, Justices Frankfurter, Harlan, and others dissenting, for committing a rather technically defined offense of desertion from the armed services.[2] The question left over was whether citizenship could be taken away for fleeing the country in wartime for the express purpose of evading the draft. Dividing 5-4, but on novel and narrower grounds, the Court, in February, 1963, held that it could not be. The dissenters were Justices Clark, Harlan, Stewart, and White. The great interest of these cases lies in the opinion of the majority, written by Justice Goldberg for himself, the Chief Justice, and Justices Black, Douglas, and Brennan.

The general approach of this opinion, the mood in which it attacks its problem, will, if sustained, have far-reaching consequences for the Court. The approach is to adjourn the apocalyptic debate to whose continual resumption we had become accustomed; it is to seek a mediating way between the ultimates of judicial assertion or denial of governmental power. There is significance in the fact that the new Justice Goldberg took this approach. It is even more significant that he was joined by Justice Black—the Great Thunderer himself, one may say, meaning no disrespect—and by the Chief Justice and Justice Douglas. This is an opinion in which the philosophical clash of old is present, but as the sound of a distant battle. The path of decision leads away from the battle. And what is offered in the end is, to be sure, not a resolution of the conflict but a moment of respite. It is altogether, in the intent and in the execution, a skillful performance, the prototype—may one hope?—of others to come. For the Court needs some respite, and so does the country. Nobody should wish to take mind out of the Supreme Court, as Namier was accused of taking it out of history. But there can be too much of stark ideological struggle, too much forcing of choices between mutually exclusive ideological ultimates, especially with respect to problems as to which no satisfactory choice between such ultimates seems possible.

Such a problem is the power of government, or the lack of it, to denationalize natural-born citizens who commit acts that may be thought to be in contravention of the duties of citizenship. The issue turns initially on whether denationalization is a punishment. If it is, in the same sense in which a fine, imprisonment, or deprivation of civil rights for the commission of a crime is a punishment, then the Constitution commands that it may not be imposed without a jury trial and other safeguards applicable to the administration of criminal justice. Some might not allow it even then, holding it to be forbidden as a cruel and unusual punishment—the ancient cruelty of banishment. Be that as it may, the statute denationalizing expatriate draft dodgers provides for civil proceedings only, not criminal safeguards, and so if the denationalization that it imposes is punishment, the statute is unconstitutional for this procedural reason, whether or not one deems the punishment cruel and unusual. This much is common ground.

But how do we tell whether denationalization is punishment? It is not enough that it hurts, that it may be seen as a sanction, for if anything is clear it is that we are not willing to surround all actions of government that fall painfully on the individual with the expensive and cumbersome panoply of criminal safeguards. Thus many forms of taxation hurt as much as, or more than, many criminal fines, but they are imposed administratively or by other civil process. What we call a punishment—for lack of a better and more precise criterion —is only a sanction whose dominant purpose is retributive and deterrent. A sanction is not punishment if, like taxes, even though it hurts, it serves some dominant purpose other than merely to hurt. But punishment is also meant, in the end, to serve a social purpose separate from its own infliction, and to achieve this larger purpose, in this or that degree, on the individual concerned, and on others through its *in terrorem* effect. The distinction is that to qualify as not punitive a sanction must have a conclusive regulatory effect on the individual on whom it falls, doing to him all that is necessary, but only what is necessary, to achieve the immediate purpose, and not using him to deter others. But if a regulatory sanction falls on conduct the individual can avoid, as many taxes do, then every time it falls it will cause others to avoid that conduct. Thus punishment is in some measure a regulatory sanction, and all sanctions are in some measure punishment.

We are in a circle. A regulatory sanction is defined as something that is not punishment, which is defined as something that is not a regulatory sanction. We have simply not developed conceptual tools that are precise enough to tell us when we require use of the criminal process and when we may dispense with it. And there is no help in a functional realism that purports to cut through the concepts and look for its criterion of decision to the actual consequences of the governmental action. This method either works out as more circular than anything else, holding that a sanction is punishment if a criminal stigma attaches to it—which, of course, it will not if we do not call it punishment; or it flounders about trying to determine which of many things that hurt, hurt worst: e.g., does deportation of aliens hurt less than denationalization of citizens? As to denationalization, however, there is a way out of the circle. But it leads into the frying pan. If there is no power in the federal government to regulate native-born citizenship, to define it and the conditions of its tenure, then denationalization cannot be a regulatory sanction, and may perhaps not even be imposed as a punishment. It cannot then be a suitable regulatory sanction, for there is nothing which it is suited to regulate that may legitimately be regulated. Seen this way, the issue loses its merely procedural aspect—"merely," because procedural defects can be cured; Congress can in future provide for jury trials. The issue then becomes one of ultimates, of ends, of the powers of government and their limitation by the Court. This is the ground on which the battle of constitutional philosophies was fought out in the past.

Justice Goldberg left this ground. He made no attempt to determine, by deduction from a priori judgments of permissible governmental purposes, whether denationalization is always, or even just generally, a regulatory sanction or a punishment, and whether there is power to impose it as either. He asked, rather, an empirical question: whatever the other possible uses of the sanction of denationalization may be, was it perhaps clear in this instance, as a matter of actual legislative intent, that the dominant purpose in denationalizing wartime expatriate draft dodgers was punitive? This is itself generally a difficult question, most often, indeed, an unanswerable one, for the Court has no means of psychoanalyzing a past Congress and arriving at a judgment of its motives, and Congress' own debates do not often shed light on so subtle a question. The difficulty is indeed illustrated by the immediate statute here involved, which Congress passed with very little debate in 1944, at the behest of Attorney General Francis Biddle. But there is in this instance also, as it happens, an illuminating prior history. The 1944 statute is the last in a series dating back to the Civil War. Ample debates and other historical materials demonstrate that all the earlier ones were plainly thought of on all sides as punitive—retributive and deterrent. And Justice Goldberg persuasively—even if not conclusively—argued the continuity of the latest from the earlier statutes.

The upshot was procedural, implying no final judgment about the powers of government. What is more, even the procedural judgment is applicable only in the peculiar circumstances of the present statute, which fell because it was demonstrably meant to be punitive and yet did not provide the procedural safeguards suitable to the infliction of punishment. But does Congress have power, without providing criminal safeguards, but also without retributive or deterrent intent, to regulate native-born citizenship and to decree that one who flees the jurisdiction to avoid a wartime draft has so far forgotten himself in the duties of that citizenship as to be deemed to have forfeited it? Congress has that power neither more surely nor more dubiously than it did before Justice Goldberg's opinion. May Congress, subject to the proper procedural safeguards, inflict loss of citizenship as a punishment for expatriate draft dodging? Again, the decision does not answer this large question. For the moment, the debate is in recess. The ball is in Congress' court, not the Court's. Congress is free to address itself to these issues and speak its will.

There is one incidental aspect of these citizenship cases that should not go unmentioned, though no doubt it is sheer sentimentality to emphasize it. It is far from unique. What it suggests is indeed a commonplace of our system. If its particular manifestation is relatively rare, that is because only a certain coincidence can bring it about just so. For very ordinary procedural reasons, the parties in these cases were, in the one, *Robert F. Kennedy* [then Attorney General] *v. Francisco Mendoza-Martinez*, and, in the other, *Dean Rusk v. Joseph Henry Cort*. Well, Kennedy and Rusk lost, of course, and their defeat was handed them by one who under the robes was their Cabinet colleague of just the day before, Arthur Goldberg. This so meets our expectations that we are not startled, but it is rather nice.

Supreme
Court
Fissures

13

As the Supreme Court concluded its October Term 1963 late in June, 1964, and rose for the summer vacation, it seemed that the Court was under the dominion of a new majority. A Hugo Black majority, one might well call it, for in this second half of Justice Black's third decade of service, the Court was overturning many a precedent that had entered the books over his dissent.[1] Holmes once referred to "the subtile rapture of a postponed power," which was the secret joy of the thinker. And it was remarked of Chief Justice Harlan Stone in the 1940's that he had the privilege of being present in the postponed time. The analogy is an ominous one from Justice Black's point of view, for Stone's triumph soon disintegrated into further discord, but a measure of the present rapture of previously postponed power is being afforded to Justice Black, too, by the new Supreme Court majority.

That majority generally consists, in addition to Justice Black, of Chief Justice Warren and Justices Douglas, Brennan, and Goldberg. Justice Harlan is a consistent dissenter, often joined by Justice Clark, and not infrequently by either Justice White or Justice Stewart, or by both. This is a generalization, of course, and valid only as such. All nine of the Justices are charged with the duty of independent judgment, and that is what they exercise. Yet they must also reach a collective judgment in each case, and hence they tend to coalesce, submerging nuances of individual philosophy. But the law is seldom settled in a single case. Clusters of cases are decisive in the long run, and as they accrete, issues converge and crisscross, and nuances of individual philosophy, hardly visible to the naked eye at first, or suppressed in face of a given dissent taking a particular line, emerge and are magnified. Centrifugal as well as centripetal forces are ever at work within a Court majority. In a series of sit-in cases[2] and a passport case[3] decided on June 22, 1964, the last day of the 1963 Term, there was evidence not only of the new accord but also of the seeds of discord within it.

An oddly aligned majority of five—Warren, Clark, Brennan, Stewart, and Goldberg—disposed of the sit-in cases on various narrow grounds without reaching the ultimate issue, which is whether the Fourteenth Amendment of its own force forbids the owner of a public accommodation such as a lunch counter or drugstore to exclude Negroes. The result was that trespass convictions of various Negro sit-in demonstrators in Maryland, Florida, and South Carolina were vacated, but the constitutional issue was left undecided. Justices Black, Harlan, Douglas, and White felt strongly that the constitutional issue ought to have been decided then and there. It was an inexcusable default on the part of the Court, said Justice Douglas, not to "put our decision into the mainstream of the law at this critical hour." And Justice Black thought it "unfair to demonstrators and property owners alike as well as against the public interest not to decide [the issue] now."

However, what the two Justices thought it unfair to withhold from the parties and the mainstream were two different things. Justice Douglas believes that the Fourteenth Amendment forbids discrimination in public accommodations, and in this view he was joined by Justice Goldberg and the Chief Justice, who spoke only because the issue had been broached, although they agreed with the majority that it should not be decided. Justice Black, with whom Justices Harlan and White agreed, believes that the Fourteenth Amendment leaves the owners of private property free to pick their customers in accordance with their own prejudices. Congress and state legislatures may have power to decree otherwise, said Justice Black, but the Fourteenth Amendment of its own force applies only to discrimination by agencies or officers of a state, not to private discriminations.

As the Court was considering the issue, so, of course, was Congress in what became the Civil Rights Act of 1964, and so were some states and municipalities. One of the restaurant cases was from Maryland, and while it was pending, Maryland passed a public accommodations statute forbidding discrimination. The fact that the issue was in the process of political settlement was surely a preponderant consideration in the majority's decision to avoid a decision. Another consideration was the extreme difficulty of the issue as a constitutional matter, the utter inconclusiveness of the usual materials of judgment, the grave doubt whether any judicially imposed rule could work satisfactorily in all parts of the country in great varieties of situations, the lack of any moral or ethical standard sufficiently clear cut, well tried, and widely accepted to support a distinction between places where access must constitutionally be free and those where the owner's prejudices may constitutionally prevail.

The opinions reaching the constitutional issue serve better than anything else to support the majority's disposition of the sit-in cases, for these opinions are about equally unpersuasive, almost equally self-refuting on either side. Justice Douglas solved the problem more or less by stating it as if it solved itself. He kept referring to it, in italics, as *apartheid.* Justice Goldberg, who also joined the Court and thus did not really want to decide, attempted to convince himself that it was the intention of the framers of the Fourteenth Amendment to outlaw discrimination in public accommodations. Anyone who has read the debates of the Reconstruction Congress (see Appendix) knows how dubious a proposition that is. Justice Black, himself the notable author of some dubious readings of Fourteenth Amendment history on other issues, rejected this one, and emerged with the conclusion that the line between the right to liberty and equal protection that the Fourteenth Amendment guarantees to people and the right to private property that it guarantees to both people and corporations is drawn at the restaurant door.

But the Court, with Justice Black joining, has applied the Equal Protection Clause to private racial covenants affecting privately owned land, and by implication to a company town.[4] The distinctions on which Justice Black would rest those cases have been traditionally taken, but they seem trivial now. So do other indicia of "state action," as the Court has called the criterion for deciding whether or not the Equal Protection Clause applies to a given discrimination. Realistically, "state action" is present in all these situations, the old standard ones and the newer ones, for we are indeed committed, as Justice Black remarks, to "rule by law," and law, whether permissive or coercive, is what makes discrimination enforceable. The question is what sort of discrimination should be forbidden, not by state legislatures and not by Congress but by the Supreme Court in the name of the Constitution. It is a very difficult question, and none of the Justices has solved it.

The sit-in cases demonstrate that very often the problem for the Court is not only how to decide but whether to decide. Judges may share a general constitutional outlook, but that does not mean that they are equally ready to put their decisions into the "mainstream" at every "critical hour"; it does not mean that they are all equally anxious to seize the initiative on issues with which the political process also is grappling; it does not mean, in sum, that they are all equally confident of the permanent validity of the constitutional judgments they reach in common, or equally sure that the best sort of rule by law is rule by judges. There is a new and fairly steady majority on the Supreme Court concerning many of the old questions over which the Court has divided during the past two decades or so. But there is no steady majority when the questions are new, as the conflict between the Equal Protection Clause and the rights of property is relatively new for the modern Court, and when one of the questions is not what to decide but whether and how much.

This is confirmed as well by the passport case decided the same day as these sit-in cases. The Subversive Activities Control (McCarran) Act of 1950, which has been so deservedly whittled down by the courts before now, provides that no member of a Communist, "Communist-front," or "Communist-infiltrated" organization that has been ordered to register under the act may apply for a passport, or get one, or use it. A majority of the Court, in an opinion by Justice Goldberg, held that, while Congress might well have authority to regulate individual travel in the interests of national security, this blunderbuss statute, reaching large numbers of miscellaneous people purely on the basis of their formal associations, regardless of their particular purposes and commitments, regardless even of the purposes for which they wish to travel—this statute is invalid. If Congress wished to forbid travel that runs counter to the national interest, it would have to be more specific, and the question of whether and under what conditions Congress might forbid travel did not need to be decided now.

Justices Black and Douglas joined the majority, but they would each have decided much more now. Justice Black thought that the statute violated the First Amendment and was a Bill of Attainder to boot, as he has said in the past. Justice Douglas thought that a prohibition on travel such as laid down by the McCarran Act was flatly unconstitutional, except perhaps in time of war. Justices Clark and Harlan, on the other hand, in dissent, thought that on the whole the statute was quite constitutional. Justice White joined them to the extent of believing that the statute was valid as applied to leading figures in the Communist party rather than the rank and file, and that the overhanging threat it represented for the rank and file (it is made a criminal offense, punishable by five years in jail, for "any member" to so much as apply for a passport, or for anyone to issue him one) was no good reason for striking it down. Thus in this case the Hugo Black majority—if one may use that shorthand in honor of the Court's senior Justice—held together handsomely, but on the question of whether and how much to decide it again revealed its subsurface fissures.

REAPPORTIONMENT
AND
LIBERAL
MYTHS

V

First
Round:
Baker v. Carr

14

Baker v. Carr,[1] the Supreme Court's reapportionment decision of March, 1962, marked a sharp break with precedent. Previously the Court had turned aside all attacks on state or Congressional apportionments and on kindred political arrangements either by declining to take jurisdiction or by briefly and inscrutably indicating that the system under attack did not violate any constitutional principle.[2] This was, on the whole, an unsatisfactory situation. The Court's position, never precisely or comprehensively stated, carried the fault of an apparent inner contradiction. To say that some apportionments do not violate constitutional principle is to imply rather strongly that there exists such a principle which is applicable to apportionment problems. And it is to leave open a haunting question. Why are some apportionments approved, while others are neither approved nor disapproved, the Court declining to take jurisdiction? May it not be that the failure to approve or disapprove is itself a form of approval? Thus, chiefly because the Court articulated its own position only once, and then only partly and not very coherently,[3] and in some measure because of misapprehension on the part of the public, the

Court was in actual effect lending an aura of constitutional validity to existing malapportionments. Moreover, not all malapportionments exist because somebody deliberately wants them that way. Many are the simple product of indecision and inertia, and as such the problem they present to the judicial process is rather a different one. But the Court treated obsolete apportionments no differently than deliberately contrived malapportionments. Normally when the Court declines to say whether or not a given practice conforms to constitutional principle, the intended and actual effect is to allow free play to the political process. Sometimes, indeed, the Court's rhetoric or the technique it employs to dispose of the case will be calculated to provoke a renewed consideration by the political institutions. Devices so calculated are employed with particular vigor if the practice that is in issue is the product of inertia rather than of a recent deliberate legislative decision. But with respect to the apportionment problem, all these distinctions were ignored. Willy-nilly, the Court was helping to entrench the status quo.

The decision in *Baker v. Carr*—the fact of the decision and also some passages in the opinions of the Justices—cleared the air. The previous decisions, and all intimations that existing apportionments, obsolete or fresh, are necessarily constitutional were swept away. The case itself concerned not a recent willful malapportionment but rather a sixty-year-old apportionment that had been rendered obsolete and oppressive by sheer inaction in face of radical shifts of population. The decision erased any supposed stamp of constitutional validity from this situation. Predictably enough, the Tennessee legislature at long last acted. Elsewhere as well, whether under pressure of impending lawsuits or even before any were filed, the most widespread initial response to *Baker v. Carr* was a flurry of legislative activity looking to fresh apportionments.

Seen as just described, the decision in *Baker v. Carr* was unexceptionable. The trouble is that one can see the result in this fashion, with heavy emphasis on the age of the Tennessee apportionment, and one can welcome it as such, but one cannot so read Justice Brennan's majority opinion. An opinion to this effect could well have been written, and there are hints of it in a special concurrence by Justice Clark. But what the Court in fact said is something else again. The Supreme Court held that the constitutionality of all apportionments, recent or ancient, is henceforth to be passed on as a matter of course, in much the same fashion in which, say, laws regulating racial practices or criminal procedures are generally brought to ultimate judgment in the Supreme Court. This reading rests on the following passage in Justice Brennan's opinion:

> Nor need the appellants, in order to succeed in this action, ask the Court to enter upon policy determinations for which judicially manage-able standards are lacking. Judicial standards under the Equal Protec-tion clause are well-developed and familiar, and it has been open to courts since the enactment of the Fourteenth Amendment to determine, if on the particular facts they must, that a discrimination reflects *no* policy, but simply arbitrary and capricious action.

Taking this passage as prescribing their function, numerous lower federal and state courts began to strike down fairly recent appor-tionments on the ground that they were somehow irrational and unconstitutional. Some courts even set their hand or threatened to set their hand to the task of themselves constructing new and con-stitutional apportionments. But the standard of judgment enunciated by Justice Brennan, which lower courts purported to apply in all directions, though it falls soothingly on the ear, is almost wholly meaningless.

The requirement of rationality invoked by Justice Brennan is, to be sure, a familiar standard in American constitutional law. It stems from a celebrated paragraph of John Marshall's in *McCulloch v. Maryland* (1819), written with reference to the powers of Congress, but applicable as well to judicial review of acts of state legislatures:

> We admit, as all must admit, that the powers of the government are limited, and that its limits are not to be transcended. But we think the sound construction of the Constitution must allow to the national [or State] legislature that discretion, with respect to the means by which the powers it confers are to be carried into execution, which will enable that body to perform the high duties assigned to it, in the manner most beneficial to the people. Let the end be legitimate, let it be within the scope of the Constitution, and all means which are appropriate, which are plainly adapted to that end, which are not prohibited, but consist with the letter and spirit of the Constitution, are constitutional.[4]

The test was restated just before the turn of the century in a famous paper entitled, "The Origin and Scope of the American Doctrine of Constitutional Law," by the constitutional scholar James Bradley Thayer.[5] A statute is to be declared unconstitutional, Thayer said, "when those who have the right to make laws have not merely made a mistake, but have made a very clear one,—so clear that it is not open to rational question." The Supreme Court is to be "the ultimate arbiter of what is rational and permissible."

More concretely, Marshall and Thayer were talking about a method of constitutional construction—that is, a method of interpreting the written document—which would result in the free exercise by the representative institutions of broad and effective powers of government, but not unlimited ones. Marshall and Thayer spoke for the main tradition, that of loose rather than strict construction, which they strove nevertheless to reconcile with the idea of limited powers conferred on separate branches of government by an organic charter. Addressing themselves to the common case of a novel legislative action, not specifically provided for in the Constitution, they argued that the action must be upheld if it can be rationally related to an established head of legislative power. Thus—in an illustration of Marshall's—the federal power to establish a postal system being conceded because it is one of those enumerated in the Constitution, it follows rationally that there should be power to punish interference with the movement of the mails. By the same token, if the states have the power to protect the morals of their citizenry or to protect themselves against subversion and insurrection, it will follow rationally that they may forbid the use of devices of contraception or ensure the loyalty to themselves and their institutions of public employees. But it may not follow that because the federal government is empowered to regulate "commerce among the several States" it is empowered also to establish a uniform law of divorce. At least we should have to know more about the relation of divorces to the operation of a national economy before we could call this connection rational.

There is also a second, related, but analytically separate, sort of application of the test of rationality. In exercising any of its powers, government, state or federal, will be permitted to make only those choices which rest on an intelligible and plausible view of reality. And as in the first set of illustrations, what is here in question is not really a requirement of rationality so much as a requirement of the absence of demonstrable irrationality. For, obviously, there are myriad legislative choices that are not rationally compelled, as indeed the very word "choice" implies. But experience has demonstrated that perfectly sane men assembled in democratic legislatures are also capable of making choices that are demonstrably irrational. Thus a legislature may act on the belief that a man who is an active member of the Communist party at the very least does not look with disfavor upon the violent overthrow of existing American institutions. But should a legislature be allowed also to conclude that once a man is a Communist he will always remain one, no matter what present disclaimers he may enter? The first conclusion, though one may find it disagreeable, can hardly be thought irrational, given what is known of Communist doctrine. The second, in light of common experience, is irrational and has been held so;[6] it is irrational in the same sense in which a requirement that all state employees must have blond hair, because blond people are more trustworthy than dark-haired ones, would be irrational. Or, again, a state may conclude that members not only of the Communist party but also of organizations shown to have close connections with that party are in some sense disloyal. But it is surely irrational to conclude, and has been held so,[7] that persons who joined and left an organization before it had any connection with the Communist party, or who joined not knowing about the connection, have given similar evidence of disloyalty.

I have gone on at length with this general description of the test of rationality as it is established in American constitutional law. The test is not, of course, invulnerable to certain lines of philosophical attack, and I am not here concerned to defend it, aside from remarking that it has found a substantial practical utility in the working of the American constitutional scheme. But I am concerned with the obvious omission in this test—namely, the question, not whether a legislative choice is rational (whatever the tacit value judgment that may be implicit in that word) but whether it is good. Confronted, for example, with the issue whether the federal government should be able to punish interference with the free movement of mails, it is quite satisfactory to most of us to be told that the power is one that can be rationally deduced from the undoubted authority of the federal government to own a post office. It is similarly satisfactory to rest a requirement of literacy for government employees on the judgment that it is rational. These are, as Thayer called them, questions of "mere power." But when it comes to excluding members of a Communist-front organization—let us assume for the moment that we know what that means—from government employment or from the bar, it does not in the same fashion suffice to be informed that the action is rational. One wants to know also whether it is good, whether, in other words, it is consistent with principles of political freedom. The question is not merely one of power; it is also a question of liberty. Again, it does not quite do to be told that an antibirth control statute is rational; the question is also one of a private sphere of moral decision. It is possible to answer that legislatures should be free to make the choice of values involved, just as they are free to make other choices that are not irrational. The late Judge Learned Hand rather inclined to this view, though it can scarcely be said that he acted on it consistently. But such a plenary legislative freedom has never quite characterized our constitutional system. By means of a complex, itself not unrestricted and ultimately not uncontrolled process, the Supreme Court has at the very least participated in making many such fundamental value choices for our society.

Let me now return to the apportionment problem and my assertion that application of the rationality test to this problem, as suggested by Justice Brennan, is very nearly meaningless. Applying the first branch of the test obviously leads nowhere. It is conceded all around that the power to apportion, to create constituencies, and otherwise to regulate the manner in which public officials and legislators are elected is a legitimate function of government. The question then becomes whether this or that apportionment, restricting the electorate in this or that fashion, or favoring this or that portion of it with more or less influence, is rational—or rather, whether it is *ir*rational; the question, as always, is not whether reason compels the legislative choice but whether reason is repelled by it. Now most, if not all, malapportionments favor rural interests of one sort or another over urban and suburban, allocate more strength proportionately to sparsely populated areas than to densely populated ones, and make other similar discriminations. Who can say that this is irrational? Undesirable, perhaps; but irrational? More irrational than a farm policy that favors farmers or an antitrust policy that favors small enterprise? Are such policies more irrational, indeed, than a policy that forces the majority to listen to ideas that it fears and hates or to tolerate the possibility that its young will read Henry Miller? Justice Clark, concurring specially in *Baker v. Carr*, looked for an internal consistency in the apportionment system in Tennessee, and finding none, held it irrational. But whence is the premise derived that an apportionment must not only be rational in the choices that it makes, but must proceed toward a single coherent objective? There may be a legislative preference for rural districts in general, but not for all alike. The choice may be made with an eye to the maintenance of party balance and hence to particular political traditions in this or that district; it may be influenced by prophecies as to rates of growth, by preference for cotton interests over tobacco interests, or vice versa, or by a judgment that this or that interest already finds sufficiently powerful representation from another district.

In sum, while there may conceivably be exceptions, particularly in highly obsolete apportionments, it seems plain that the conventional test of rationality cannot lead anywhere in this field. A near analogy may perhaps render the point even plainer. No doubt, given the present state of scientific knowledge, a legislature which acted on the premise that Negroes are inherently less intelligent than whites or that Jews are less likely to be honest than Gentiles would be held to have acted irrationally. There is no foundation for such a premise in the common experience of informed, rational men, although there might be in common prejudice. But for a legislature to conclude that racial tension is an existing fact of life and that it is therefore best to segregate the races; or for it to conclude that most Negroes are not likely to go on to a university and that it is therefore not economical to maintain one for them—these are certainly not irrational acts. The Constitution is held to forbid them because they are bad on principle, because it is morally reprehensible for government to treat people in this unequal fashion, no matter what the rational reason for doing so. The question, therefore, with apportionment, as with race relations, is not one of rationality. It is, rather, what principles restrict otherwise rational choices that a legislature might make?

This is the question that the Court not only left unanswered in *Baker v. Carr*, but rather went out of its way to obscure. One does not expect a full and complete answer to such a question to spring into life from a court's first opinion on a problem, but one does expect the question to be faced, and one expects it certainly not to be willfully obfuscated.

The problem of apportionment seems to call forth in many people the most naïve notions concerning the nature and functioning of representative democratic government. The root idea seems to be one stated by President Kennedy at a news conference on March 29, 1962, shortly after the decision in *Baker v. Carr*. "Quite obviously," said the President, "the right to fair representation, that each vote count equally is, it seems to me, basic to the successful operation of a democracy." Mr. Kennedy went on to remark, forgetting perhaps where once he had sat, that there "is no sense of a Senator representing five million people sitting next to a Senator representing ten thousand." But what does this imply? One person, one vote? And how? Proportional representation? At large elections? Is districting to be allowed? What is the use of a second House, or must we all become unicameral, like Nebraska? It is very well to maintain that the federal Senate and the federal Electoral College are the products of an historical compromise, which is explained by particular historical circumstances, and which is not applicable to the composition of the House of Representatives or of state legislatures. But are we to believe that our federal government lacks a feature that is "basic to the successful operation of a democracy"—that, indeed, it contains an inconsistent feature, and is therefore not a successfully operating democracy?

President Kennedy, of course, in the nicest and most innocent way possible, did not mean what he said. He was merely expressing "the democratic creed," as Professor Robert A. Dahl calls it in his recent work, *Who Governs?* This creed is a set of vague beliefs existing "at a high level of abstraction." What President Kennedy said—and other persons of equal sophistication are capable of saying the same thing when the mood of high-level abstraction is upon them—describes some sort of town meeting democracy, but not anything that has ever existed in this country on any larger scale, and certainly not anything that exists today. If the Supreme Court has undertaken to make reality conform to the one person, one vote principle, it has indeed set for itself quite a task, to whose performance it will have to return decade after decade, with the regularity of the census. But that is not really the point. If a one person, one vote democracy is the goal toward which we should strive, then it would be the function of the Court to define it and set it before us. The question is, should we adhere to the goal of absolute voting equality? Is it what we are now certain we want? Is the true meaning of representative democracy to be found within it?

The principle of equality of representation proceeds from the premise that the representative institutions are something like animated voting machines, engineered to register decisions made by the electorate. The representative institutions are seen as a rather poor substitute for a decision-making process that works by direct vote of the people. No doubt, occasional new matters will arise that were not settled at a prior election, and the representative institutions are authorized, as delegates of the people, to dispose of such unforeseen matters. But these decisions are to be ratified or rejected at the next election, and if possible sooner. And above all, as the French say, not too much zeal. Legislatures should meet infrequently and for short periods. The initiative and referendum movement, which engaged the enthusiasm of Progressives in the first decade or so of this century, but which can scarcely be said to have left an enduringly significant mark on our political system, proceeded from this sort of premise. And, indeed, on no other premise is equality of representation supportable as the overriding, all-important principle. For if the representative institutions are to exercise a relatively independent, deliberate decision-making function, elections and the vote are matters of a different order of importance. The problem becomes one of access to, participation in, influence on the process of decision, and only ultimately and in necessarily attenuated fashion one of ensuring at election time the legislature's fidelity to the popular will.

This is, of course, how modern political science sees the problem. It has been a long time since serious students have professed to believe that elections are occasions when the electorate disposes of the common run of issues that governments are confronted with.

The equal-vote premise ignores all that we have learned in a generation of fresh inquiry and reflection. And it ignores not only the laws
of probability but also—in a highly developed, complex, pluralistic
society—all the laws of possibility. Is this to say that elections are
practically meaningless, a show trial of democracy, a spectacle, an
emotional binge, a morality play, or a what-have-you? There have
been those who have come close to arguing as much, particularly
when in the throes of defending that plainly countermajoritarian
institution, the Supreme Court—which is a point of some little irony.
But this simplicity is not the truth either. Some elections do sometimes turn on issues, although few and general, and no one knows
ahead of time which issues they may turn on or how. This is a
factor in the process by which democratic government makes decisions, for in an indeterminate measure decisions are influenced in
this fashion. But the heart of democratic government, and the
morality which distinguishes it from everything else, is that it rests
on consent. And the secret of consent is only in part a matter of
control, of the reserve power of a majority to rise up against
decisions that displease it. It is, perhaps more importantly, the sense
shared by all that their interests were spoken for in the decision-
making process, no matter how the result turned out. Government
by consent requires that no segment of society should feel alienated
from the institutions that govern. This means that the institutions
must not merely represent a numerical majority, which is a shifting
and uncertain quantity anyway, but must reflect the people in all
their diversity, so that all the people may feel that their particular
interests and even prejudices, that all their diverse characteristics,
were brought to bear on the decision-making process.

We have thus, and ought to have, majoritarian government in the
sense that an essentially numerical majority has, and knows it has,
the reserve power to turn out discredited decision makers, putting
in others who will in future resist what has displeased it. But we
have also, and ought to have, *reflective* government, which represents in the sense that it reflects, and so government to which general
consent is given, government which is legitimate and stable. To
achieve all this, we have constructed not one but a number of
institutions, and their constituencies are different. It is commonly
true that the executive, who has, of course, great powers of initiative

as well as approval in the legislative process, is the instrument through which numerical majorities express and make effective such concrete wishes as they may be able to generate. It is also true that the legislature carries the burden of reflecting the people, and that this is a function it could not well perform if it were constructed strictly on the one person, one vote principle. And where no such function is performed, where no reflective institutions have power that is shared in this or that measure by all groups, interests, factions, and other configurations in society, what we are accustomed to call democracy does not obtain. No matter how freely a strong majoritarian executive like General de Gaulle may be elected— although in his instance it is not even true that he is freely elected by a majority—and no matter how frequently he may put how many major decisions to a free majoritarian vote by referendum, the result will not be democratic government so long as no reflective institutions share power.

It is argued that legislatures can be arranged to perform the reflecting function simply by being districted, as all ours are, without necessitating substantial voting inequality, which is created only by unequal districts. But the people's diversities are not all conveniently contained in equal contiguous districts; many interests and other configurations, far from being so clustered, would form permanent minorities throughout any number of equal districts. One need not believe that malapportionment, so called, always serves important, legitimate ends and is never used to obtain unjust partisan advantage, or for other undesirable purposes. It is enough justification for unequal districting that it *sometimes* serves legitimate ends. For the illegitimate ones can be attained as well under the most absolute one man, one vote requirement, which must therefore be seen as forbidding what should be allowed and even encouraged, and permitting all that anyone can wish to forbid. But perhaps the saving grace of the one man, one vote rule is that it would forbid nothing very effectively. As Dean Phil C. Neal, of the University of Chicago Law School, has pointed out in an important paper on the subject,[8] a requirement of equal districting would very likely prove self-defeating, since it is possible to achieve all the malapportionment in the world by careful gerrymandering of perfectly equal districts. Those who have been complaining will then have a magnificently equal vote which will never elect anyone. Proportional representation is a mathematically perfect way out, but, as has been demonstrated time and again, it is a method that so fragments legislative institutions as to make them incapable of coherent and responsible government. Our institutions are over-fragmented as is; their capacity for inaction is one of the ills attributed to malapportionment. We tend to cure this through the party system, and justly complain because the cure is imperfect. Who, then, would want proportional representation, which rings the death knell of any manageable two- or even three-party system and leads invariably to a spectrum of parties, thus forcing the legislature to engage in the very initial coalition-building process that needs to have taken place before the legislature is formed, if effective government is to ensue?

It is far from clear, writes Dean Neal, that the one person, one vote idea "suggests a principle which even the interests represented by the urban plaintiffs [in *Baker v. Carr* and like cases] could consider satisfactory under all circumstances, and even less clear that it is a principle which assures fair treatment to other interests equally entitled to fair treatment." That states the upshot of the foregoing analysis. It also follows from the same analysis, however, that some institution—and, perhaps one may even posit, an institution that has independent powers of initiative as well as a veto—must be available as an effective voice of the majority. That institution is the executive, including the federal President. To be sure, the man from Mars reading our Constitution would think otherwise, just as, in an opposite sense, he would have received a strange impression of reality from a reading of the Soviet constitution of 1936. For the Electoral College seems to deflect the majoritarian character of the Presidency. Actually, however, not since 1888 have we elected a President in a two-party contest who had fewer popular votes than his opponent, and then Benjamin Harrison lost the popular vote by about the same tiny margin (although, of course, it was greater relatively) by which John F. Kennedy won it. In circumstances of such even balance, a toss of the coin, the Electoral College, or, as recently in Minnesota, a three-judge recount serves, one about as well as another, to make a decisive choice and render it legitimate. Moreover, the Electoral College actually works to strengthen the majoritarian influence, because its distortion of a true majority counterbalances precisely the distortion to be found in the malapportioned legislature. A President views his constituency as being weighted to the place where the major population centers are. Even Harrison won because he carried New York.

All governors are straight-out majoritarian. Until recently, Georgia constituted an exception, but no longer. The state provisionally abandoned the county-unit system in the 1962 election under pressure from a lower federal court, and on March 18, 1963, the Supreme Court made it final.[9] Unfortunately, however, the Court, in an opinion by Justice Douglas, offered no tenable principle in support of its conclusion that election of governors and other statewide officials by the county-unit method is unconstitutional. Justice Douglas' peroration gave voice to the familiar "creed" at the highest possible level of abstraction:

> The conception of political equality from the Declaration of Independence, to Lincoln's Gettysburg Address, to the Fifteenth [no racial restrictions on voting], Seventeenth [popular election of senators], and Nineteenth [women's vote] Amendments can mean only one thing—one person, one vote.

Earlier in the opinion—evidently in deference to some members of his majority, for there is reason to think that Justice Douglas somehow means exactly what he said in the peroration—the principle is qualified in such a way as to make it not necessarily applicable to the election of a districted legislature. It is to be one person, one vote within a given constituency from which an official is elected, once that constituency has been defined. But what is a constituency? Is not the whole state the legislature's constituency and his district, however unequal, that of any member? And would it be all right if Georgia had its governor chosen by a malapportioned legislature or by one chamber of it? The result of the case can be justified in terms of the analysis here put forward. But the result is given the benefit of no coherent explanation in the Court's opinion, save only as it is rested on the one person, one vote principle, which the Court did not bother to justify either generally or in the particular circumstances.

It remains to ask whether we have evolved or can see emerging some other operative principle—other than equal representation—which is capable of general application. Neither the Supreme Court nor any of the other courts that have been busily tackling the problem has come within shouting distance of such a principle. All we have been vouchsafed have been plays on words, plays on statistics, and meaningless figures arbitarily picked out of thin air. One court, for example, held with a straight face that the ratio of population disparities between districts must be no more than 4-1. And why not, a commentator asked, 5-1 or 3-1? Indeed, why not? Well, the answer may be, because the court said 4-1, not 5 or 3, and somebody has got to decide these things. But when things are to be decided on hunch or out of thin air, because there is no other way, it is a fixed characteristic of our system that we let the political institutions do it. The political institutions reflect the people, even if imperfectly, and they include a governor responsive to the majority. Malapportioned though they may be, they are more easily subject to correction and more nearly responsible and responsive than courts, which do not suffer from malapportionment, because they are not apportioned, nor are they representative. It is an irony to which I alluded earlier that the superdemocrats look to the unrepresentative courts for an arbitrary decision which they resent when it is made by a faultily representative legislature, acting in concert with a majoritarian governor.

Courts are fit to render judgment on questions of principle, which we do not, in our tradition, relegate to the political market place, to be disposed of on the basis of one of those not irrational, but it may be intuitive or otherwise unverifiable, choices. Principle is what is expected of courts. Perhaps some principle applicable to apportionment can be worked out, which goes beyond the requirement merely that the executive be majoritarian. If so, the first wisdom is to look at the reality of our allocations of power to govern, not at paper provisions and statistical nightmares. What does it mean to juggle ratios or to bewail the fact that 20 per cent of a state's population can elect a majority of its legislature, X per cent of the population of the United States can elect the President, and X minus 10 per cent can elect the Senate? This is no fact; it isn't what ever happens. The malapportioned Senate, for example, is more nearly majoritarian than the House, because Minneapolis and even Atlanta are coming to resemble New York and Cleveland more than they do their neighboring counties, and in state-wide elections Minneapolis and Atlanta count heavily, and count even beyond the mere numbers of their people. If a tenable principle is ever to emerge, it will proceed from an understanding of the realities of power, of the role of parties and how they are run, of the role of money and of various relevant skills, of the state-wide influence of urban home rule governments and of various groups and factions, and so forth and so on. When we know, to revert to Dahl's question, "Who Governs?", we may begin to be in a position to lay down a constitutional principle that tells us who should govern. Until then our imperfect representative institutions are better fitted than courts to tinker with the system.

The political arena is messier than the judicial, to be sure, but that is where all of us who feel under- or mis-represented should be exerting every ounce of power and influence. We may be right, but it may also be, especially if we lose, that we were after all wrong. For years now malapportionment has been the cynosure of assorted muckrakers—a common, catchall grievance, the supposed cause of urban rot and the obsolescence of federalism, the real reason, for all we know, why "wealth accumulates, and men decay." But it is quite possible that malapportionment has been held responsible for too many ills, and that the responsiveness of our legislatures has been more gravely impaired by antiquated committee and seniority systems, and by other institutional habits that are seldom brought to light. Let a major political effort, led by majoritarian executives, be tried in that direction. So far as Congress is concerned, it may also be that it fails to act when it does because it *is* truly representative. The country, we should not forget, was very closely divided in 1960. This may be a deplorable fact, but it is scarcely undemocratic. As to state legislatures, urban rot, and the obsolescence of federalism, it may be that the real causes of our discontent are fiscal. The federal government has pre-empted the sources of public finance. State governments subsist in substantial measure on federal handouts. It is therefore somewhat less than surprising to find them relatively inert and irresponsible. Moreover, there is a finite amount of political energy and even attention in the people, and what there is the federal government, again, pre-empts more and more.

It is therefore question-begging to ask how we can obtain re-apportionment, and a consequent solution of our problems, from a minority entrenched through malapportionment. The supposed minority may not be a minority at all; malapportionment may not be what entrenches it; and our problems may be rooted elsewhere anyway. If, nevertheless, we beg these questions and assume a minority entrenched in the legislature through malapportionment, the answer is that the remedy lies with the majoritarian executive, whom we can influence, and whose own bargaining power can very properly be heightened by federal judicial holdings striking down obsolete apportionments and requiring legislatures to act affirmatively. The courts may be in no position to do more, but this much they can do. Beyond this, we should expect of the courts only that they permit the play of political forces to be free either of unexplained constitutional inhibitions or of pacifying assurances that the status quo is necessarily constitutional.

Congress

15

THE SUPREME COURT HELD on February 17, 1964, that Congressional districts must be as nearly equal in population as is practicable, so that in any given nation-wide Congressional election, one man's vote for a representative is roughly equal to another's.[1] "Mathematical precision" may, perhaps, be unattainable, the Court said, but substantial equality of districts is the "standard of justice and common sense," which federal courts throughout the country will hereafter enforce. The state immediately affected was Georgia. The opinion of the Court was by Justice Black for a majority of six, consisting also of Chief Justice Warren, Justices Douglas and Brennan, and the two appointees of President Kennedy, Justices White and Goldberg. (These latter two, incidentally, made the majority. It is a certainty that Justice Goldberg's predecessor, Justice Frankfurter, would have dissented, and it is at least questionable whether Justice White's predecessor, Justice Whittaker, would have signed this majority opinion.) The dissenters were three: Justices Clark, Harlan, and Stewart.

Many years of agitation and litigation culminated in 1962 in

Baker v. Carr, which asserted federal jurisdiction over the apportionment of state legislatures. This decision was a second climax. The forces behind the agitation and behind the court cases have been, generally, the liberals, the Northern Democrats, urban and labor interests, in short, all those who want to get America moving again, and who since the earliest New Deal have felt frustrated by Congress. Yet this decision found as much favor with the chairman of the Republican as with the chairman of the Democratic National Committee. For nobody knows now where the advantage will lie when the smoke of litigation clears, let us say, in 1968 or conceivably 1966.

Those who feel so sure that the country wants to move forward in their sense and would do so but for malapportioned legislatures forget that John Kennedy carried the popular vote in 1960 by a margin not visible to the naked eye, and that when, under the impact of Barry Goldwater, the mood changed, a still malapportioned Congress registered the fact. Many a suburb and exurb that has burgeoned in the past decade is at least as underrepresented as many a city. Two of the most populous and underrepresented districts in the nation are Maricopa County (Phoenix), Arizona, and Dallas County, Texas. John J. Rhodes, an ardent Goldwaterite, represents Phoenix. Reapportionment in Arizona is as likely as not to hurt two Democrats, Morris K. Udall and George F. Senner, Jr., who represent the malapportioned second and third districts. As for Dallas, nearly a million people there for a decade sent the antediluvian Bruce Alger (Rep.) to the House, and after reapportionment we may as well expect half a million people each to send us two Algers. Unless, of course, the reapportionment is accompanied by a skillful gerrymander, which nothing in this decision will prevent, and which can come near to making the whole thing a farce. What Eric Goldman has said of the initiative, the referendum, the recall, and other Progressive reforms of the early 1900's may prove true as well of the ultimate, over-all political effect of apportionment reform in the 1960's: "The most conspicuous result was the lack of any result."[2]

But if the decision is right on principle, then presumably it is right regardless of whom it helps or hurts in the next election or in the next two decades. The reader of Justice Black's majority opinion will find himself unaided in the effort to decide whether the Court's decision is right or wrong. Justice Black argues only that his conclusion follows from the language and the history of the Constitution. The language is that of Article I, Section 2: "The House of Representatives shall be composed of Members chosen every second Year by the People of the several States." This provision is part of the Constitutional Convention's Great Compromise between the small and the large states. The quid for this quo is Section 3 of the same article, providing that each state shall have two senators, to be chosen by its legislature. Thus the large states could exert the force of their numbers in the House (and also, incidentally, in the election of the President), and the small were guaranteed equality in the Senate. No matter how often one intones the phrase "chosen by the People of the several States," there is nothing in it that seems necessarily to refer to equality of districts. Article I apportions to the states voting power in the national institutions. It does not spell out the ways in which a state should make internal distribution of the power it has thus gained. Indeed, Section 2 of Article I goes on to say quite plainly that the states may decide for themselves who shall vote for members of the national House of Representatives, except that the qualifications cannot differ from those established by the state for the more numerous branch of its own legislature. And in fact nothing in this article has prevented the states from imposing property qualifications, poll taxes till just the other day, when the Twenty-fourth Amendment became effective, and disabilities based on sex till the Nineteenth Amendment was enacted in 1920.

The historical context to which Justice Black devotes the better part of his opinion also proves nothing. If one assumes that every time a Founding Father spoke the word "people" he had in mind the Georgia Congressional Apportionment Act of 1931, the case for the majority's result is made out. But if the intensity of one's convictions does not quite lead one to this daring assumption, various remarks by Madison and James Wilson and others remain at best ambiguous, and there is left in any event the question whether the views of these men were adopted by the Convention. For if the language of Article I, Section 2, expresses these views, it expresses them most inartistically; it would have been easy to say that all votes must count equally. The historical case is utterly unconvincing, and very probably, as Justice Harlan said in dissent, "demonstrably unsound."

Yet inquiry merely begins, it does not end with history and with the text of Article I. And so, although there is nothing in Justice Black's majority opinion to support such a surmise, it is possible nevertheless that the decision may establish a sound and wise principle. Is substantial, if not altogether mathematical, equality of representation such a principle? The way to begin answering this question is to realize that it need not be put in this qualified form. There is no practical obstacle to the attainment of perfect mathematical equality. Either proportional representation or state-wide at-large elections will attain mathematical equality for every vote cast. But proportional representation encourages small parties and ends invariably in unstable or paralyzed multi-party government. At-large elections tend to the other extreme; the losing party loses everything, not only the power to make its views prevail in the national House but also the right to make them heard. No state in recent times has willingly adopted either system, nor does Justice Black's opinion advocate either system.

It is thus apparent that no one, no matter how strong his attachment to the notion of equal votes, regards equality of representation as the single overriding objective to be attained in the construction of representative institutions. On reflection, we all acknowledge other goals as well: stability, enhancement of the two-party system, representation of the losers as well as the winners, and representation also of isolated and even alienated interests. That is why we now almost universally district, and that, sometimes, is why we district unevenly. The House is not just the register of 1962's majority will—and why, after all, should that govern us in 1964, and who imagines that there was such a thing as a majority will in 1962 on, let us say, the Rivers and Harbors Appropriation Bill of 1964? The House is a deliberative representative institution, charged with making many a judgment that cannot be related to the last election or even the next. It is at least as important that the largest possible variety of interests in this immense country be reflected in the House, have access to it, have some share, however small, of power, and thus gain, in the late Judge Learned Hand's phrase, a sense of common venture in government—all this is at least as important in our great, heterogeneous Republic as the simple notion of one man, one vote.

Perhaps it is true, as every aggrieved liberal will argue, that the disparity between the Atlanta Congressional district and the smallest rural one in Georgia is evidence not of regard for legitimate considerations of any sort but of entrenched and inequitable rural power. But to recognize the existence of an evil is not automatically to prove the value of any and all suggested cures. The cure imposed by the Court is either fatuous, because gerrymanders, of which the Court said and is likely to say nothing, can nullify all that the cure can reasonably be intended to accomplish; or it is worse than the disease, because if taken seriously as stressing equality of representation to the exclusion of other legitimate considerations, it misunderstands and may ultimately ruin representative institutions. Until the Supreme Court succeeds in working out some principle of representation which, instead of distorting the past and over-simplifying the present, takes some account of all the objectives that properly play a role in the construction of deliberative, representative institutions—until then it is not possible to rejoice that the federal courts will have the last word in apportioning the House of Representatives.

One Man,
One Vote,
More
or Less

16

In STRIKING DOWN the Georgia county-unit system in 1963, Justice Douglas coined the slogan, "one person, one vote." In February, 1964, the Court held that this slogan defined the standard applicable to Congressional districting. Four months later the Court decided that it was to be "one person, one vote," more or less, in the apportionment of seats in both houses of state legislatures as well.[1]

The Court's rulings on apportionment have been popular. They seem—and emerge from newspaper reports—simple, straightforward, obviously just. They favor majority control, and there is hardly a strain of opinion in American political life which does not think that it represents or can represent a majority. Hence the Court's rulings seem to offer large promises of success to everyone, urban Democrats and suburban Republicans, supporters of medicare and opponents of open housing, and so forth and so on. It is as if the Court had pronounced a piety no more controversial than the common appeal to bring out the vote on election day.

But the Court's ruling is not so simple and straightforward as it is made to appear, and it would not be obviously just even if it were

196

that simple. Stable, effective, good government is a product of more than merely the application of the majoritarian principle. The legislature is a deliberative institution, which should ensure, as Justice Stewart said in dissent in June, 1964, "a fair, effective, and balanced representation of the regional, social, and economic interests within a state." Persons, said Chief Justice Warren for the majority, "not history or economic interests . . . people, not land or trees or pastures, vote." But people, replied Justice Harlan, "are not ciphers" and "legislators can represent their electors only by speaking for their interests—economic, social, political—many of which do reflect the place where electors live."

Despite its rhetoric, the majority of the Court recognized the limitations of the strict majoritarian principle. In the interstices of his opinion it becomes clear that the Chief Justice is demanding only substantially equal districts, only deviations from a strict population basis that are not "too egregious," only that "a state make an honest and good faith effort to construct districts, in both houses of its Legislature, as nearly of equal population as is practicable."

Who is to decide what is substantial or egregious, good faith or bad? Not an electoral majority, in which the Chief Justice places such heartfelt reliance, for in Colorado a majority approved the apportionment by direct vote in a referendum, and yet the Chief Justice struck it down. The judges of the lower federal courts, rather, are to decide, under what must necessarily be only occasional supervision by the Supreme Court. These judges are given no criteria for their decisions. The only thing the Chief Justice does for them is to exclude from consideration the criteria that have been most commonly used. The judges are plunged into second-guessing the expedient, empirical, political judgments of fifty state legislatures decade after decade. This they are unfitted to do—by experience, by access to relevant information, and by responsiveness to the interests affected—and the attempt can only bring them and the tasks that they are fitted to perform into disrepute.

In an earlier day of misguided judicial effort, two generations ago, the Supreme Court charged federal judges with speaking the last word on, among other things, labor policy[2] and rates to be charged by public utilities.[3] This seems hard to believe now, but it was so. Only "good" and "legitimate" strikes and picketing and boycotts were to be permitted, and not "bad"; only rates which allowed a gas or water or electric company a "fair" return on its investment might be set by a state, and not "unfair" rates. There were no criteria. Federal judges were simply charged with deciding. And so they picked and chose the strikes they liked, if any. And no state could set a utility rate without then conducting five or ten years of litigation to a totally unpredictable outcome.

The situation became intolerable, and it was not cured without endangering the entire place of the federal judiciary in the American system, with all its many valuable functions. The issues, it will be said, were different then. But they only seem so on the surface. The root of the trouble was that judges were deciding, in their uncharted discretion and ultimately according to whim—in a word, lawlessly—questions that mattered deeply to many people, that were not felt to be governed by immutable principles peculiarly within the province of judges, and that *were* felt to be the proper concern of officials responsive (however imperfectly, but through other devices also in addition to the franchise) to the people and to the interests affected. It was not satisfactory then and it will not prove satisfactory now to leave final decision of such pragmatic questions to lifetime federal appointees responsible only to other lifetime appointees in Washington.

RELIGION
AND THE
SCHOOLS

VI

Federal
Aid to
Education

17

SHOULD FEDERAL AID TO EDUCATION BE EXTENDED to parochial schools? The issue always carries a grave threat to the enactment of any sort of aid to education program at all; it defeated President Kennedy's and inhibited the drafting of President Johnson's; and it gives one the eerie feeling of having tumbled head over heels through time and space into a parliamentary crisis in the Third or Fourth French Republic. But the crisis is real here and now, and the issue is constitutional as well as political. The adjective "constitutional" signifies that the policy choices open to the President and Congress are not altogether free, since the Supreme Court may foreclose some by invoking the First Amendment's prohibition against laws "respecting an establishment of religion."

President Kennedy was convinced that one form of aid to parochial schools—"across-the-board loans"—was unconstitutional. This was a sound and wise judgment, but as a prediction of what the Court would do in fact it was daring. The *Everson* case of 1947,[1] on which President Kennedy relied, is inconclusive as a precedent, although the Court did say: "No tax in any amount, large or small, can be levied to support any religious activities or institutions, whatever they may be called." It is even far from certain that if Congress extended across-the-board loans to parochial schools a case could be contrived to give the Court jurisdiction to pass on the constitutionality of the statute. But, as Mr. Kennedy recognized, the Supreme Court is not the only institution of our federal government required to construe and apply, which is to say, "preserve, protect and defend the Constitution of the United States." That is a function also and first of the President and of Congress. They also must be guided by the history of the American disestablishment, of which, as the late Justice Rutledge said, the First Amendment "is at once the refined product and the terse summation."[2] This is not to suggest, of course, that Madison's illustrious Memorial and Remonstrance Against Religious Assessments neatly applies itself to the conditions of our day. We must work out our own prudential solutions still. But we are admonished that certain solutions touch fundamental values, if not the very meaning, of our society. Therefore—quite aside from any specific prediction of what the Court may do in fact—policy and constitutional law merge inextricably here.

We are often reminded of how complex a society we have become, in the technological and economic sense, and of the delicate adjustments from which we depend, as by a thread. At least as much is true of us politically and culturally, of the tension of federalism and of the balance between nationalizing and pluralistic forces. Culturally, no doubt the most significant nationalizing, egalitarian force, by which we have set immense store for a hundred years, has been the free public school system. Without one, Britain was two nations. We should have been twenty. And today, by virtue of the Court's school desegregation decisions, it is chiefly through our system of public education that we have set about completing the equalizing work begun by the Emancipation Proclamation. Yet when this great nationalizing force threatened to engulf pluralistic influences by making public school education not only compulsory but exclusive of private schooling, the First Amendment prevented, for in addition to forbidding "an establishment of religion" it also protects "the free exercise thereof." The Court intervened in 1925, in *Pierce v. Society of Sisters*.[3] Two years earlier the Court had foreclosed state control of a parochial school's curriculum.[4]

Such is the adjustment. The state is secular, unifying, egalitarian. But it is bound to suffer centrifugal cultural influences, and to subject them to no direct control, let alone prohibition. We misunderstand the scheme, however, if we think of the state as neutral. It is neutral as it may prefer none of our many religions and cultural strains. But it is itself committed to exerting a secular, unifying force. Only the state has this commitment. No other group does, and if the state abandons it, it is gone. The state, therefore, while required impartially to accept the presence in society of other influences, is nevertheless itself a party in the contest of cultures.

But public school secularism is not just another among our many sects. It has cohesive national content. That is the whole of its content, and its function is unique. It is what we render unto Caesar and what we get from Caesar. To offer equal support throughout to public and private schools would be effectively to abandon the mission of the state, for it would be to surrender the sole means by which the state is permitted to draw people to its schools and away from centrifugal ones. The churches all have a powerful ally in the protected institution of the family. The state, responsible for our nationhood, is forbidden to compel and must rely entirely on the inducement of its free public schools.

This inducement may be reduced in various ways, to be sure, short of being given up altogether. There may be pressing reasons for reducing it in order to satisfy other needs, such as those of national defense, or in order to remedy, in the general public interest, this or that critical shortage of skills. And, as the churches themselves are well aware, the importance of the mission—their own or the state's —is not the same in colleges as it is in elementary and secondary schools. There are questions of the conflict of purposes and of degree here as elsewhere. Hence one need not be overly troubled by assistance extended to private as well as public universities by the National Defense Education Act and similar statutes, or by President Johnson's program, contained in the Elementary and Secondary Education Act of 1965, which makes grants for the purchase of books to parochial as well as public schools, and makes available to parochial as well as public school students remedial and other special instruction. Even across-the-board loans or grants for general use, extended to parochial as well as public schools, would not immediately signal the end of public education. Yet they would surely invite the beginning of the end of the primacy of that system.

Unless they were to be the beginning of the end of the privateness of private schools. That, as the law of the Constitution now stands, is a more than possible development. Private schools that draw on public funds might be considered public to the extent of being required, as the state is, to admit pupils without regard to race or religion, and conceivably to offer either no or all religious teachings. This is, of course, preposterous. But it bespeaks the tenacity with which the law holds the state to its egalitarian mission in all its activities. The incongruity of the result just supposed is itself an indication of the revolution that would be worked in our system by involving the state with parochial schools. No one can foresee all the wide-ranging adjustments that would be necessitated were the existing state-church balance to be violently disturbed.

It remains to say a word about the supposed inequity of forcing some parents to pay taxes for the support of the public schools, while barring them from access to the public funds so accumulated and remitting them to their own resources in supporting their private schools. The burden is undeniable, but its justification is plain. The nationalizing work of the state is in everyone's ultimate interest, within the limits set on the state by the Free Exercise of Religion Clause of the First Amendment. We pay for the work of the state and we benefit from it, whether or not conscience permits us to partake of public schooling. This, as Holmes said of all taxes, is payment for the American civilization. Separate paths within it, which are allowed, are the particular concern of those who pursue them.

The
School
Prayer
Cases

18

In THREE CASES, one from New York in 1962[1] and one each from
Pennsylvania and Maryland in 1963,[2] the Supreme Court forbade
religious exercises in the public schools. Religious observances
sponsored or conducted by school boards or their agents are unconstitutional, the Court held, because under the First and Fourteenth
Amendments government, state or federal, and all its subdivisions
and representatives "shall make no law respecting an establishment
of religion." Prescribed school prayers, the Court concluded, are an
establishment of religion.

Anyone who values American public education as perhaps the
single most important nationalizing, and therefore secular, force in
our pluralistic society must have regarded it as a near disaster if the
Supreme Court had validated the prayers in the New York case, let
alone those in the Pennsylvania and Maryland cases that followed a
year later. For such an act of legitimation would have given enormous impetus to Heaven knows (!) what insistent and pervasive
incursions into the public school system by organized religion. In
the end the system might well have been fragmented into regions

and schools dominated by one or another of the churches, each tending to attract only the communicants of the dominant church—that is to say, public parochial schools. But it does not follow on this premise that one must view the Supreme Court's actual decisions as right, proper, and beneficial. Legitimation of religious incursions was not the sole course of action open to the Court. The cases need not have been decided when they were, they need not have been decided in the order in which they were decided, and decision need not have rested on the ground chosen by the Court. All of which makes quite a difference, if one is interested not merely in abstract doctrine but in an actual effective school system that comes somewhere near to the heart's desire.

The decision in the New York case was unfortunate and should have been avoided altogether, as it could have been by a simple denial by the Court of the petition to review. The so-called prayer involved was this sentence composed by the New York Board of Regents:

Almighty God, we acknowledge our dependence upon Thee, and we beg Thy blessings upon us, our parents, our teachers and our Country.

This, obviously, is not so much religion as a sort of mass-media religiosity. It represents the kind of accommodation observable on almost every occasion in our public life, when a priest, a minister, and a rabbi are given equal time, and are expected to sound—and at any rate to be heard—as if there were no differences among them. The Regents' prayer was not prescribed. It was made available to school boards in New York that wanted to use it, and some, but by no means all, directed teachers to start class by leading this prayer. Quite evidently, pressures against a wholly secular school system are severely felt at the local level in many places. And here was a clumsy attempt to find some vacuous common denominator that would satisfy such pressures without unduly offending anyone. If this is unconstitutional as an establishment of religion, then just about anything with the word "God" in it would also be. Hardly any qualification of the holding of unconstitutionality seems possible, and the Court hardly offered any, except to remark in a footnote, without explanation, that it was not passing judgment on references to the Deity in the Declaration of Independence or on other "patriotic or ceremonial" "manifestations in our public life of belief in God."

The Court's footnoted disclaimer—Justice Stewart, in dissent, called it an "unsupported *ipse dixit*"—was not very convincing. The immediate reaction to the decision pretty well disregarded it, and not unjustly so. That reaction can be ranged as follows, in descending order of apocalyptic vision. Justice Douglas concurring, and Justice Stewart dissenting, both thought—one approvingly, the other with regret—that all invocations of the Deity on official occasions are, or are soon to become, unconstitutional. The Justices spared nothing, not the hope daily expressed by the Court's own crier that God will "save the United States and this Honorable Court," nor the third stanza of "The Star-Spangled Banner," nor the engraving on the coin of the realm. An Alabama congressman observed somewhat less comprehensively that the Supreme Court, having put the Negro in the schools, had now driven God out. Cardinal Spellman was not only "shocked" but "frightened," and various Protestant divines feared for "the basic moral supports of free democracy," although other Protestant clergymen and many rabbis hailed the decision as shoring up the so-called constitutional wall of separation between church and state, thus ensuring the freest play of conscientious religious observance.

All the alarms about "The Star-Spangled Banner" and what the Court's crier has been in the habit of saying since the day of John Marshall may have been so many debating points, but they were debating points which the Court itself had made available. Seen more closely in its own school context, the Court's decision is also not free from doubt. Even as applied solely to schools (if this were logically possible), an absolute rule of the sort announced by the Court could be enforced—that is, could be made effective in the reality of the American public school system—only by a massive effort, requiring organized litigation, the backing of public opinion, and the support, at least, of the federal executive; an effort, in other words, such as was eventually mounted to realize the Court's decision in the *School Segregation Cases*. This is hardly to be expected; we are, after all, capable of one such effort at a time. And failing all this, the Court would fail, and would impair future possibilities of more limited effective action in this field. This was the Court's experience with an attempt, begun in 1948 and soon abandoned, to abolish released-time programs of religious instruction.[3]

Even assuming, however, that the absolute, unqualified standard adopted by the Court could be realized, and that it is desirable in principle, what would be its effect, not on some ideal public school system but on ours, now, in this moment of transition and crisis? And would the end result be worth the probable cost? To be sure, the public schools, by and large, and in recent times, have tried to be not only nondenominational and otherwise cohesive but secular, and it is a worthy and important objective to keep them so, resisting the *nouvelle vague* of the religious revival. But the great office of the American public school system has been to serve as a unifying, egalitarian force in a vast and diverse society; one of the centripetal forces without which we would be in danger of being sundered by our pluralistic stresses. To continue giving this service in the exploding circumstances of the post-World War II generation, the system must be renewed and strengthened in many ways, not least of all economic, not all of equal immediacy or importance. As the Alabama congressman rudely remarked, the public schools are, for one thing, in process of assimilating the Negro to the general level of education. Although there are exceptions, the schools, at least in urban areas, are in awful shape. They stand, indeed, in the gravest possible danger for a system with the objectives of ours, namely, the danger of being deserted by the middle class, and of becoming the schools of the poor, the colored, the newly arrived. This is a catastrophic prospect, and too little is being done to avert it. We need desperately to multiply and improve our schools, to disperse homogeneous neighborhood groups through the system, to draw those who have left the public schools back into them.

Complete secularization of the public schools is for many of us—who may be a minority, but who hold what many more may find on reflection to be the true principle of our tradition—an ultimate ideal. But is this the time to ventilate the issue of religion in the sort of absolute terms that are certain to alienate many of those whose patronage and support of the public schools is especially needed, because they possess the means to seek an alternative? Principle is one thing, no matter how worthy and valid, but the wise and effective government of a free society is sometimes quite another. School officials may in perfectly good faith conclude—in the present unsettled state of educational policy and in light of other pressing needs of the school system—that the time and the problem call for accommodation and compromise.

Something—but not enough—of these considerations seems to have been borne in on the Justices in the year that passed between the New York case and the later Pennsylvania and Maryland cases. The decision and the opinions in 1963 seemed to mark, in a discreet way, a barely perceptible retreat from the New York case, which is on all accounts best forgotten. What was involved in Pennsylvania and Maryland was Bible reading, Old Testament and New, and the saying of the Lord's Prayer. The possibilities of sectarian differences and of their classic disruptive effect are obviously heightened in these circumstances. They were present, also, of course, in the New York case, no matter how innocuous the prayer, if for no other reason than that agnostics are also a sect, not to speak of professing atheists. But the point is that to a public which is largely neither agnostic nor atheist, the potential disruptive effect, which presumably nobody desires, of publicly sponsored religion can be made more persuasively clear where Bible reading and Lord's Prayer saying are involved than in the circumstances of the New York case. There is more of a tendency to recognize and respect differences between the King James and Douay Bibles, and between Jews and Christians, and Unitarians and orthodox Christians, than between agnostics and believers. This may be—it is—deplorable, but it is so, and agencies of government, including the Supreme Court, are not obliged to close their eyes to it as a relevant tactical consideration.

The Court in the more recent cases placed some emphasis on the factor of practical coercion. In neither Pennsylvania nor Maryland did the regulations as such coerce children to participate. But in practice, the pressure on nonconformist children is well-nigh irresistible, and in neither state was anything positive done to counteract it. Justice Stewart, in an able dissent, urged that the factor of coercion be made decisive. He would have returned the cases to the lower courts for the taking of more concrete evidence on this issue. Whether or not that additional step should have been taken—or could have been taken without wholly repudiating the New York decision of the year before—it is much to be regretted that the Court did not rest wholly on the ground of the practical coercion of nonconformist children. Again, that would surely have been a more persuasive ground to many who otherwise might find the decision disagreeable. And it is a ground that would have allowed, at least temporarily, for a variety of adjustments to be made by school boards facing a variety of conditions across the country. Still, though it took the broader ground that these prayers, whether or not coercive, are unconstitutional as an establishment of state-sponsored religion, the Court this time did not seem bent, either in its holding or in the tone of its opinion, on banishing from the public schools, and perhaps from public life, too, at once and absolutely, all recognition of religion.

The Original
Understanding
and the
Segregation
Decision*

Appendix

BEFORE SETTING OUT on the direct and noble march to the Court's conclusion in the *School Segregation Cases*,[1] Chief Justice Warren took care to post a rear guard. The history of the adoption of the Fourteenth Amendment, to which reargument in these cases had been largely addressed, though casting some light, was, the Chief Justice said, "inconclusive" at best. "The most avid proponents of the post-War Amendments undoubtedly intended them to remove all legal distinctions among 'all persons born or naturalized in the United States.' Their opponents, just as certainly, were antagonistic to both the letter and the spirit of the Amendments and wished them to have the most limited effect. What others in Congress and the state legislatures had in mind cannot be determined with any degree of certainty."[2] Three pages later, as befits a commander in mid-advance, the Chief Justice, having made his

* I was one of two law clerks to Justice Frankfurter during the Supreme Court's October Term, 1952. At that term the Court heard the first argument in the *School Segregation Cases* and handed down the order for reargument; the cases were reargued and decided at the following term. My interest in pursuing an investigation into the original understanding of the Fourteenth Amendment was prompted by the events which took place during my service at the Court.

dispositions, had no further thought for the rear: "In approaching this problem, we cannot turn the clock back to 1868 when the Amendment was adopted, or even to 1896 when *Plessy v. Ferguson* was written. We must consider public education in the light of its full development and its present place in American life throughout the Nation. Only in this way can it be determined if segregation in public schools deprives these plaintiffs of the equal protection of the laws."[3]

The *School Segregation Cases* were extensively briefed and argued at two terms of Court. Their importance, judged by every criterion relevant to the Court's work, is difficult to overestimate, and plainly the Court itself did not underestimate it. Yet the cases were disposed of in the end by a relatively brief opinion which hit only the high spots of issues necessarily involved.[4] The Court knew, of course, that its judgment would have an unparalleled impact on the daily lives of a very substantial portion of the population, and that the response of many of those affected would be in varying degrees hostile. It was necessary, therefore, if ever it had been, to exert to the utmost the prestige, the oracular authority of the institution. To this end, it was desirable that the Court speak unanimously, with one voice from the deep. And the less said the less chance of internal disagreement. By the same token, it was wise to present as small a target as possible to marksmen on the outside. In sum, without imputing to the Court aspirations to a form of art it does not profess to practice, one may be entitled to surmise that here was a decision which, like a poem, "should not mean / But be," and that the Court saw this and acted on it. Considerations of this order, applicable only to so extraordinary a case, are sufficient, in any event, to explain the brevity of the reference to the history of the Fourteenth Amendment's adoption and the briskness of the transition from an apparent assumption of that history's relevance to the statement that the clock cannot be turned back.

Beneath the brevity and beneath the briskness lies the pervasive problem of the weight to be accorded in constitutional adjudication to evidence of the framers' original understanding.[5] Reliance on such evidence is subject to caveats applicable to the use of legislative history as an aid in statutory construction.[6] What is more important, it may raise a fundamental question concerning the Court's function in construing the Constitution. This difficulty is best posed by quotation of two extreme judicial utterances, both advocating meticulous adherence to original intent, so called:

1. No one, we presume, supposes that any change in public opinion or feeling, in relation to this unfortunate race, in the civil-

ized nations of Europe or in this country, should induce the court to give to the words of the Constitution a more liberal construction in their favor than they were intended to bear when the instrument was framed and adopted. Such an argument would be altogether inadmissible in any tribunal called on to interpret it. If any of its provisions are deemed unjust, there is a mode prescribed in the instrument itself by which it may be amended; but while it remains unaltered, it must be construed now as it was understood at the time of its adoption. . . . Any other rule of construction would abrogate the judicial character of this count, and make it the mere reflex of the popular opinion or passion of the day.

2. The whole aim of construction, as applied to a provision of the Constitution, is to discover the meaning, to ascertain and give effect to the intent, of its framers and the people who adopted it. . . . As nearly as possible we should place ourselves in the condition of those who framed and adopted it.

Of course, such views, when they prevail, threaten disaster to government under a written constitution. No further proof need be adduced than that the first quotation—could anything contrast more strikingly with the opinion of the Court in the *School Segregation Cases?*—comes from the judgment of Chief Justice Taney in *Dred Scott v. Sandford*,[7] and the second from Justice Sutherland's dissent in 1934 in *Home Bldg. & Loan Ass'n v. Blaisdell*.[8] But it is a long way from rejection of the Taney-Sutherland doctrine to the proposition that the original understanding is simply not relevant.[9] For arguments based on that understanding have a strong pull. They have decided cases for judges who held the views represented by the passages quoted.[10] But the Court has also employed them without intentionally connoting, indeed while disavowing, such views.[11] And evidence of the original understanding has been relied on by judges well aware that it was *a constitution* they were expounding.[12]

The original understanding forms the starting link in the chain of continuity which is a source of the Court's authority, and it is not unnatural that appeals to it should recur as consistently as they do.[13] Happily, finding the original understanding, like applying the Constitution itself, is, at best, "not a mechanical exercise but a function of statecraft" and of historical insight.[14] And what is relevant is not alone the origin of constitutional provisions but also "the line of their growth," the further links in the chain of continuity.[15] This being so and our law not being given to following hard and fast theoretical formulations on questions of the scope of this one, it is possible, in the

Chief Justice's words, for historical materials to cast some light although they are inconclusive and although, in any event, the clock cannot be turned back. But only an examination in some detail of the relevant materials themselves can make clear just how this has proved possible in the *School Segregation Cases*.

The Thirty-Ninth Congress and the Fourteenth Amendment

The discussion, by the parties and by the United States as amicus, of the Fourteenth Amendment's history, which took place in response to questions propounded by the Court in its order for reargument of the *School Segregation Cases*,[16] must surely have amounted to the most extensive presentation of historical materials ever made to the Court. The briefs and appendices are book-size and shelf-length. The heart of this mass of evidence is to be found in the reported debates of the first session of the 39th Congress, which convened on December 4, 1865,[17] and sent the Fourteenth Amendment to the country on June 13, 1866,[18] shortly before it adjourned to go home and face the electorate. Other materials have a bearing, of course. But the debates of the Congress which submitted, and the journals and documents of the legislatures which ratified, the amendment provide the most direct and unimpeachable indication of original purpose and understanding —to the extent, of course, that any such indication is to be found. Of these two sets of materials, the Congressional debates are in this case the richer, and they rank, in any event, first in importance. It may perhaps be said that whatever they establish constitutes a rebuttable presumption. For it is not unrealistic, in the main, to assume notice of Congressional purpose in the state legislatures. A showing of ratification on the basis of an understanding different from that revealed by Congressional materials must carry the burden of proof. And, of course, the ratifying states are a chorus of voices; a discordant one among them proves little.

Very much the better part of the first session of the 39th Congress was devoted to discussing, in one connection or another, the subject matter of the Fourteenth Amendment: the governance of the South, readmission of the Southern states, loyalty to the Union, a place under the sun for the newly freed Negro race, distribution of powers (in the context of these problems) between the states and the federal government. The bulk of this session-long debate may conveniently be analyzed as it related to four measures: The Freedmen's Bureau Bill, which President Andrew Johnson vetoed and which the Radicals failed to pass over his veto; the Civil Rights Act of 1866,[19] enacted over a veto; an abortive proposal for a short constitutional amendment, whose sponsor was John A. Bingham of Ohio; and the Fourteenth Amendment itself.

To obtain a proper understanding of the relevant Congressional purpose, it is necessary to concentrate not only on statements dealing specifically with public school education of the Negro race but also on remarks going to subjects which were deemed to be closely allied—though the relationship may not have survived as clearly to this day. It will become plain that the right, if any, to an unsegregated public school education resided for most men who spoke at this session in a fringe area, where its companions were, among other less well-defined rights, suffrage, jury service, and intermarriage. The first two debates to be reviewed—those on the Freedmen's Bureau Bill and on the Civil Rights Bill—were, of course, debates looking to legislation rather than to a constitutional amendment, and they dealt with an issue of constitutionality as well as one of policy. The former arose under the Thirteenth Amendment, which had gone into effect not long before the 39th Congress convened. The two issues are not always easy to separate and must often be examined in tandem. Finally, it is important to form an impression of the political atmosphere of the session. The Democrats were a small and—with a few exceptions—cowed minority. The dominant Republicans consisted of three groups: Radicals, Moderates, and Conservative supporters of President Johnson. The first two factions were to form an alliance which was to wage in 1866 a bitter and successful campaign against the President. That coming event cast an unmistakable and significant shadow over the session.

The Freedmen's Bureau Bill

The bill to enlarge the powers of the Freedmen's Bureau[20] provided in its section 7:

> That whenever, in any State or district in which the ordinary course of judicial proceedings has been interrupted by the rebellion, and wherein, in consequence of any State or local law, ordinance, police, or other regulation, custom, or prejudice, any of the civil rights or immunities belonging to white persons, including the right to make and enforce contracts, to sue, be parties and give evidence; to inherit, purchase, lease, sell, hold, and convey . . . property, and to have full and equal benefit of all laws and pro-

ceedings for the security of person and estate, are refused or denied to negroes . . . or wherein they . . . are subjected to any
. . . different punishment . . . for the commission of any act . . .
than are prescribed for white persons . . . it shall be the duty of
the President . . . to extend military protection . . ."[21]

On the passage of this bill (on January 25 and February 8 in the
Senate,[22] and on February 6 and 9 in the House[23]) the Republican
party, with one exception in the House,[24] and with the notable absence
in the Senate of Edgar Cowan, the Pennsylvania Conservative, stood
together. Senators Norton of Minnesota and Van Winkle of West Virginia, who, with Cowan, later voted against the Civil Rights Bill and
against the Fourteenth Amendment, were recorded for this bill. So
was Senator Doolittle of Wisconsin, who was absent for the vote on
the Civil Rights Bill but voted against the Fourteenth Amendment.
These votes for the Freedmen's Bureau Bill may seem inconsistent
with Conservative actions later in the session. For the enumeration
in section 7 of "civil rights and immunities" was not exclusive. The
bill's coverage depended, therefore, on the meaning of those terms.
In the subsequent debate on the Civil Rights Bill, Conservatives and
others attacked similar general language as susceptible of a "latitudinarian" construction, and the leadership deemed it wise to strike
it. But there are a number of explanations for these Conservative Republican votes in favor of the Freedmen's Bureau Bill. For one thing,
this bill drew constitutional validity from a source—the war power—
not open to the later Civil Rights Bill, which applied throughout the
country. Constitutional scruples to the side, the fact that the Freedmen's Bureau Bill did not apply in the North meant that there was no
occasion to worry about federal interference with practices in that
part of the country, which was where constituents lived. Finally, it was
not until after the vote on this bill—certainly not until after the Senate
vote on January 25—that the struggle between President and Radical
Congress was publicly joined. Conservative Republicans who later
sided with the President, and many Moderates as well, still entertained
at this time some hope of averting the conflict. They felt that if they
gave in to Radical opinion on the Freedmen's Bureau Bill their hand
would be strengthened in attempts to find common ground with the
Radicals, and they had reason to believe that the President would
pursue the same strategy. It was for a time commonly expected that
Johnson would sign the Freedmen's Bureau Bill.[25] The President, however, vetoed it on February 19, and the Senate, on the following day,
failed to override.[26] The President's supporters—the party whip and
illness were to deplete their ranks later—rallied around him.

In the course of debate on the Freedmen's Bureau Bill and on a predecessor proposal which was briefly before the Senate,[27] Charles Sumner and Henry Wilson of Massachusetts, Radicals of abolitionist antecedents, as well as John Sherman of Ohio and Lyman Trumbull of Illinois, Moderates, spoke in general terms of measures that would have to be taken and existing practices that would have to be eliminated, both now and in the long run, in order to better the condition of the Negro in the South. They referred, among other things, to the Negro's need for, and right to, education. In the House, Ignatius Donnelly of Minnesota moved an amendment to empower the bureau to offer to refugees and freedmen "a common-school education."[28] These remarks and the Donnelly amendment are evidence of a real concern in Congress with education of the Southern Negro, of which we shall see more. But, except perhaps for Sumner's speech,[29] none of them can be read as advocating unsegregated schools or as assuming that the bill would lead to their establishment.* Nor, apart from a broadside Democratic attack in the House aimed more at future Radical objectives than at this particular bill, did the opposition so assume or argue.[30]

---

* Wilson enumerated the rights listed in the bill and added the freedman's right to "go into the schools and educate himself and his children." (*Globe,* 111.) But he was speaking of rights which would obtain if Southern Black Codes, denying, as he believed, any schooling at all, were annulled by passage of this bill. And he was speaking against the background of a report on conditions in the South by a Republican politician and Union major general, the former German revolutionary Carl Schurz, which the Senate had requested from the President and had had printed. (*Globe,* 30, 78–80.) This report dealt with "Education of the Freedmen" and discussed the opposition to it of Southern whites. It recommended education for the Negro "as an integral part of the educational systems of the States," but spoke throughout of "negro education," "colored schools," "school-houses in which colored children were taught," and the desirability only of supporting schools for freedmen out of general tax funds to which Negroes contributed and from which white schools benefited. There were no references to unsegregated schools, even as an ultimate objective, in the Schurz Report. (*S. Exec. Doc.* No. 2, 39th Cong., 1st Sess. 2, 25–27 [1865]. The problem to which Wilson was addressing himself was the establishment and maintenance of segregated schools for freedmen, which he believed to be a matter of some difficulty in the South of that day. The same is true of a reference by Sherman to "the right to be educated" (*Globe,* 42), and by Trumbull to the need "to educate, improve, enlighten, and Christianize the negro" (*Globe,* 322). Donnelly, arguing for his amendment, spoke of the value of education for both the white and colored races. Conceiving, obviously, of the separate education of the Negro, he said it would "shame the whites into an effort to educate themselves." He noted that Tennessee excluded Negroes from white schools, "while it makes no provision for their education in separate schools," that, evidently, being what he found objectionable. (*Globe,* 586, 587, 589.)

The Civil Rights Bill

On January 29, 1866, before passage in the House of the Freedmen's Bureau Bill, Lyman Trumbull of Illinois brought up in the Senate the Civil Rights Bill. Section 1 of the bill contained, as had section 7 of the Freedmen's Bureau Bill, a general prohibition of "discrimination in civil rights or immunities," which preceded a specific enumeration of such rights. Section 1, after conferring citizenship on native-born Negroes, provided:

> That there shall be no discrimination in civil rights or immunities among the inhabitants of any State or Territory of the United States on account of race, color, or previous condition of slavery; but the inhabitants of every race and color, without regard to any previous condition of slavery or involuntary servitude, except as a punishment for crime whereof the party shall have been duly convicted, shall have the same right to make and enforce contracts, to sue, be parties, and give evidence, to inherit, purchase, lease, sell, hold, and convey real and personal property, and to full and equal benefit of all laws and proceedings for the security of person and property, and shall be subject to like punishment, pains, and penalties, and to none other, any law, statute, ordinance, regulation, or custom to the contrary notwithstanding.

Section 2 provided, by way of enforcement power:

> That any person who under color of any law . . . or custom, shall subject . . . any inhabitant of any State or Territory to the deprivation of any right secured or protected by this act . . . shall be deemed guilty of a misdemeanor, and on conviction shall be punished by fine not exceeding $1,000, or imprisonment not exceeding one year, or both.[31]

In opening debate, Trumbull, who was no Radical, said that the bill was intended to "secure to all persons within the United States practical freedom." It was, he said, a question of securing "privileges which are essential to freemen." He reviewed the Slave Codes which had fallen with the proclamation of the Thirteenth Amendment. They restricted the movements of Negroes; they forbade them to own firearms; they punished the exercise by them of the functions of a minister of the gospel; they excluded them from other occupations; and they made it "a highly penal offense for any person, white or colored, to teach slaves." In lieu of Slave Codes, Trumbull said, the South now had Black Codes and these "still impose upon [Negroes] . . . the very restrictions which were imposed upon them in consequence of the existence of slavery, and before it was abolished. The purpose of the bill under consideration is to destroy all these discriminations." Section 1, Trumbull continued, was the heart of the bill; it was there that "civil liberty" was secured to the Negro, "civil liberty" being what was left of "natural liberty" after the latter had, necessarily, been circumscribed to make possible life in society. It was of the essence of civil liberty that laws be brought to bear on all persons equally, "or as much so as the nature of things will admit."

Trumbull concluded his remarks on section 1 by repeating that it would ensure for the Negro "the rights of citizens. . . . The great fundamental rights set forth in this bill: the right to acquire property, the right to go and come at pleasure, the right to enforce rights in the courts, to make contracts, and to inherit and dispose of property. These are the very rights that are set forth in this bill as appertaining to every freeman." When Trumbull had finished, James A. McDougall of California, a Democrat, asked him to return to section 1. What, again, was meant by "civil rights"? Trumbull answered by reading the enumeration of rights in section 1. That was the definition. Was there any reference to political rights? McDougall pursued. No, said Trumbull.[32]

With the single exception of Lot M. Morrill of Maine, a Radical who, looking beyond the bill at hand, expounded a theory of the equality of the races,[33] others—Radicals and Moderates alike—who spoke in favor of the bill were content to rest on the points Trumbull had made. The rights to be secured by the bill were those specifically enumerated in section 1, and the necessity for extending the protection so defined was demonstrated by the Black Codes enacted by Southern legislatures.[34] On its merits, this argument had one or two weaknesses. It disregarded the general civil rights guaranty which preceded the enumeration of rights in section 1, and, in directing attention only to evils existing in the South, it ignored the fact that the bill was to apply throughout the nation. These weaknesses were to be skillfully seized upon. The argument probably had another, which the opposition let pass, and which does not affect the search for Congressional purpose. It is very likely that Trumbull and his fellows exaggerated the severity of the Black Codes. The picture— of which this exaggeration was a feature—of a willful reign of terror instituted or threatened by fire-eating Southerners who had learned nothing and were unreconciled to defeat and to all its consequences served Radical purposes and was, with varying degrees of sincerity and of unwitting assistance from some Southern politicians, being spread broadcast by the Radical leadership. This educational campaign, as the

Radicals called it, was to continue throughout the session and beyond. But no one maintains that the impression of conditions in the South fostered by the Radicals was completely unjustified. And, in any event, what is important here is the fact of its existence and of its effectiveness, not the truth of the matter asserted. This impression is incorporated by reference into Congressional statements of objectives; it plays a large part in defining those objectives, regardless of the extent to which it was founded in reality and regardless of the motives which underlay its creation.[35]

Of the remarks in opposition in the Senate, those of three men—two of them Democrats, the other a nominal Republican, but an avowed supporter of the President—must be noted.[36] Willard Saulsbury of Delaware, a Democrat who had once described himself wistfully as perhaps the last slaveholder in the nation, declared that the bill was "one of the most dangerous that was ever introduced into the Senate of the United States." He attacked its constitutionality, then asked whether the bill conferred the right to vote. Certainly, he said, Trumbull might have no intention of conferring that right. But:

> The question is not what the senator means, but what is the legitimate meaning and import of the terms employed in the bill. . . . What are civil rights? What are the rights which you, I, or any citizen of this country enjoy? . . . [H]ere you use a generic term which in its most comprehensive signification includes every species of right that man can enjoy other than those the foundation of which rests exclusively in nature and in the law of nature.[37]

Edgar Cowan, Republican of Pennsylvania, who was wholly at odds with the Radical leadership, also took a broad view of the effect of the bill. He said:

> Now, as I understand the meaning and intent of this bill, it is that there shall be no discrimination made between the inhabitants of the several States of this Union, none in any way. In Pennsylvania, for the greater convenience of the people, and for the greater convenience, I may say, of both classes of the people, in certain districts the Legislature has provided schools for colored children, has discriminated as between the two classes of children. We put the African children in this school-house . . . and educate them there as best we can. Is this amendment [the Thirteenth; the proponents of the Civil Rights Bill argued that it implemented this amendment] to the Constitution of the United States abolishing slavery to break

up that system which Pennsylvania has adopted for the education of her white and colored children? Are the school directors who carry out that law and who make this distinction between these classes of children to be punished for a violation of this statute of the United States? To me it is monstrous.[38]

It was quite a different thing, Cowan continued, to grant to everyone "the right to life, the right to liberty, the right to property." This he was willing to do. But it had to be by amendment to the Constitution.

Reverdy Johnson, Democrat of Maryland, one of the great lawyers of his time, offered an analysis of the bill which came to the same point Saulsbury had made. The states, in the exercise of their police power, had always, and had, in Johnson's opinion, properly taken account of the prejudices of the people. When legislators failed to do that, they created the sort of situation which had resulted from the passage of the Fugitive Slave Act; they passed unenforceable legislation. "I mention that," said Johnson, "for the purpose of applying it to one of the provisions of this bill." Most states had legislated against miscegenation. Yet this bill, Johnson believed, would wipe all such legislation off the books. Trumbull, and William Pitt Fessenden of Maine, like Trumbull a Moderate, interrupted to dispute this interpretation. Negroes could not marry whites and whites could not marry Negroes, they argued; hence there could be no discrimination in an antimiscegenation statute. But neither Fessenden nor Trumbull answered Johnson's broader point, which was that even if his interpretation was wrong, the error was not "so gross a one that the courts may not fall into it."[39]

The vote on the passage of the Civil Rights Bill in the Senate, on February 2, was 33 ayes, 12 nays. Three Republicans—Cowan, Norton of Minnesota, and Van Winkle of West Virginia—were recorded against.[40]

James F. Wilson of Iowa, from the House Committee on the Judiciary, managing the bill in the House, brought it up there on March 1. This was after the President's veto of the Freedmen's Bureau Bill had been upheld. Wilson addressed himself to section 1:

> This part of the bill . . . provides for the equality of citizens of the United States in the enjoyment of "civil rights and immunities." What do these terms mean? Do they mean that in all things civil, social, political, all citizens without distinction of race or color, shall be equal? By no means can they be so construed. Do they mean that all citizens shall vote in the several States? No. . . . Nor do they mean that all citizens shall sit on the juries, or that

their children shall attend the same schools. These are not civil rights or immunities. Well, what is the meaning? What are civil rights? I understand civil rights to be simply the absolute rights of individuals, such as—

> "The right of personal security, the right of personal liberty, and the right to acquire and enjoy property." "Right itself, in civil society, is that which any man is entitled to have, or to do, or to require from others, within the limits of prescribed law." *Kent's Commentaries*, vol. 1, p. 199.

. . . .

> But what of the term "immunities"? . . . It merely secures to citizens of the United States equality in the exemptions of the law. A colored citizen shall not, because he is colored, be subjected to obligations, duties, pains . . . This is the spirit and scope of the bill, and it goes not one step beyond.

. . . .

> . . . Laws barbaric and treatment inhuman are the rewards meted out by our white enemies to our colored friends. We should put a stop to this at once and forever.[41]

Wilson thus presented the Civil Rights Bill to the House as a measure of limited and definite objectives. In this he followed the lead of the majority in the Senate. Indeed, his disclaimers of wider coverage were more specific than those made in the Senate. And the line he laid down was followed by others who spoke for the bill in the House. Again the Black Codes were referred to, and again the point was made that the term "civil rights" was defined by section 1, which enumerated the rights in question.[42]

The Democratic assault on the bill commenced when George S. Shanklin of Kentucky asked Wilson to allow an amendment stating explicitly that nothing in the bill conferred the right to vote. Wilson, though he was soon to give in, refused to agree to such a provision, "as it is in the bill now."[43] Next came Andrew Jackson Rogers of New Jersey, a member, as we shall see, of the Joint Committee on Reconstruction, and, though under forty, a prominent figure in the 39th Congress. Because his views were sometimes extreme and his language frequently vehement, some of the House Democrats resisted Rogers' leadership, and the Radicals, on the other hand, were often pleased to act on the bland assumption that Rogers was the official Democratic leader in the House, though he held no such position.* A few days previously Rogers had had occasion to take note of the Civil Rights Bill as passed in the Senate. At that time he had seemed to favor most of what he took to be the objectives of section 1. His attack had been constitutional:

> Negroes should have the channels of education opened to them by the States, and by the States they should be protected in life, liberty, and property, and by the States should be allowed all the rights of being witnesses, of suing and being sued . . . .
>
> . . . .
>
> Who gave the Senate the constitutional power to pass that bill guarantying equal rights to all . . . ?[44]

In this debate he made the same constitutional point. But he took a broader and less benign view of the effect of section 1:

> In the State of Pennsylvania there is a discrimination made between the schools for white children and the schools for black. The laws there provide that certain schools shall be set apart for black persons, and certain schools shall be set apart for white persons. . . . [T]here is nothing in the letter of the Constitution which gives . . . authority to Congress [to interfere] . . . .
>
> . . . .

* E.g.: "Mr. Windom [a Radical]. . . . I was somewhat surprised yesterday in listening to the argument of the gentleman who, I believe, is the recognized leader of the Democratic party of the House—the gentleman from New Jersey. . . .
Mr. Rogers. Mr. Speaker—
Mr. Windom. Have I done him too much honor?
Mr. Rogers. Mr. Speaker, I hope nobody . . . will make that assertion again. The object . . . is only to create dissatisfaction on this side of the House.
. . . .
Mr. Marshall. I wish merely to say that we do not recognize him as our leader.
. . . .
Mr. Windom. . . . I think every member upon this side of the House and every modest member upon the other side accords to the gentleman from New Jersey the position I assign him. [Laughter.]
. . . .
Mr. Niblack. I desire simply to say that we on this side do not need any 'leader.' There are not enough of us. [Laughter.] Therefore every man carries on a kind of guerrilla fight." (Globe, 1157–58.)

> ... As a white man is by law authorized to marry a white woman, so does this bill compel the State to grant to the negro the same right of marrying a white woman ....

> .   .   .   .

> All the rights that we enjoy, except our natural rights, are derived from Government. Therefore, there are really but two kinds of rights, natural rights and civil rights. This bill, then, would prevent a State from refusing negro suffrage under the broad acceptation of the term "civil rights and immunities."[45]

These charges, with particular reference to suffrage, were pressed home for the Democrats by Anthony Thornton of Illinois:

> It is said that the words "civil rights" do not include the right of suffrage, because that is a political right. . . . I do not assume . . . that [they] do . . . but with the loose and liberal mode of construction adopted in this age, who can tell what rights may not be conferred by virtue of the terms as used in this bill? Where is it to end? Who can tell how it may be defined, how it may be construed? Why not, then, if it is not intended to confer the right of suffrage upon this class, accept a proviso that no such design is entertained?[46]

The leadership, which was to be unsure of its majority, and hence sensitive on the issue of suffrage throughout the session, had had enough of this. Wilson moved to amend by adding a new section:

> That nothing in this act shall be so construed as to affect the laws of any State concerning the right of suffrage.

He said:

> Mr. Speaker, I wish to say [that] . . . that section will not change my construction of the bill. I do not believe the term civil rights includes the right of suffrage. Some gentlemen seem to have some fear on that point.

The House adopted the amendment by voice vote.[47]

The Democrats were, of course, not pacified by this concession. Their concluding shot was fired by Michael C. Kerr of Indiana. Power to enact this bill was sought, he said, in the amendment abolishing slavery. But:

> Is it slavery or involuntary servitude to forbid a free negro, on account of race or color, to testify against a white man? Is it

either to deny to free negroes, on the same account, the privilege of engaging in certain kinds of business . . . such as retailing spirituous liquors? Is it either to deny to children of free negroes or mulattoes, on the like account, the privilege of attending the common schools of a State with the children of white men?

These were all matters, apparently, in Kerr's mind, with which the bill might be thought to deal. He himself favored letting Negroes testify and "providing facilities for the education of their children." But he thought Congress was powerless to attain these ends. And the construction which might in practice be given to the term "civil rights" was quite unpredictable and would not be controlled by disclaimers made on the floor of the House.[48]

Despite its vigor, this Democratic attack might well have gone unheeded, as had the similar one in the Senate, and changes in the Senate draft might have ended with the suffrage amendment accepted by Wilson, had it not been for misgivings in the regular Republican ranks in the House as well. These came from three fairly distinct quarters. Henry J. Raymond of New York, publisher of the *New York Times*, and not a Radical, favored extending to Negroes the "rights and privileges" of citizens. By that he understood the right of free passage, to bear arms, to testify, "all those rights that tend to elevate [the Negro] and educate him for still higher reaches in the process of elevation." Giving the Negro the rights of citizenship "will teach all others of his fellow-citizens of all races to respect him more, and to aid him in his steps for constant progress and advancement in the rights and duties that belong to citizenship."[49] But Raymond thought that the bill's penal enforcement provisions rendered it unconstitutional, and he therefore opposed it as a whole, though he did not seem to subscribe to the alarmist view of the scope of section 1. Perhaps it was simply that the position he took made a close analysis of that section unnecessary.

Columbus Delano of Ohio, a Moderate, shared Raymond's constitutional difficulties. He inclined to the belief that these might be removed if the general civil rights language at the head of section 1 and the penal provisions further on were struck. But, unlike Raymond, Delano feared that the bill might be construed to outlaw a wide variety of practices prevalent in the North as well as in the South. This was a question of policy, and Delano was concerned about the entire first section, not just the sentence at the beginning. He asked Wilson whether the provision in the body of section 1 entitling Negroes "to full and equal benefit of all laws and proceedings for the security of person and property *as is enjoyed by white citizens*" (the italicized phrase was not in the bill as passed by the Senate but was added in committee in the House and appears in the statute as enacted) would not confer "upon the emancipated race the right of being jurors." Wilson thought not.

> Mr. Delano. I have no doubt of the sincerity of the gentleman, and . . . I have great confidence in his legal opinions. . . .
> But, with all this, I must confess that it does seem to me that this bill necessarily confers the right of being jurors. . . .
>
> . . . .
>
> Now, sir . . . I presume that the gentleman himself will shrink from the idea of conferring upon this race now, at this particular moment, the right of being jurors, or from so wording this bill as to leave it a serious question and render it debatable hereafter in the courts or elsewhere.

Moreover:

> [W]e once had in the State of Ohio a law excluding the black population from any participation in the public schools. . . . That law did not, of course, place the black population upon an equal footing with the white, and would, therefore, under the terms of this bill be void.[50]

Here Wilson broke in with "I desire to ask the gentleman," but Delano had no further time for interruptions, and so there was no argument on this point. It is to be noted that Delano was not suggesting that Ohio would be forced to provide unsegregated schools; he was predicting only the fall of laws which excluded Negroes from schools of any sort. Despite these views, which were not met by amendment in so far as they related to provisions in the body of section 1, Delano ended up voting for the bill and to override the President's veto.

The final expression of Republican misgivings was the most formidable, and it was decisive. It came from John A. Bingham of Ohio, a Radical, and one of the most influential men in the 39th Congress. Bingham was speaking in support of a motion he had offered to recommit with instructions to strike the sentence at the head of section 1 which forbade all "discrimination in civil rights or immunities," and to substitute for the penal enforcement provisions of the bill language permitting a civil action by aggrieved parties.[51] He tried at the start to meet an argument which he knew would be advanced against him, as indeed it was:

> Mr. Speaker . . . I beg leave . . . to say, that although the

objections which I urge against the bill must, in the very nature of the case, apply to the proposed instructions, I venture to say no candid man, no rightminded man, will deny that by amending as proposed the bill will be less oppressive, and therefore less objectionable. Doubting, as I do, the power of Congress to pass the bill, I urge the instructions with a view to take from the bill what seems to me its oppressive and I might say its unjust provisions.

Bingham then proceeded to examine the civil rights provision which he proposed to delete. "What are civil rights?" he asked. It seemed that

the term civil rights includes every right that pertains to the citizen under the Constitution, laws, and Government of this country. . . . [A]re not political rights all embraced in the term "civil rights," and must it not of necessity be so interpreted?

. . . [T]here is scarcely a State in this Union which does not, by its constitution or by its statute laws, make some discrimination on account of race or color between citizens of the United States in respect of civil rights.

.   .   .   .

By the Constitution of my own State neither the right of the elective franchise nor the franchise of office can be conferred . . . save upon a white citizen of the United States.

Coming to the specific rights enumerated in that part of section 1 which his motion would have left untouched, Bingham noted that they had been denied by many states, and said: "I should remedy that not by an arbitrary assumption of power, but by amending the Constitution of the United States, expressly prohibiting the States from any such abuse of power in the future." He had made no such statement about civil rights in general. He went on then to attack the penal enforcement provisions as unwise as well as unconstitutional. The federal government, by constitutional amendment, could protect the rights of life, liberty, and property in the manner Bingham had just described. State officials would then take an oath to observe such a prohibition as he envisioned, and Congress could somehow enforce the oath. But Congress had never—it could not and it should not—employ "the terrors of the penal code within organized States." The Freedmen's Bureau Bill had been carefully worded to apply only in territories under military occupation. Bingham quoted de Tocqueville: " 'centralized government, decentralized administration.' That sir, coupled with your declared purpose of equal justice, is the secret of your strength and power."

That should be the rule in peacetime. He quoted also from Chancellor Kent on the powers that properly belong to the states. Then occurred these passages:

> Now what does this bill propose? To reform the whole civil and criminal code of every State government by declaring that there shall be no discrimination between citizens on account of race or color in civil rights or in the penalties prescribed by their laws. I humbly bow before the majesty of justice, as I bow before the majesty of that God whose attribute it is, and therefore declare there should be no such inequality or discrimination even in the penalties for crime; but what power have you to correct it? . . . You further say that . . . there shall, as to qualification of witnesses, be no discrimination on account of race or color. I agree that . . . there should be no such discrimination.
>
> But whence do you derive power to cure it by a congressional enactment? There should be no discrimination among citizens of the United States in the several States, of like sex, age, and condition, in regard to the franchises of office. But such a discrimination does exist in nearly every State. How do you propose to cure all this? By a congressional enactment? How? Not by saying, in so many words, which would be the bold and direct way of meeting this issue, that every discrimination of this kind . . . is hereby abolished. You propose to make it a penal offense for the judges of the States to obey the constitution and laws of their States. . . . I deny your power to do this. You cannot make an official act, done under color of law . . . and from a sense of public duty, a crime.[52]

Such was Bingham's position, and it is not lacking in ambiguity. Like Raymond, he thought the bill was unconstitutional, but he did not take the narrow ground of section 2 only; the bill for him was unconstitutional from top to bottom. Hence, unlike Delano, he made no pretense that his motion would cure the constitutional defect. With Delano, apparently unlike Raymond, and certainly unlike Wilson and his supporters, he read the general term "civil rights" broadly, or at any rate thought it was of uncertain reach. In the first half of his speech, it is perfectly clear that Bingham, while committing himself to the need for safeguarding by constitutional amendment the specific rights enumerated in the body of section 1, was anything but willing to make a similar commitment with respect to "civil rights" in general. The second half of the speech, in which Bingham bore down heavily on penal sanctions as provided in section 2, ends in some ambiguity. Bingham said first that he wanted no such sanctions applied to violations of rights which he was ready to enshrine in the Constitution. He mentioned the rights of life, liberty, and property, and the ideal of equal justice: the sort of thing enumerated in the body of section 1. Then, in the last two paragraphs, while still pressing his fight against penal sanctions, he referred both to rights specifically listed in section 1 and to at least one other which in his view was covered by the term "civil rights." And he went on record as opposed on principle to discriminations with respect to all these rights. But was he, in these two final paragraphs, spoken just before the hammer fell, hastening to say something he had rather carefully and gingerly refrained from saying before, namely, that he was prepared to write what he considered to be the substance of a general "civil rights" provision into the Constitution? On their face, and following as they do a lecture on federalism, these remarks are quite consistent with a belief that some discriminations, practiced in the North as well as in the South, though objectionable on moral principle, to be sure, should be cured by state rather than federal action. Bingham's professions here are high-flown. They call on God and the majesty of justice, and they differ rather markedly from his earlier flat and specific declaration concerning the evils he would remedy by amending the Constitution. Are these not the sort of soothing but vague and vacuous concessions Bingham was likely to offer to his Radical colleagues while trying to induce them to rebel against at least one feature of a leadership bill? Similarly, in denouncing criminal sanctions imposed, as he thought, against state officials for denying the franchise to Negroes, Bingham may seem in this passage to suggest that he would have approved a "bold and direct" Congressional enactment declaring "that every discrimination of this kind . . . is hereby abolished." Yet if his speech as an entirety means anything at all, it means that he would have considered such a "bold and direct" Congressional enactment unconstitutional.

These are words spoken in debate by a man not normally distinguished for precision of thought and statement. Perhaps judgments may differ about them, though they must not be taken out of context. One makes out their meaning as best one can. They are important because of Bingham's role in drafting section 1 of the Fourteenth Amendment and his avoidance in all his drafts of the term "civil rights." Whatever the ambiguities of his speech, one thing is certain. Unless one concludes that Bingham entertained apprehensions about the breadth of the term "civil rights" and was unwilling at this stage, as a matter of policy, not constitutional law, to extend a federal guaranty covering all that might be included in that term, there is no rational explanation for his motion to strike it. There was no illusion in Bingham's mind of removing a constitutional infirmity in this fashion. He was endeavoring merely to make the bill less "oppressive," less "unjust." Constitutional scruples to the side, he wanted a bill that would at least be satisfactory on policy grounds. That was the object of his attempt to remove the penal provisions. What other object could he have had in mind in trying also to eliminate the comprehensive civil rights guaranty, which in his opinion would force a change in the law of his own state?

Wilson, the manager of the bill, who rose to answer Bingham, had understood the latter as objecting to the breadth of the "civil rights" provision. He defended the term "civil rights" in accordance with the line he had laid down at the beginning of debate. Bingham, he said,

> tells the House that civil rights involve all the rights that citizens have under the Government . . . that this bill is not intended merely to enforce equality of rights, so far as they relate to citizens of the United States, but invades the States to enforce equality of rights in respect to those things which properly and rightfully depend on State regulations and laws. My friend . . . knows, as every man knows, that this bill refers to those rights which belong to men as citizens of the United States and none other; and when he talks of setting aside the school laws and jury laws and franchise laws of the States by the bill . . . he steps beyond what he must know to be the rule of construction which must apply here, and as a result of which this bill can only relate to matters within the control of Congress.

This misrepresented Bingham's statement in that it had him referring specifically to school and jury laws, which Bingham had not done. Wilson also implied that Bingham had argued, as Bingham had not, that his motion would remove the constitutional infirmity he saw in the bill. It could not, said Wilson. If any part of section 1 was unconstitutional, all of it had to be.[53]

Bingham complained generally, in one sentence, that "the gentleman from Iowa has taken advantage of me by misstating my position."[54] The voting then began. Wilson asked whether it was in order for him to accept Bingham's motion to recommit with instructions. He was told that he could do so only by unanimous consent. "Mr. Stevens and others objected." Bingham's motion was then defeated by a large majority. But the House voted to recommit the bill without instructions. This vote was close: 82–70. Bingham, of course, voted to recommit. So did the Democrats; also Raymond, Delano, and Thomas T. Davis of

New York, a Republican who shared Raymond's view. So did many
Radicals such as Justin Morrill of Vermont, member of the Joint Com-
mittee on Reconstruction, and even one of the leaders of the House,
Robert C. Schenck of Ohio. Thaddeus Stevens voted against and
Wilson followed him, as did most Radicals.[55]

Wilson brought the bill back four days later, on March 13. He reported a committee amendment striking from section 1 the civil rights
provision Bingham had objected to. Wilson said:

> Mr. Speaker, the amendment which has just been read proposes
> to strike out the general terms relating to civil rights. I do not
> think it materially changes the bill; but some gentlemen were
> apprehensive that the words we propose to strike out might give
> warrant for a latitudinarian construction not intended.

The House concurred by voice vote. Wilson noted, in response to a
question, that the bill as it now stood contained no proviso excluding
suffrage from its application; but he thought the committee amendment just reported should take care of any apprehensions on that score.
He then pressed for a vote. Bingham and others asked that the bill be
printed and allowed to lay over so gentlemen could read it again. Wilson
would not give in, however, and the vote was taken. The majority for
passage was large. Bingham and five other Republicans were recorded
against. Raymond and a few others did not vote.[56]

Two days later the Senate concurred in the House amendments.[57]
The President vetoed the bill on March 27. In discussing section 1, he
conceded that the only rights safeguarded by it were those enumerated.
He did not attack the section on the basis of any alarmist "latitudinarian"
construction. His objections were constitutional.[58] The Senate took up
the veto on April 4, having had a recess on account of the death of
Senator Solomon Foot of Vermont. There were speeches by Trumbull,
Reverdy Johnson, Cowan, and Garrett Davis, Democrat of Kentucky,
who was still maintaining that the bill would abolish antimiscegenation
statutes and mark the end of segregation in hotels and railroad cars and
churches. Finally the Senate overrode the veto, five Republicans voting
to uphold.[59] On April 9 the House also overrode, without debate. Seven
Republicans, including Henry J. Raymond, voted to uphold the President. Bingham was paired in support of the veto.[60]

The Bingham Amendment

While the Senate was passing the Freedman's Bureau and Civil
Rights Bills, but before the President had vetoed the former and before the House had taken up the latter, the Joint Committee on Recon-

struction worked out and reported a proposed constitutional amendment dealing with the "privileges and immunities of citizens" and with "equal protection." The principal author of this proposal, and its manager in debate, was John A. Bingham of Ohio.

The Joint Committee, known popularly as the Committee of Fifteen, came into being under a resolution of December 13, 1865. The father of the Committee was Thaddeus Stevens, one of the most powerful Congressional leaders in our history, the frail but indomitable incarnation of Radical revolutionary fervor and partisan passion. Stevens possessed, as he once understated it to the House, "some will of my own," and he was at no time animated by a desire to compromise with the new President. Conservatives and Moderates in his party were. But not Stevens. He would either rule the President or fight him. He conceived of the Joint Committee as a sort of Politburo, governing the South with, or without, or against the President. The resolution creating the Committee was a veiled reflection of Stevens' purpose. It struck the dominant political note which, on the whole, was to characterize the work of the session. And it was in some measure a poor forecast of the business the Committee was in fact to deal with. It instructed the Committee to "inquire into the condition of the States which formed the so-called confederate States of America, and report whether they, or any of them, are entitled to be represented in either House of Congress, with leave to report at any time, by bill or otherwise." But, as its journal shows, the Committee was never entirely Stevens' creature. There were nine members from the House and six from the Senate, three of the total being Democrats.[61]

The Committee convened on January 6, 1866, and discussed the basis upon which the former Confederate states might again be given representation in the federal government, and the related question of Negro suffrage. At the third meeting, on January 12, a subcommittee was appointed and charged with reporting on the basis of representation. It consisted of William Pitt Fessenden, the Moderate senator from Maine, Thaddeus Stevens, Senator Jacob Howard of Michigan, a Radical, Roscoe Conkling of New York, then in the House, who generally acted with the leadership but was not a doctrinaire Radical, and Bingham. Into the hopper of the Subcommittee went the following draft, proposed by Bingham as an amendment to the Constitution:

> The Congress shall have power to make all laws necessary and proper to secure to all persons in every state within this Union equal protection in their rights of life, liberty and property.

Stevens, in addition to a proposal on the basis of representation, submitted the following:

All laws, state and national, shall operate impartially and equally on all persons without regard to race or color.

On January 20 Fessenden, reporting to the full Committee from the Subcommittee, brought forth three proposed articles of amendment to the Constitution,

the first two as alternative propositions, one of which, with the third proposition, to be recommended to Congress for adoption:

· · · · · · · · · · · · ·

Article A.

Representatives and direct taxes shall be apportioned among the several States within this Union, according to the respective numbers of citizens of the United States in each State; and all provisions in the Constitution or laws of any State, whereby any distinction is made in political or civil rights or privileges, on account of race, creed or color, shall be inoperative and void.

Or the following:

Article B.

Representatives and direct taxes shall be apportioned among the several States which may be included within this Union, according to their respective numbers, counting the whole number of citizens of the United States in each State; provided that, whenever the elective franchise shall be denied or abridged in any State on account of race, creed or color, all persons of such race, creed or color, shall be excluded from the basis of representation.

Article C.

Congress shall have power to make all laws necessary and proper to secure to all citizens of the United States, in every State, the same political rights and privileges; and to all persons in every State equal protection in the enjoyment of life, liberty and property.

As is apparent, the combination of articles A and C amounted to an immediate grant of Negro suffrage, while that of articles B and C was a prospective grant, to be realized when and if Congress felt so inclined, probably later than sooner, since an interim scheme was provided. As regards other rights, article A again acted directly and immediately, but negatively, on the states, with a reserve implementing power being lodged in Congress by article C, whereas article B made no provision but rather left the whole matter to Congress through article C. Articles A and C differed in that the latter struck at discriminations, in suffrage and other rights, whether or not based on color; that is, article C covered all classes of "citizens" and "persons," whereas article A did not. As regards the extent of the rights protected, the two articles were coterminous in the matter of suffrage, both using the words "political rights and [or] privileges." But were they intended to be otherwise coterminous also? That is to say, in the view of the Subcommittee, did the power to protect the enjoyment of "life, liberty and property" granted by article C go the same length as the prohibition of distinctions in "civil rights or privileges" written into article A? If so, the Subcommittee's draftsmanship was, of course, terrible. This is not conclusive against the hypothesis, but it gives pause. Moreover, reasoning from the position Bingham, the author of the "life, liberty and property" language, took on the Civil Rights Bill, it is fair to conclude that he for one saw a difference between the term "civil rights" and his own formula. On the assumption that the Subcommittee understood civil rights protection to reach further than the Bingham proposal, articles A and C taken together reveal a rational purpose rather than monumentally bad draftsmanship, the purpose being to strike broadly and immediately at discriminations based on color, leaving to Congress the less urgent problem of other unequal laws, and at the same time to make the affirmative function of Congress to take over legislative powers hitherto reserved to the states narrower than a negative provision, limiting state power but substituting no other. Again, comparing the two packages, one would expect the proposal which went the whole way on suffrage to protect a greater range of other rights, and the one which embodied the more conservative approach to the suffrage question to be satisfied with the grant of narrower—and prospective—additional protection. On this hypothesis, the alternative proposals presented the full Committee with a real choice all the way down the line.

It is more than likely that Thaddeus Stevens personally favored the alternative which included article A. But the old gentleman was a confirmed practitioner of the art of the possible. And so he moved that article C be severed from the other two, and then that article B be considered in preference to article A. This was done. Article B, with minor changes, was reported out as the Committee's first product. It was doomed to defeat, largely because it was unacceptable to Charles Sumner, who was at this time unable to abandon the principle of immediate suffrage, though he eventually saw the light.[62]

At the Committee's next meeting, on January 24, article C was tackled.

A couple of unsuccessful attempts were made to tinker with the provision concerning political rights. Finally, by a vote of 7–5, it was decided to refer the proposal to a select committee consisting of Bingham, Representative George S. Boutwell of Massachusetts, a Radical, and Andrew Jackson Rogers, for redrafting. Three days later, Bingham reported it back in this form:

> Congress shall have power to make all laws which shall be necessary and proper to secure all persons in every State full protection in the enjoyment of life, liberty and property; and to all citizens of the United States in any State the same immunities and also equal political rights and privileges.

The two parts of the article had been turned around; equal protection had become full; the same political rights had become equal; and the word "immunities" appears for the first time. These would seem to be largely matters of style, though it may be remarked that "full" is presumably something different than "equal." Stevens tried to get this proposal reported out, but could not do it. Four Republicans were absent and three voted nay. When consideration was resumed on February 3, Bingham proposed the following substitute:

> The Congress shall have power to make all laws which shall be necessary and proper to secure to the citizens of each State all privileges and immunities of citizens in the several States (Art. 4, Sec. 2); and to all persons in the several States equal protection in the rights of life, liberty and property (5th Amendment).

Protection in this draft had reverted back to "equal." The more notable change, however, is the elimination of any reference to political rights. The substitution was agreed to by a vote of 7–6, Stevens and Fessenden voting against. On February 10 it was decided, 9–5, to report this proposal out. Senator Ira Harris of New York, an inconspicuous Moderate, and Conkling were the only Republicans who voted nay.[63]

Debate began in the House on February 26. Bingham in a brief opening aired the notion indicated by the parenthetical references to the Constitution. He said:

> Every word of the proposed amendment is to-day in the Constitution of our country, save the words conferring the express grant of power upon the Congress of the United States.
>
> .   .   .   .
>
> Sir, it has been the want of the Republic that there was not an express grant of power in the Constitution to enable the whole

people of every State, by congressional enactment, to enforce obedience to these requirements of the Constitution.[64]

A number of Radicals who spoke in support of Bingham also gave vent to the idea that the proposal was in some way declarative, merely enabling Congress to enforce rights already guaranteed by the Constitution as it stood.[65] William D. ("Pig-Iron") Kelley of Pennsylvania even expressed the opinion that the amendment would add no new powers whatever to those Congress already possessed, though he recognized that reasonable men might have doubts on this score which it was worthwhile to remove. Kelley at the same time appeared to think that the proposal dealt with suffrage.[66] Aside from him, however, and from Bingham, later, when he was responding to attacks, the supporters of the amendment had little if anything specific to say about the kind of state action to which it was directed. This contrasts with the speeches made in behalf of the Civil Rights Bill. The opposition was bipartisan, as in the case of the Senate draft of the Civil Rights Bill, and it was to prove effective.

For the Democrats, Rogers, having noted that the need which Bingham professed for his amendment proved that the Civil Rights Bill—then about to come up in the House—was unconstitutional, addressed himself to the equal protection clause. He for one evidently saw no difference between this formula and the comprehensive civil rights provision in the Senate draft of the Civil Rights Bill. Under this clause, he said,

Congress can pass . . . a law compelling South Carolina to grant to negroes every right accorded to white people there; and as white men there have the right to marry white women, negroes, under this amendment, would be entitled to the same right. . . .

Further:

In the State of Pennsylvania there are laws which make a distinction with regard to the schooling of white children and the schooling of black children. . . . Under this amendment, Congress would have power to compel the State to provide for white children and black children to attend the same school, upon the principle that all the people in the several States shall have equal protection in all the rights of life, liberty, and property, and all the privileges and immunities of citizens in the several States.

. . . .

Sir, I defy any man upon the other side of the House to name to me any right of the citizen which is not included in the words "life, liberty, property, privileges, and immunities," unless it should be the right of suffrage. . . .[67]

The speech which was very likely decisive against the Bingham amendment was delivered by Robert S. Hale of New York, a lawyer and former judge, and a man who was able to make the House sit up and listen. Hale was a regular Republican. Though he was to be recorded absent for the vote on passage of the Civil Rights Bill, he was to vote to override the veto of that bill, and eventually for the Fourteenth Amendment. This proposal seemed to him, however, to entrust Congress with the most extraordinary powers. To begin with, Hale paid his respects to Bingham:

Listening to the remarks of the distinguished member of the committee who reported this joint resolution to the House, one would be led to think that this amendment was a subject of the most trivial consequence. He tells us, and tells us with an air of gravity that I could not but admire, that the words of the resolution are all in the Constitution as it stands, with the single exception of the power given to Congress to legislate. A very important exception, it strikes me. . . .

. . . .

What is the effect of the amendment . . . ? I submit that it is in effect a provision under which all State legislation, in its codes of civil and criminal jurisprudence and procedure, affecting the individual citizen, may be overridden . . . and the law of Congress established instead.

This roused Thaddeus Stevens. He asked:

Does the gentleman mean to say that, under this provision, Congress could interfere in any case where the legislation of a State was equal, impartial to all? Or is it not simply to provide that, where any State makes a distinction in the same law between different classes of individuals, Congress shall have power to correct such discrimination and inequality?

The first proposition stated by Stevens was, of course, what Hale had meant, and he said so. This was much more than just a "provision for the equality of individual citizens before the laws of the several States." Moreover, it was important to realize the reach of this language. For example, said Hale, all states distinguished between the property rights of married women, on the one hand, and of *femmes sole* and men, on the other. Such distinctions would be outlawed by this proposal. No, said Stevens, propounding a theory of reasonable classification under the equal protection clause:

> When a distinction is made between two married people or two *femmes sole,* then it is unequal legislation; but where all of the same class are dealt with in the same way then there is no pretense of inequality.

Hale disagreed. The proposal, he said, "gives to *all persons* equal protection." If what Stevens had said were the correct construction, it would be sufficient also to extend the same rights to one Negro as to another in order to satisfy the amendment. There was no further reply from Stevens. Hale next drew Bingham's fire. The latter put up to him the fact that property rights and procedural rights in courts of law had been denied by some states. (Here at last we return to the Black Codes.) Was not some protection needed? This was weak ground for Hale. The states should provide it, he said, and if Bingham found that the state of Ohio could not protect its citizens, he ought to come to New York, where things were different. Bingham pursued the matter:

> I do not cast any imputation upon the State of New York. The gentleman knows full well, from conversations I have had with him, that so far as I understand this power, under no possible interpretation can it ever be made to operate in the State of New York while she occupies her present proud position.
>
> .   .   .   .
>
> . . . It is to apply to other States [than those which seceded] . . . that have in their constitutions and laws to-day provisions in direct violation of every principle of our Constitution.
>
> Mr. Rogers. I suppose the gentleman refers to the State of Indiana?
>
> Mr. Bingham. I do not know; it may be so. It applies unquestionably to the State of Oregon.[68]

This is an interesting passage. Bingham here specified state enactments which his proposal would strike down. He refused to commit himself on Indiana. The reference there, as Professor Charles Fairman has pointed out, was probably to the provision of the Indiana constitution denying suffrage to Negroes and mulattoes.[69] His own state, as Bingham remarked in the Civil Rights Bill debate, made a similar discrimination. The Oregon constitution at that time, as has also been pointed out, forbade free Negroes or mulattoes not residing in the state at the time of its adoption to come into the state, reside there, hold real estate, contract, or sue.[70] This sort of thing Bingham wanted to strike down. As for the state of New York in her then proud position, whether or not Bingham knew it, her laws permitted the establishment of separate but equal schools for colored children in the discretion of local districts. Segregated schools in fact existed at least until the year 1900. And it seems quite possible, on the face of her statutes, that New York maintained her proud position in respect of permissive segregation in rural districts till 1938.[71]

The next day, Thomas T. Davis, another New York Republican, took up where Hale had left off. He, too, thought that this was an extraordinary grant of power to Congress, and he feared that the power would be used "in the establishment of perfect political equality between the colored and the white race of the South." The Negroes, he said,

> must be made equal before the law, and be permitted to enjoy life, liberty, and the pursuit of happiness. I am pledged to my own conscience to favor every measure of legislation which shall be found essential to the protection of their just rights [Davis was to vote for the Civil Rights Bill], and I shall most cheerfully aid in any plan for their education and elevation which may reasonably be adopted.
>
> . . . .
>
> Give them protection, teachers, education, and hold out to them inducements to self-improvement . . .

But this amendment meant "centralization of power in Congress" and very likely political rights—and that was going too far.[72]

The proposal was clearly in trouble, and Bingham, in a long speech, attempted a rescue operation. Among other things, he said:

> The proposition pending before the House is simply a proposition to arm the Congress . . . with the power to enforce the bill of rights as it stands in the Constitution today. It "hath that extent—no more."
>
> . . . .
>
> . . . [R]equirements of our Constitution have been broken; they are disregarded to-day in Oregon; they are disregarded to-day, and have been disregarded for the last five, ten, or twenty years in every one of the eleven States recently in insurrection.
>
> . . . .
>
> . . . Gentlemen who oppose this amendment oppose the grant of power to enforce the bill of rights. Gentlemen who oppose this amendment simply declare to these rebel States, go on with your confiscation statutes, your statutes of banishment, your statutes of unjust imprisonment, your statutes of murder and death against men because of their loyalty to . . . the United States.[73]

Bingham, though with singular lack of clarity, was suggesting to those of the members who were alarmed that he had some definite evils in mind, limited and distinct in their nature. His peroration pulled out all stops in an appeal to due process, "law in its highest sense."[74] But the assurances, the magic of somewhat windy eloquence, and even a political rallying cry, which Bingham also employed—all failed. Hale's argument had sunk in and was going to prevail. Bingham was followed by another New Yorker, Giles W. Hotchkiss, a Radical, who read the proposal as had his colleague Hale, and who, according to his own lights, also feared "the caprice" of future Congresses:

> As I understand it . . . [Bingham's] object in offering this resolution . . . is to provide that no State shall discriminate between its citizens and give one class of citizens greater rights than it confers upon another. If this amendment secured that, I should vote very cheerfully for it to-day; but . . . I do not regard it as permanently securing those rights. . . .
>
> . . . I am unwilling that Congress shall have [the] power [this amendment confers]. . . . The object of a Constitution is not only to confer power upon the majority, but to restrict the power of the majority. . . . It is not indulging in imagination to any great stretch to suppose that we may have a Congress here who would establish such rules in my State as I should be unwilling to be governed by.
>
> .   .   .   .
>
> Mr. Speaker, I make these remarks because I do not wish to be placed in the wrong upon this question. I think the gentleman from Ohio [Mr. Bingham] is not sufficiently radical in his views upon this subject. I think he is a conservative. [Laughter.] I do not make the remark in any offensive sense. But I want him to go to the root of this matter.
>
> .   .   .   .
>
> . . . Why not provide by an amendment to the Constitution that no State shall discriminate against any class of its citizens; and let that amendment stand as part of the organic law of the land, subject only to be defeated by another.[75]

Roscoe Conkling, who had voted against reporting this proposal out of the Joint Committee, was quick to point out that he was against it for reasons "very different . . . from, if not entirely opposite to" those given by Hotchkiss. Conkling certainly thought the proposal went far enough and was sufficiently radical. He moved to postpone consideration of it to a day certain, the second Tuesday of April. A vote was first taken on a Democratic motion to postpone indefinitely. This was defeated by a party line-up, with, however, somewhat more than normal defections. Thus Davis and Hale voted with the Democrats. The Conkling motion, taken up next, carried 110–37. The Republican leadership was solidly behind it. Bingham himself voted for it. Six Republicans voted consistently against any kind of postponement—Democratic or Republican. Davis decided that if he could not have indefinite postponement, he wanted none, no doubt expressing the judgment, indicated also by the position of the leadership, that the proposal could be beaten then and there. The date of this vote was February 28.[76] The second Tuesday in April came and went with no further mention of the Bingham amendment. It was never brought up in the Senate, nor ever again in the House.

The Fourteenth Amendment

Having reported out Bingham's draft, the Joint Committee on Reconstruction did not resume consideration of proposed constitutional amendments till April 16.[77] On that day the Committee heard Senator Stewart, Republican of Nevada, expound a reconstruction plan which he and other Moderates had hoped might yet provide a basis for peaceful coexistence between the Radicals and the President. The Stewart plan turned on a constitutional amendment granting equal "civil rights" to Negroes, as well as limited suffrage. The South was offered, among other things, an amnesty and the power to restrict Negro suffrage so long as it did so without using race as a sole or explicit criterion.[78] Stewart and his hopes got a hearing, but nothing more, from the Joint Committee. At its next meeting on April 21,

Mr. Stevens said he had a plan of reconstruction, one not of his own framing, but which he should support, and which he submitted to the Committee for consideration.

It was read as follows:

. . . .

Whereas, It is expedient that the States lately in insurrection should . . . be restored to full participation in all political rights; therefore,

Be it resolved . . . that the following Article be proposed . . . as an amendment to the Constitution . . . :

Article—

Section 1. No discrimination shall be made by any state, nor by the United States, as to civil rights of persons because of race, color, or previous condition of servitude.

Sec. 2. From and after the fourth day of July, in the year one thousand eight hundred and seventy-six, no discrimination shall be made by any state, nor by the United States, as to the enjoyment . . . of the right of suffrage. . . .

Sec. 3. [Excluded all persons who were denied suffrage from the basis of representation, till 1876.]

Sec. 4. [Confederate debt and compensation for slaves.]

Sec. 5. Congress shall have power to enforce by appropriate legislation, the provisions of this article.

And be it further resolved, [former Confederate states which ratified this amendment and enacted legislation in compliance with it, to be readmitted to the Union, when ratification of the amendment was complete.]

Provided, [that certain "rebels" be excluded from office till 1876.][79]

As Stevens said, this proposal was not his own. It had been placed before him in March by Robert Dale Owen, reformer son of a reformer father. Owen, some nine years later, described his meeting with Stevens. The latter objected to prospective suffrage, as provided in section 2. This was a frank recognition, said Owen, of the fact that the Negro was not yet ready to vote or hold office. "I hate to delay full justice so long," said Stevens. But suffrage was not now the Negro's immediate need, the younger man answered. "He thirsts after education, and will have it if we but give him a chance, and if we don't call him away from the school-room to take a seat which he is unfitted to fill in a legislative chamber." Stevens then made a quick decision in favor of the proposal. He said there was not a majority for immediate suffrage, and this could pass. Owen, as he recalled, also took his amendment around to other members of the Joint Committee. Fessenden; Representative Elihu Washburne of Illinois, Grant's friend, who was briefly to be his Secretary of State; Roscoe Conkling; Senator Jacob Howard of Michigan and Representative George S. Boutwell of Massachusetts, two Radicals—all approved with varying degrees of enthusiasm, though none with the decisiveness of Stevens. "So, qualifiedly [these are Owen's words], did Bingham, observing, however, that he thought the first section ought to specify, in detail, the civil rights which we proposed to assure; he had a favorite section of his own on that subject."[80]

The Committee went at the Owen proposal section by section. Bingham moved that section 1 be amended by adding the following:

nor shall any State deny to any person within its jurisdiction the equal protection of the laws, nor take private property for public use without just compensation.

This motion was lost, 7–5. Stevens voted with Bingham. So did Rogers and Reverdy Johnson, though not Grider, the other Democrat. The Committee then voted 1C–2 (Grider and Rogers) to adopt section 1 as it stood. Sections 2, 3, and 4 were also adopted. When the Committee reached section 5, Bingham moved the following as a substitute:

Sec. 5. No State shall make or enforce any law which shall abridge the privileges or immunities of citizens of the United States; nor shall any State deprive any person of life, liberty or property without due process of law, nor deny to any person within its jurisdiction the equal protection of the laws.

This is, of course, language which now appears unchanged in the Fourteenth Amendment. The Committee adopted it, 10–2 (Grider and Rogers). Section 5 of the original proposal was renumbered and also accepted. Throughout this meeting Fessenden and Conkling as well as Senator Ira Harris of New York were absent.

Two days later the Committee, Fessenden still absent, modified the final provisions of the proposal following the numbered articles, which it severed, intending to report them out separately. At the next meeting, on April 25, Senator George H. Williams of Oregon, a Radical, moved to strike section 5, that is, the substitute which Bingham had got accepted at the meeting before last. Williams had voted for the substitution. His present motion carried, 7–5. Stevens was with Bingham in opposition. So was Rogers, who had voted with Bingham for equal protection language in section 1, a vote Bingham had lost, but against the substitution of the section he was now supporting. So far Rogers favored equal protection only as a losing cause. Harris, Howard, Johnson, Williams, Grider, Conkling, and Boutwell voted to strike the section. Fessenden was still absent. The Committee then voted, 7–6, to report the entire package. Conkling, Boutwell, and Representative Henry T. Blow of Missouri were the Republicans voting nay. Bingham, nothing daunted, promptly moved the adoption of his deleted section 5 as a separate proposed amendment to the Constitution. He was again defeated, 8–4, even Stevens leaving him on this one. The three Democrats were with Bingham. Williams then moved that the vote to report out the package be reconsidered. This carried 10–2, the only nays being Howard and Stevens. With that the Committee adjourned.

The Committee was in session again on April 28, three days later, with Fessenden now present. This time the entire proposal was reported out, but with major changes. Instead of granting suffrage prospectively, it was now decided to write a new section 2, simply eliminating from the basis of representation persons to whom the vote was denied, and a new section 3 disfranchising, for purposes of federal elections, large numbers of Southerners till the year 1870. That done, Bingham, still trying, moved to substitute for section 1 (the civil rights section) his privileges and immunities, due process, and equal protection language, which had once been substituted for section 5 and then been struck. This motion carried 10–3. All three Democrats voted for it, as did Stevens and Roscoe Conkling. The opposition consisted of Howard and Representative Justin Morrill of Vermont, both stout Radicals, and Senator James W. Grimes of Iowa, a moderate Republican of the Fessenden sort. Fessenden himself and Harris abstained. On the vote to report the resulting amendment out, only three Democrats were opposed. The Committee also reported a bill readmitting, upon the ratification of the amendment, states which had voted to ratify it, and a bill excluding from office certain Confederate officials.[81]

One of the puzzles to which this course of events in the Joint Committee gives rise is solved by the recollections of Robert Dale Owen. As Thaddeus Stevens told Owen, it was Fessenden's absence at the meetings of April 21, 23, and 25 which caused the Committee not to report out the draft it had approved, including a civil rights provision in section 1 and a grant of prospective suffrage in section 2, and excluding Bingham's formula. Fessenden, who was sick of the varioloid, a mild and euphonious form of smallpox which no longer distracts our politics, was chairman of the Committee on the part of the Senate. It seemed to most members (but not to Stevens and Howard, as we have seen) a lack of courtesy to report out the Committee's most important and final product in his absence. Hence the decision to do so was left in abeyance for three days. That gave a chance to the New York, Illinois, and Indiana Congressional delegations to caucus and to decide that it was politically inadvisable to go to the country in 1866 on a platform having anything to do with Negro suffrage, immediate or prospective. On that issue, these delegations felt, the Republicans might lose the election. This view was communicated to the Committee. As a result, when it met again, the Committee fell to rewriting section 2.[82] Why it proceeded to redo section 1 as well, Owen was, however, unable to explain. Nor did he explain the on-again-off-again attitude toward the Bingham formula.

Section 1, as originally proposed by Owen and Stevens, was framed in terms of the sentence the House had struck from the Civil Rights

Bill to avoid a "latitudinarian" construction. The language Bingham at first proposed to add to section 1 had two apparent effects: it protected, as his own defeated amendment had done, against discriminations other than just those based on color, and it added a special property safeguard not dependent on discrimination. As regards Negro rights, there is no internal indication whether the "equal protection of the laws" formula (*nota bene*—"of the laws," not "in the rights of life, liberty and property," as in the earlier Bingham amendment) was thought by the Committee to imply greater or lesser coverage than the term "civil rights." In either event, it must have been realized that the two provisions overlapped. Yet Bingham at first seemed to want both in, and the Committee, when at one point it accepted Bingham's substitute for section 5, might seem to have been prepared to submit them together. The answer to this oddity may lie in the mechanics of Committee drafting. Inconsistencies, redundancies, and the vestiges of tactical maneuvers appear at some stages and remain to be combed out later. The Committee never actually gave final approval to both the civil rights provision and the Bingham proposal as parts of the same measure.

On April 30, 1866, Fessenden in the Senate and Stevens in the House introduced the Committee draft. They both announced that a report as well as testimony taken before the Committee would soon be printed and distributed.[83] Debate started in the House first, on May 8, under a thirty-minute rule.[84] Stevens opened. The founders, he said, had not been able to build on the uncompromising foundation of the Declaration of Independence. They had decided to wait for "a more propitious time. That time ought to be present now." Now should have been the time to build "upon the firm foundation of eternal justice." But "the public mind has been educated in error for a century. How difficult in a day to unlearn it." The new constitutional structure the Committee was erecting, Stevens said, was defective still, but it made it possible to "trust to the advancing progress of a higher morality and a purer and more intelligent principle." The proposition "falls far short of my wishes, but it fulfills my hopes. I believe it is all that can be obtained in the present state of public opinion. . . . I will take all I can get in the cause of humanity and leave it to be perfected by better men in better times. It may be that that time will not come while I am here to enjoy the glorious triumph; but that it will come is as certain as that there is a just God."

In all probability, the disappointment of Thaddeus Stevens centered on the failure to make any provision for Negro suffrage, immediate or prospective. It was for this reason that he had called the final Committee draft a "shilly-shally, bungling thing" in conversation with Robert Dale

Owen.[85] On the other hand, while he supported Bingham's formula at various drafting stages in committee, Stevens had himself proposed language (directed specifically at racial distinctions) which he might well have regarded as more sweeping, and which, as he had early had occasion to tell the House, was "the genuine proposition," "the one I love."[86] And he spoke his disappointment to the same House now in general terms. He went on then to "refer to the provisions of the proposed amendment":

> The first section prohibits the States from abridging the privileges and immunities of citizens of the United States, or unlawfully depriving them of life, liberty, or property, or of denying to any person within their jurisdiction the "equal" protection of the laws.
>
> I can hardly believe that any person can be found who will not admit that every one of these provisions is just. They are all asserted, in some form or other, in our Declaration or organic law. But the Constitution limits only the action of Congress, and is not a limitation on the States. This amendment supplies that defect, and allows Congress to correct the unjust legislation of the States, so far that the law which operates upon one man shall operate *equally* upon all. Whatever law punishes a white man for a crime shall punish the black man precisely in the same way. . . . Whatever law protects the white man shall afford "equal" protection to the black man. Whatever means of redress is afforded to one shall be afforded to all. Whatever law allows the white man to testify in court shall allow the man of color to do the same. These are great advantages over their present codes. . . . I need not enumerate these partial and oppressive laws. Unless the Constitution should restrain them those States will . . . crush to death the hated freedmen. Some answer, "Your civil rights bill secures the same things." That is partly true, but a law is repealable by a majority.[87]

It will be noted that Stevens, in passing, suggested the argument with which Bingham had supported his earlier amendment, that is, that the provisions now proposed were "asserted" elsewhere in the Constitution. But he went on to mention evils to which the proposal was directed, harking back to those which had been pointed to in support of the Civil Rights Bill. In the debate which followed, many members were heard from. But only two on either side of the aisle devoted more than the briefest sort of generality to section 1. These two were Bingham, whose generalities were not brief, and Rogers, who specified his objections. For the rest, speakers on both sides identified section 1 with the Civil Rights Act. Republicans added, following Stevens' lead, that that great enactment would now be placed beyond the power of future Congresses to repeal,[88] or remarked on the self-evident justice of the proposal, the better part of which was in the Constitution as it stood anyway.[89] One or two regretted that suffrage was not conferred.[90] Democrats gibed that in bringing forth this proposal the Radical leadership had admitted the unconstitutionality of the Civil Rights Act,[91] or charged rather vaguely that the Radicals had far-reaching ultimate aims, including political equality for the Negro.[92] But the bulk of the debate turned on other sections, principally section 3. A number of the Republicans who spoke failed even to mention section 1.[93]

To Andrew Jackson Rogers, who at least in this respect saw further than most, section 1 was the heart of the matter. He said:

> Now sir, I have examined these propositions . . . and I have come to the conclusion different to what some others have come, that the first section of this programme of disunion is the most dangerous to liberty. It saps the foundation of the Government . . . it consolidates everything. . . .
>
> This section . . . is no more nor less than an attempt to embody in the Constitution . . . that outrageous and miserable civil rights bill. . . .
>
> .   .   .   .
>
> . . . What are privileges and immunities? Why, sir, all the rights we have under the laws of the country are embraced under the definition of privileges and immunities. The right to vote is a privilege. The right to marry is a privilege. The right to contract is a privilege. The right to be a juror is a privilege. The right to be a judge or President of the United States is a privilege. I hold if that ever becomes a part of the fundamental law of the land it will prevent any State from refusing to allow anything to anybody embraced under this term of privileges and immunities. . . . It will result in a revolution worse than that through which we have just passed.

Rogers did not deal specifically with the equal protection clause. He proceeded to attack section 2, which, he said, was intended to exert indirect pressure on the South to grant Negro suffrage. Then:

> Sir, I want it distinctly understood that the American people believe that this Government was made for white men and white women. They do not believe, nor can you make them believe—the edict of God Almighty is stamped against it—that there is social equality between the black race and the white.

I have no fault to find with the colored race. . . . I wish them
well, and if I were in a State where they exist in large numbers I
would vote to give them every right enjoyed by the white people
except the right of a negro man to marry a white woman and the
right to vote. But, sir this . . . [is an] indirect way to inflict upon
the people of the South negro suffrage.[94]

Bingham spoke just before some few final remarks by Stevens, which,
in turn, immediately preceded a vote. Bingham said:

The necessity for the first section . . . is one of the lessons that
have been taught . . . by the history of the past four years. . . .
There . . . remains a want now, in the Constitution . . . which the
proposed amendment will supply. . . . It is the power in the people
. . . to protect by national law the privileges and immunities of all
the citizens of the Republic and the inborn rights of every person
within its jurisdiction whenever the same shall be abridged or denied
by the unconstitutional acts of any State.
    . . . [T]his amendment takes from no State any right that ever
pertained to it. No State ever had the right . . . to deny to any freeman the equal protection of the laws or to abridge the privileges
and immunities of any citizen of the Republic, although many of
them have assumed and exercised the power, and that without
remedy. The amendment does not give, as the second section shows,
the power to Congress of regulating suffrage. . . .
    . . . But, sir, it has been suggested, not here, but elsewhere, if
this section does not confer suffrage the need of it is not perceived.
To all such I beg leave again to say, that many instances of State
injustice and oppression have already occurred in the State legislation of this Union, of flagrant violations of the guaranteed privileges
of citizens of the United States, for which the national Government
furnished and could furnish by law no remedy whatever. Contrary
to the express letter of your Constitution, "cruel and unusual punishments" have been inflicted under State laws . . . not only for crimes
committed, but for sacred duty done. . . .
          .   .   .   .

    . . . That great want of the citizen and stranger, protection by na-
tional law from unconstitutional State enactments, is supplied by
the first section of this amendment. That is the extent that it hath, no
more; and let gentlemen answer to God and their country who
oppose its incorporation into the organic law of the land.[95]

Bingham went on to discuss section 3, about which he was more lucid and less enthusiastic.

It was to section 3 that Thaddeus Stevens addressed his closing remarks. He noted dissension about it, and pleaded for its adoption, to save the Republican party and through it the country. Unless section 3 was passed, Stevens could see "that side of the House . . . filled with yelling secessionists and hissing copperheads." Section 3 was actually "too lenient for my hard heart. Not only to 1870, but to 18070, every rebel who shed the blood of loyal men should be prevented from exercising any power in this Government." Stevens conjured up the scene in the House before the war when "the men that you propose to admit" through a milder section 3 occupied the other side, among them "the mighty Toombs, with his shaggy locks . . . when weapons were drawn, and Barksdale's bowie-knife gleamed before our eyes. Would you have these men back again so soon to reënact those scenes? Wait until I am gone, I pray you. I want not to go through it again. It will be but a short time for my colleague to wait." With these searing words in its ears, the House, though by a close vote (84–79) in which some Democrats, who sought to keep the proposal as obnoxious as possible, provided the winning margin, obeyed Stevens and cut off amendments. (James A. Garfield had one changing section 3.) By a vote of 128–37 the House then adopted the draft as reported by the Joint Committee. Lovell Rousseau of Kentucky and a few other Conservatives were in the opposition.[96] This was the afternoon of May 10. The final vote in committee had been had twelve days before.

The proposal was brought up in the Senate on May 23. Before debate started Charles Sumner made a point which had also been raised by a Democrat in the House. The testimony taken before the Joint Committee, he said, had not been published as a whole, and no report drawing the Committee's conclusions had been submitted. He thought it was a "mistake that we are asked to proceed . . . under such circumstances." Fessenden answered saying there was nothing to be gained by waiting longer.[97] Debate itself was opened by Jacob Howard, the Michigan Radical. Fessenden, victim of the varioloid, was not feeling well enough to speak at length. Howard paid due and reasonably loyal attention to section 1, whose inclusion in its present form he had opposed in committee:

> To these privileges and immunities, whatever they may be—for they are not and cannot be fully defined in their entire extent and precise nature—to these should be added the personal rights guarantied and secured by the first eight amendments of the Constitution.

As for the equal protection clause:

> This abolishes all class legislation in the States and does away with
> the injustice of subjecting one caste of persons to a code not ap-
> plicable to another. It prohibits the hanging of a black man for a
> crime for which the white man is not to be hanged. It protects the
> black man in his fundamental rights as a citizen with the same
> shield which it throws over the white man. . . .
> But, sir, the first section of the proposed amendment does not
> give . . . the right of voting. The right of suffrage . . . is merely the
> creature of law. It [is] . . . not regarded as one of those fundamental
> rights lying at the basis of all society and without which a people
> cannot exist except as slaves.[98]

Speakers who followed Howard did not address themselves to section
1, except that Benjamin F. Wade, the Ohio Radical, and one or two
others wondered whether section 1 should not define national citizenship. Stewart of Nevada made a last extended plea for the plan he had
advocated before the Joint Committee and elsewhere.[99] Further debate
was then postponed. It had so far gone on for parts of two days. It was
not resumed till four days later, on May 29, when Howard, "after consultation with some of the friends of this measure," presented some
amendments which, "it has been thought . . . will be acceptable to both
Houses of Congress and to the country."[100] In other words, a Republican
caucus had been in session and had straightened out differences among
the Republicans, which, as debate had revealed, centered around section
3. It was agreed to forgo disfranchising Southern whites. Instead a
provision was inserted disqualifying certain Southerners for federal office;
section 2, though modified, remained essentially the same; and United
States citizenship was defined in section 1. Thus the amendment assumed
its present form. The proceedings of the caucus were, as Thomas A.
Hendricks, Democrat of Indiana, charged, so secret that "no outside
Senators, not even the sharp-eyed men of the press, have been able to
learn one word that was spoken, or one vote given."[101] They have remained secret to this day.

The Senate now engaged in a debate which lasted for several days.
But, as had been the case in the House and earlier in the Senate itself,
proportionately little was said about section 1 by either Democrats or
Republicans. It was charged that the section gave citizenship to "savage"
Indians and Gypsies and that it embodied the Civil Rights Act.[102] Luke
Poland, Republican from Vermont and a former chief justice of that
state, drew attention to state laws, "some of them of very recent enact-

ment," at which the Civil Rights Act had struck. This amendment, he implied, was also directed at the Black Codes.[103] The same implication was left with the Senate by John B. Henderson of Missouri, a Republican who enjoyed much respect, and who was no doctrinaire Radical. It would be "a loss of time," he said, "to discuss the remaining provisions of the section [other than the citizenship clause, which he held to be simply declaratory of existing law], for they merely secure the rights that attach to citizenship in all free Governments." Nevertheless, Henderson did mention the Black Codes, which formed a "system of oppression" rendering the Negro a "degraded outcast" deprived of the "commonest rights of human nature," the right to hold property, to sue, to confront witnesses, to have the process of the courts. The Freedmen's Bureau and Civil Rights Bills and, Henderson implied, section 1 of this amendment, were all intended to cure this situation.[104] Timothy O. Howe of Wisconsin, a Radical, spoke in the same vein, but in richer detail. Negroes, he said, had been denied elementary rights:

> The right to hold land . . . the right to collect their wages by the processes of the law . . . the right to appear in the courts as suitors . . . the right to give testimony . . .
> . . . [B]ut, sir, these are not the only rights that can be denied. . . . I have taken considerable pains to look over the actual legislation [in the South] . . . I read not long since a statute enacted by the Legislature of Florida for the education of her colored people. . . . They make provision for the education of their white children also, and everybody who has any property there is taxed for the education of the white children. Black and white are taxed alike for that purpose; but for the education of colored children a fund is raised only from colored men.

Howe described the colored school system in Florida, which was, of course, segregated, without pointing out that fact; what he stressed was the inadequacy of the poorly supported colored schools. He implied that section 1 would render this legislation illegal, but he gave no indication that he believed its vice to lie in segregation.[105]

Aside from a parting shot by Reverdy Johnson, nothing else was said in the Senate about section 1, and it is perhaps noteworthy that conservative Republicans like Cowan and Doolittle, Democrats like Johnson, and even Democrats of the stripe of Garrett Davis of Kentucky spoke at some length, but refrained from raising alarms concerning the reach of section 1 and the sort of local practices it would outlaw.[106] This contrasts with Senate and House debates on the Civil Rights Act, and with Rogers' and even some of his colleagues' more recent statements in the House. But the absence of purported alarm must be understood in the light of the paucity of attention generally devoted to section 1, which in turn is doubtless attributable to the evident greater political vulnerability of the Republicans with respect to other sections of the amendment. Just before the vote, Reverdy Johnson, who had spoken at length on the basis of representation,[107] remarked that while he saw no objection to the due process clause, he simply did not understand what would be the effect of the privileges and immunities clause, and wished it might be deleted. No one made a closing speech for the proponents. The vote followed immediately. It was 33–11; the date, June 8. Four Republicans—Cowan, Doolittle, Norton of Minnesota, and Van Winkle of West Virginia, the hard core of Conservatives—voted nay.[108]

On June 13 the House, under a fifteen-minute rule, took up the amendment as returned from the Senate.[109] Rogers spoke first. The burden of his remarks was a complaint that the amendment had been ill-considered by a Congress cringing under the party whip. He referred in passing to section 1, repeating that it "simply embodied the gist of the civil rights bill." His heavy artillery was concentrated on the manner in which the amendment had been pushed through the Senate by command of the secret Radical caucus.[110] A few others spoke without mentioning section 1. Then Thaddeus Stevens moved the previous question, thus bringing on the vote. But first he had a few words to say, which are worth quoting extensively, both for their characteristic bite and because they were the launching words, the last spoken before the Fourteenth Amendment slid down the ways. The implacable old man was not happy:

> In my youth, in my manhood, in my old age, I had fondly dreamed that when any fortunate chance should have broken up for awhile the foundation of our institutions, and released us from obligations the most tyrannical that ever man imposed in the name of freedom, that the intelligent, pure and just men of this Republic, true to their professions and their consciences, would have so remodeled all our institutions as to have freed them from every vestige of human oppression, of inequality of rights, of the recognized degradation of the poor, and the superior caste of the rich. In short, that no distinction would be tolerated in this purified Republic but what arose from merit and conduct. This bright dream has vanished "like the baseless fabric of a vision." I find that we shall be obliged to be content with patching up the worst portions of the ancient edifice, and leaving it, in many of its parts, to be swept through by the tempests, the frosts, and the storms of despotism.

Do you inquire why, holding these views and possessing some will of my own, I accept so imperfect a proposition? I answer, because I live among men and not among angels.

Perhaps more strenuous effort might have resulted in a better plan. But Congress had had to face the hostility of the President, and this proposal met in some measure the danger of "tyranny" emanating from the White House, "the danger arising from the unscrupulous use of patronage and from the oily orations of false prophets, famous for sixty-day obligations and for protested political promises." Stevens lightly reviewed some of the changes made in the Senate. The principal one was, of course, section 3, and he disapproved. He ended by urging speedy adoption of the imperfect product. "I dread delay," he said. Then:

The danger is that before any constitutional guards shall have been adopted Congress will be flooded by rebels and rebel sympathizers. . . . Whoever has watched the feelings of this House during the tedious months of this session, listened to the impatient whispering of some and the open declarations of others; especially when able and sincere men propose to gratify personal predilections by breaking the ranks of the Union forces and presenting to the enemy a ragged front of stragglers, must be anxious to hasten the result and prevent the demoralization of our friends. Hence, I say, let us no longer delay; take what we can get now, and hope for better things in further legislation; in enabling acts or other provisions.

I now, sir, ask for the question.

The vote which followed immediately and which sent the Fourteenth Amendment to the country was 120 yeas, 32 nays. There were no Republican votes against. Rousseau of Kentucky and a few other Conservatives were recorded absent. Eldridge, the Democrat, said: "I desire to state that if Messrs. Brooks and Voorhees had not been expelled, they would have voted against this proposition. [Great laughter.]" And Schenck, of the Radical leadership, retorted: "And I desire to say that if Jeff. Davis were here, he would probably also have voted the same way. [Renewed laughter.]"[111]

Summary and Conclusions

As we have seen, the first approach made by the 39th Congress toward dealing with racial discrimination turned on the "civil rights" formula. The Senate Moderates, led by Trumbull and Fessenden, who sponsored this formula, assigned a limited and well-defined meaning to it. In their view it covered the right to contract, sue, give evidence in court, and inherit, hold, and dispose of real and personal property; also a right to equal protection in the literal sense of benefiting equally from laws for the security of person and property, including presumably laws permitting ownership of firearms, and to equality in the penalties and burdens provided by law. Certainly able men like Trumbull and Fessenden realized that each of the seemingly well-bounded rights they enumerated carried about it, like an upper atmosphere, an area in which its force was uncertain. Thus it is clear that the Moderates wished also to protect rights of free movement, and a right to engage in occupations of one's choice. They doubtless considered that their enumeration somehow accomplished this purpose. Similarly, the Moderates often argued that one of the imperative needs of the time was to educate, to "elevate," to "Christianize" the Negro; indeed, this was an almost universally held doctrine, from which even Conservatives like Cowan and Democrats like Rogers did not dissent. Hence one may surmise that the Moderates believed they were guaranteeing a right to equal benefits from state educational systems supported by general tax funds. But there is no evidence whatever showing that for its sponsors the civil rights formula had anything to do with unsegregated public schools; Wilson, its sponsor in the House, specifically disclaimed any such notion. Similarly, it is plain that the Moderates did not intend to confer any right of intermarriage, the right to sit on juries, or the right to vote.

Civil rights protection was first extended by the Freedmen's Bureau Bill. This was not a closely debated measure, because it was limited in duration and territorial applicability. The Conservative votes cast in its favor mark it as a sacrificial offering on the altar of Radicalism, not seriously considered on its own merits. When the same formula was next brought forth in the Civil Rights Bill, it evoked warnings from the Democratic and Conservative opposition in the Senate, which argued that the phrase "civil rights" might well be construed to include more rights than its sponsors intended to affect. One of the warnings related to segregation. The Moderates were unmoved, and the bill was carried in the Senate.

The Joint Committee in the meantime was dealing with the same problem. It elected not to use the civil rights formula and offered instead, in the Bingham amendment, equal protection "in the rights of life, liberty and property," plus a privileges and immunities clause. Given the evils represented by the Black Codes, which were foremost in the minds of all men, it must be supposed that this language was deemed to protect all the rights specifically enumerated in the Civil Rights Bill.

But it is difficult to interpret the deliberate choice against using the term "civil rights" as anything but a rejection of what were deemed its wider implications.

The Bingham amendment did not act directly on the states. It was an unconditional grant of power to Congress, like the older grants of legislative power; and like them it was bolstered by a necessary and proper clause. This feature made it unacceptable to Moderates like Hale. The fact that the amendment itself gave no assurance of permanent protection cost the support of some Radicals. On these grounds the proposal went down to defeat. There were some questions raised also concerning the kind of rights covered, and Bingham rather clumsily responded by suggesting the Moderate position on the Civil Rights Bill, but this was completely secondary. Only Rogers, a partisan given to extreme accusations, spoke of this proposal as if there had been no difference between it and a "civil rights" guaranty.

The Civil Rights Bill itself, as brought from the Senate to the House, split the alliance of various shades of Moderates and Radicals which constituted the Republican majority. The bill was presented to the House as a measure of limited objectives, following Trumbull's views. But a substantial number of Republicans were troubled by the issue of constitutionality. Others were uneasy on policy grounds about the reach of section 1, but inclined to believe that the bill could be rendered constitutional by amendment, and, in any event, out of mixed motives at which one can only guess, conquered their apprehensions and voted for it in the end. Bingham, whose position was in this instance entirely self-consistent, thought the bill incurably unconstitutional, its enforcement provisions monstrous, and the civil rights guaranty of very broad application and unwise. The concession these Republicans wrung from the leadership was the elimination of the civil rights formula and thus the avoidance of possible "latitudinarian" construction. The Moderate position that the bill dealt only with a distinct and limited set of rights was conclusively validated.

Against this backdrop, the Joint Committee on Reconstruction began framing the Fourteenth Amendment. In drafting section 1, it vacillated between the civil rights formula and language proposed by Bingham, finally adopting the latter. Stevens' speech opening debate on the amendment in the House presented section 1 in terms quite similar to the Moderate position on the Civil Rights Bill, though there was a rather notable absence of the disclaimers of wider coverage which usually accompanied the Moderates' statements of objectives. A few remarks made in the Senate sounded in the same vein. For the rest, however, section 1 was not really debated. Rogers, whose remarks are always subject to heavy discount, considering his shaky position in the affections of his own party colleagues, raised "latitudinarian" alarms. One or two other Democrats in the House did so also. But more and more, debate turned on section 3 and not much else. The focus of attention is well indicated by Stevens' brief address immediately before the first vote in the House. In this atmosphere, section 1 became the subject of a stock generalization: it was dismissed as embodying and, in one sense for the Republicans, in another for the Democrats and Conservatives, "constitutionalizing" the Civil Rights Act.

The obvious conclusion to which the evidence, thus summarized, easily leads is that section 1 of the Fourteenth Amendment, like section 1 of the Civil Rights Act of 1866, carried out the relatively narrow objectives of the Moderates, and hence, as originally understood, was meant to apply neither to jury service, nor to suffrage, nor to antimiscegenation statutes, nor to segregation. This conclusion is supported by the blunt expression of disappointment to which Thaddeus Stevens gave vent in the House. Nothing in the election campaign of 1866 or in the ratification proceedings negatives it. Section 1 received in both about the attention it had received in Congress, and in about the same terms.[112] One or two "reconstructed" Southern legislatures took what turned out, of course, to be temporary measures to abolish segregation.[113] There is little if any indication of an impression prevailing elsewhere that the amendment required such action.

If the Fourteenth Amendment were a statute, a court might very well hold, on the basis of what has been said so far, that it was foreclosed from applying it to segregation in public schools. The evidence of Congressional purpose is as clear as such evidence is likely to be, and no language barrier stands in the way of construing the section in conformity with it. But we are dealing with a constitutional amendment, not a statute. The tradition of a broadly worded organic law not frequently or lightly amended was well established by 1866, and, despite the somewhat revolutionary fervor with which the Radicals were pressing their changes, it cannot be assumed that they or anyone else expected or wished the future role of the Constitution in the scheme of American government to differ from the past. Should not the search for Congressional purpose, therefore, properly be twofold? One inquiry should be directed at the Congressional understanding of the immediate effect of the enactment on conditions then present. Another should aim to discover what if any thought was given to the long-range effect, under future circumstances, of provisions necessarily intended for permanence.

That the Court saw the need for two such inquiries with respect to the original understanding on segregation is clearly indicated by the questions it propounded at the 1952 term.[114] The Court asked first whether Congress and the state legislatures contemplated that the Fourteenth Amendment would abolish segregation in public schools. It next asked whether, assuming that the immediate abolition of segregation was not contemplated, the framers nevertheless understood that Congress acting under section 5 or the Court in the exercise of the judicial function would, in light of future conditions, have power to abolish segregation.

With this double aspect of the inquiry in mind, certain other features of the legislative history—not inconsistent with the conclusion earlier stated, but complementary to it—became significant. Thus, section 1 of the Fourteenth Amendment, on its face, deals not only with racial discrimination but also with discrimination whether or not based on color. This cannot have been accidental, since the alternative considered by the Joint Committee, the civil rights formula, did apply only to racial discrimination. Everyone's immediate preoccupation in the 39th Congress —in so far as it did not go to partisan questions—was, of course, with hardships being visited on the colored race. Yet the fact that the proposed constitutional amendment was couched in more general terms could not have escaped those who voted for it. And this feature of it could not have been deemed to be included in the standard identification of section 1 with the Civil Rights Act. Again, when it rejected the civil rights formula in reporting out the abortive Bingham amendment, the Joint Committee elected to submit an equal protection clause limited to the rights of life, liberty, and property, supplemented by a necessary and proper clause. Now the choice was in favor of a due process clause limited the way the equal protection clause had been in the earlier draft, but of an equal protection clause not so limited: equal protection "of the laws." Presumably the lesson taught by the defeat of the Bingham amendment had been learned. Congress was not to have unlimited discretion, and it was not to have the leeway represented by "necessary and proper" power.[115] One would have to assume a lack of familiarity with the English language to conclude that a further difference between the Bingham amendment and the new proposal was not also perceived, namely, the difference between equal protection in the rights of life, liberty, and property, a phrase which so aptly evoked the evils uppermost in men's minds at the time, and equal protection of the laws, a clause which is plainly capable of being applied to all subjects of state legislation. Could the comparison have failed to leave the implication that the new phrase, while it did not necessarily, and certainly not expressly, carry greater coverage than the old, was nevertheless roomier, more receptive to "latitudinarian" construction? No one made the point with regard to this particular clause. But in opening debate in the Senate, Jacob Howard was frank to say that only the future could tell just what application the privileges and immunities provision might have. And before the vote in the Senate, Reverdy Johnson, a Democrat, to be sure, but a respected constitutional lawyer and no rabid partisan, confessed his puzzlement about the same clause. Finally, it is noteworthy that the shorthand argument characterizing the Fourteenth Amendment as the constitutional embodiment of the Civil Rights Act was often accompanied on the Republican side by generalities about the self-evident demands of justice and the natural rights of man. This was true both in Congress and in the course of the election that followed.[116] To all this should be added the fact that while the Joint Committee's rejection of the civil rights formula is quite manifest, there is implicit also in its choice of language a rejection—presumably as inappropriate in a constitutional provision—of such a specific and exclusive enumeration of rights as appeared in section 1 of the Civil Rights Act.

These bits and pieces of additional evidence do not contradict and could not in any event override the direct proof showing the specific evils at which the great body of congressional opinion thought it was striking. But perhaps they provide sufficient basis for the formulation of an additional hypothesis. It remains true that an explicit provision going further than the Civil Rights Act could not have been carried in the 39th Congress; also that a plenary grant of legislative power such as the Bingham amendment would not have mustered the necessary majority. But may it not be that the Moderates and the Radicals reached a compromise permitting them to go to the country with language which they could, where necessary, defend against damaging alarms raised by the opposition, but which at the same time was sufficiently elastic to permit reasonable future advances? This is thoroughly consistent with rejection of the civil rights formula and its implications. That formula could not serve the purpose of such a compromise. It had been under heavy attack at this session, and among those who had expressed fears concerning its reach were Republicans who would have to go forth and stand on the platform of the Fourteenth Amendment. Bingham, of course, was one of these men, and he could not be required to go on the hustings and risk being made to eat his own words. If the party was to unite behind a compromise which consisted neither of an exclusive listing of a limited series of rights nor of a formulation dangerously vulnerable to attacks pandering to the prejudices of the people, new language had to be found.

Bingham himself supplied it. It had both sweep and the appearance of a careful enumeration of rights, and it had a ring to echo in the national memory of libertarian beginnings. To put it another way, the Moderates, with a bit of timely assistance from Fessenden's varioloid, consolidated the victory they had achieved in the Civil Rights Act debate. They could go forth and honestly defend themselves against charges that on the day after ratification Negroes were going to become white men's "social equals," marry their daughters, vote in their elections, sit on their juries, and attend schools with their children. The Radicals (though they had to compromise once more on section 3) obtained what early in the session had seemed a very uncertain prize indeed: a firm alliance, under Radical leadership, with the Moderates in the struggle against the President, and thus a good, clear chance at increasing and prolonging their political power. In the future, the Radicals could, in one way or another, put through such further civil rights provisions as they thought the country would take, without being subject to the sort of effective constitutional objections which haunted them when they were forced to operate under the Thirteenth Amendment.

It is, of course, giving the men of the 39th Congress much more than their due to ennoble them by a comparison of their proceedings with the deliberations of the Philadelphia Convention. Yet if this was the compromise that was struck, then these men emulated the technique of the original framers, who were also responsible to an electorate only partly receptive to the fullness of their principles, and who similarly avoided the explicit grant of some powers without foreclosing their future assumption.[117] Whatever other support this theory may have, it has behind it the very authoritative voice of Thaddeus Stevens, who held it, and twice gave notice of it in speaking on the Fourteenth Amendment. It was Stevens who dutifully defined section 1 more or less in the narrow terms a Trumbull or a Fessenden would have used; it fell short of his wishes. And it was Stevens, his hopes fulfilled, who powerfully and candidly emphasized the political opportunities which the amendment gained for the Radicals, and who looked to the future for better things "in further legislation, in enabling acts or other provisions." Similarly, when it at last emerged, though too late to influence debate, the report of the Joint Committee submitted the amendment "in the hope that its imperfections may be cured and its deficiencies supplied, by legislative wisdom."[118] It need hardly be added that in view of Stevens' remarks, and in view also of the nature of the other evidence which supports it, this hypothesis cannot be disparaged as putting forth an undisclosed, conspiratorial purpose such as has been imputed to Bingham and others with regard to protection of corporations.[119] Indeed, no specific purpose going beyond the coverage of the Civil Rights Act is suggested; rather an awareness on the part of these framers that it was *a constitution* they were writing, which led to a choice of language capable of growth.

It is such a reading as this of the original understanding, in response to the second of the questions propounded by the Court, that the Chief Justice must have had in mind when he termed the materials "inconclusive." For up to this point they tell a clear story and are anything but inconclusive. From this point on the word is apt, since the interpretation of the evidence just set out comes only to this, that the question of giving greater protection than was extended by the Civil Rights Act was deferred, was left open, to be decided another day under a constitutional provision with more scope than the unserviceable Thirteenth Amendment. Some no doubt felt more certain than others that the new amendment would make possible further strides toward the ideal of equality. That remained to be decided, and there is no indication of the way in which anyone thought the decision would go on any given specific issue.[120] It depended a good deal on the trend in public opinion. Actually, one of the things the Radicals had contended for throughout the session, and doubtless considered that they gained by the final compromise, was time and the chance to educate the public. Such expectations as the Radicals had were centered quite clearly on legislative action. At least this holds true for Stevens. These men were aware of the power the Court could exercise. They were for the most part bitterly aware of it, having long fought such decisions as the *Dred Scott* case. Most probably they had little hope that the Court would play a role in furthering their long-range objectives. But the relevant point is that the Radical leadership succeeded in obtaining a provision whose future effect was left to future determination. The fact that they themselves expected such a future determination to be made in Congress is not controlling. It merely reflects their estimate that men of their view were more likely to prevail in the legislature than in other branches of the government. It indicates no judgment about the powers and functions properly to be exercised by the other branches.

Had the Court in the *School Segregation Cases* stopped short of the inconclusive answer to the second of its questions handed down at the previous term, it would have been faced with one of two unfortunate choices. It could have deemed itself bound by the legislative history showing the immediate objectives to which section 1 of the Fourteenth Amendment was addressed, and rather clearly demonstrating that it was not expected in 1866 to apply to segregation. The Court would in that event also have repudiated much of the provision's "line of growth." For it is as clear that section 1 was not deemed in 1866 to deal with jury service and other matters "implicit in . . . ordered liberty"[121] to which the Court has since applied it.[122] Secondly, the Court could have faced the embarrassment of going counter to what it took to be the original understanding, and of formulating, as it has not often needed to do in the past, an explicit theory rationalizing such a course. The Court, of course, made neither choice. It was able to avoid the dilemma because the record of history, properly understood, left the way open to, in fact invited, a decision based on the moral and material state of the Union in 1954, not 1866.

Notes

I. THE RACES IN THE PUBLIC SCHOOLS

1. The Decade of School Desegregation

1. Brown v. Board of Education, 347 U.S. 483 (1954); 349 U.S. 294 (1955).
2. Address before Pennsylvania Bar Association, June 27, 1916, 22 *Pa.B.A. Rep.* 221 (1916).
3. *Southern School News,* Dec. 1964, p. 1, cols. 1-5; Sept. 1964, p. 1, cols. 4-5; Dec. 1963, p. 1, cols. 1-5; Oct. 1963, p. 1, col. 1; Sept. 1963, p. 1, cols. 1-5.
4. Brown v. Board of Education, 349 U.S. 294, 301 (1955).
5. *Id.* at 300.
6. *Id.* at 300-301.
7. *Id.* at 300.
8. 16 *Law. Guild Rev.* 21, 22 (1956).
9. R. P. Warren, *Segregation* 112-14 (1956).
10. 24 *J. Negro Education* 397, 402-03 (1955).
11. H. H. Quint, *Profile in Black and White* 21 (1958).
12. 358 U.S. 1 (1958).
13. See A. M. Bickel, *The Least Dangerous Branch, passim* (1962).
14. 261 U.S. 525.

15. 300 U.S. 379 (1937).
16. 333 U.S. 203 (1948); see G. Patric, "The Impact of a Court Decision: Aftermath of the McCollum Case," 6 *J. Pub. Law* 455 (1957).
17. 343 U.S. 306 (1952).
18. School Dist. v. Schempp, 374 U.S. 203 (1963); Engel v. Vitale, 370 U.S. 421 (1962).
19. See Florida *ex rel.* Hawkins v. Board of Control, 350 U.S. 413 (1956), 355 U.S. 839 (1957); Sweatt v. Painter, 339 U.S. 629 (1950); Sipuel v. Board of Regents, 332 U.S. 631 (1948); Missouri *ex rel.* Gaines v. Canada, 305 U.S. 337 (1938); U.S. Comm'n on Civil Rights, *Equal Protection of the Laws in Public Higher Education, 1960* (1961); U.S. Comm'n on Civil Rights, *Education* 167-71 (1961).
20. See *New York Times,* Mar. 12, 1956, p. 19, col. 2.
21. See Carson v. Warlick, 238 F. 2d 724 (4th Cir. 1956), *cert. denied,* 353 U.S. 910 (1957); Covington v. Edwards, 264 F.2d 780 (4th Cir.), *cert. denied,* 361 U.S. 840 (1959); see R. McKay, "With All Deliberate Speed," 43 *Va. L. Rev.* 1205, 1215-20 (1957); D. Meador, "The Constitution and the Assignment of Pupils to Public Schools, 45 *Va. L. Rev.* 517, 533-34 (1959). See also Note, "State Efforts to Circumvent Desegregation," 54 *Nw. U.L. Rev.* 354 (1959); Note, "The Federal Courts and Integration of Southern Schools: Troubled Status of the Pupil Placements Acts," 62 *Colum. L. Rev.* 1448 (1962).
22. Cf. remarks of Brown, J., Transcript of Trial, Vick v. County Bd. of Educ., 205 F. Supp. 436 (W.D. Tenn. 1962), in 6 *Race Relations L. Rep.* 1001, 1003 (1962), quoted in U.S. Comm'n on Civil Rights Staff, *Civil Rights U.S.A.: Public Schools, Southern States* 3-4 (1962).
23. School Bd. v. Atkins, 246 F.2d 325 (4th Cir.), *cert. denied,* 355 U.S. 855 (1957).
24. James v. Almond, 170 F. Supp. 331 (E.D. Va.), *appeal dismissed per stipulation,* 359 U.S. 1006 (1959); Harrison v. Day, 200 Va. 439, 106 S.E.2d 636 (1959). See also James v. Duckworth, 170 F. Supp. 342 (E.D. Va.), *aff'd,* 267 F.2d 224 (4th Cir.), *cert. denied,* 361 U.S. 835 (1959).
25. Griffin v. School Bd. of Prince Edward Cty., 377 U.S. 218 (1964).
26. Griffin v. School Bd. of Prince Edward Cty. and Pettaway v. School Bd. of Surry Cty., 339 F.2d 486 (4th Cir. 1964). And see Griffin v. State Bd. of Education, 239 F. Supp. 560 (E.D. Va. 1965).
27. Shuttlesworth v. Birmingham Bd. of Educ., 162 F. Supp. 372 (N.D. Ala.), *aff'd per curiam,* 358 U.S. 101 (1958).
28. Bush v. Orleans Parish School Bd., 138 F. Supp. 337 (E.D. La. 1956), *aff'd,* 242 F.2d 156 (5th Cir.), *cert. denied,* 354 U.S. 921

(1957); Hall v. St. Helena Parish School Bd., 197 F. Supp. 649 (E.D. La. 1961), *aff'd per curiam*, 368 U.S. 515 (1962).

29. Ross v. Peterson, 5 *Race Rel. L. Rep.* 703, 709 (S.D. Tex. 1960); see Boson v. Rippy, 285 F.2d 43 (5th Cir. 1960); Borders v. Rippy, 195 F. Supp. 732 (N.D. Tex. 1961); U.S. Comm'n on Civil Rights, *Education* 18-19, 53-55 (1961); cf. Davis v. East Baton Rouge Parish School Bd., 219 F. Supp. 876, 885 (E.D. La. 1963).

30. Mannings v. Board of Pub. Instruction, 277 F.2d 370 (5th Cir. 1960); Gibson v. Board of Pub. Instruction, 272 F.2d 763 (5th Cir. 1959); Holland v. Board of Pub. Instruction, 258 F.2d 730 (5th Cir. 1958).

31. Aaron v. McKinley, 173 F. Supp. 944 (E.D. Ark.), *aff'd sub nom.* Faubus v. Aaron, 361 U.S. 197 (1959); cf. Aaron v. Cooper, 261 F.2d 97 (8th Cir. 1958), *order on remand,* 169 F. Supp. 325 (E.D. Ark. 1959) (transfer of school to private corporation enjoined; school, if reopened, must be integrated).

32. See Garett v. Faubus, 230 Ark. 445, 323 S.W.2d 877 (1959).

33. Holt v. Raleigh City Bd. of Educ., 265 F.2d 95 (4th Cir.), *cert. denied,* 361 U.S. 818 (1959). But see McCoy v. Greensboro City Bd. of Educ., 283 F.2d 667 (4th Cir. 1960).

34. Beckett v. School Bd., 185 F. Supp. 459 (E.D. Va. 1959), *aff'd sub nom.* Farley v. Turner, 281 F.2d 131 (4th Cir. 1960).

35. See Jones v. School Bd., 278 F.2d 72 (4th Cir. 1960).

36. See Brunson v. Board of Trustees, 311 F.2d 107 (4th Cir. 1962), *cert. denied,* 373 U.S. 933 (1963); *New York Times,* Oct. 22, 1963, p. 31, col. 2.

37. See cases cited note 30 *supra.*

38. Parham v. Dove, 271 F.2d 132, 135 (8th Cir. 1959); see Dove v. Parham, 282 F.2d 256 (8th Cir. 1960).

39. See Dove v. Parham, 196 F. Supp. 944 (E.D. Ark. 1961).

40. 304 F.2d 118 (4th Cir. 1962).

41. *Id.* at 124.

42. Dillard v. School Bd., 308 F.2d 920 (4th Cir. 1962), *cert. denied,* 374 U.S. 827 (1963).

43. Jeffers v. Whitley, 309 F.2d 621 (4th Cir. 1962).

44. Wheeler v. Durham City Bd. of Educ., 309 F.2d 630 (4th Cir. 1962).

45. Brunson v. Board of Trustees, 311 F.2d 107 (4th Cir. 1962), *cert. denied,* 373 U.S. 933 (1963). See also Buckner v. School Bd. of Greene Cty., 332 F.2d 452 (4th Cir. 1964); Brown v. School Dist. of Charleston, S.C., 328 F.2d 618 (4th Cir. 1964), *affirming* 226 F. Supp. 819 (E.D. S.C. 1963); Bell v. School Bd., 321 F.2d 494 (4th Cir. 1963); Jackson v. School Bd., 321 F.2d 230 (4th Cir. 1963); Bradley v. School Bd., 317 F.2d 429 (4th Cir. 1963); Marsh v. County School Bd., 305 F.2d 94 (4th Cir. 1962); Adams

v. School Dist. of Orangeburg Cty., 232 F. Supp. 692 (E.D. S.C. 1964); Randall v. Sumter School Dist. No. 2, 232 F. Supp. 786 (E.D. S.C. 1964); Brown v. School Bd. of Frederick Cty., 234 F. Supp. 808 (W.D. Va. 1964). But cf. Blakeney v. Fairfax Cty. School Bd., 231 F. Supp. 1006 (E.D. Va. 1964).

46. Northcross v. Board of Ed., 302 F.2d 818, 820, 824 (6th Cir.), cert. denied, 370 U.S. 944 (1962).

47. Note, "The Federal Courts and Integration of Southern Schools," 62 Colum. L. Rev. 1448, 1471-73 (1962).

48. Augustus v. Board of Pub. Instruction, 306 F.2d 862 (5th Cir. 1962).

49. Bush v. Orleans Parish School Bd., 308 F.2d 491 (5th Cir. 1962); and see id. 230 F. Supp. 509 (E.D. La. 1963).

50. Potts v. Flax, 313 F.2d 284 (5th Cir. 1963); Evers v. Jackson School Dist., 328 F.2d 408 (5th Cir. 1964). And see Harris v. Bullock Cty. Bd. of Education, 232 F. Supp. 959 (M.D. Ala. 1964); Youngblood v. Board of Pub. Instruction, 230 F. Supp. 74 (N.D. Fla. 1964); Carr v. Montgomery Cty. Bd. of Education, 232 F. Supp. 705 (1964).

51. Calhoun v. Latimer, 321 F.2d 302 (5th Cir. 1963), vacated and remanded, 377 U.S. 263 (1964).

52. Armstrong v. Bd. of Education, 220 F. Supp. 217 (N.D. Ala.), 323 F.2d 333 (5th Cir. 1963), cert. denied, sub nom. Gibson v. Harris, 376 U.S. 908 (1964); Davis v. Board of School Comm'rs, 219 F. Supp. 542 (S.D. Ala.), 322 F.2d 356 (5th Cir.), cert. denied, 375 U.S. 894 (1963). See also Lee v. Macon Cty. Bd. of Education, 221 F. Supp. 297 (M.D. Ala. 1963), 231 F. Supp. 743 (M.D. Ala. 1964).

53. Armstrong v. Bd. of Education, 333 F.2d 47 (5th Cir. 1964); Davis v. Board of School Comm'rs, 333 F.2d 53 (5th Cir. 1964).

54. Calhoun v. Latimer, 377 U.S. 263 (1964).

55. Stell v. Savannah-Chatham Cty. Bd. of Education, 220 F. Supp. 667 (S.D. Ga. 1963) (Scarlett, J.), rev'd, 318 F.2d 425 (5th Cir. 1963), 333 F.2d 55 (5th Cir. 1964); and see Hall v. St. Helena Parish School Bd., 233 F. Supp. 136 (E.D. La. 1964) (West, J.), mandamus issued, Hall v. West, 335 F.2d 481 (5th Cir. 1964); Evers v. Jackson Municipal School Dist., 232 F. Supp. 241 (S.D. Miss. 1964) (Mize, J.), rev'd, 328 F.2d 408 (5th Cir. 1964); Harris v. Gibson, 322 F.2d 780 (5th Cir. 1963).

56. Watson v. City of Memphis, 373 U.S. 526 (1963).

57. Goss v. Board of Educ., 373 U.S. 683 (1963).

58. See, e.g., Bush v. Orleans Parish School Bd., 308 F.2d 491, 502 (5th Cir. 1962) (New Orleans); Ross v. Peterson, 5 Race Rel. L. Rep. 703, 709 (S.D. Tex. 1960) (Houston).

59. See Maxwell v. County Bd. of Educ., 301 F.2d 828 (6th Cir. 1962) rev'd on other grounds, 373 U.S. 683 (1963); Flax v. Potts, 218

F. Supp. 254 (N.D. Tex. 1963) (Ft. Worth). For decisions requiring more speed now than in the past, see Gaines v. Dougherty
Cty. Bd. of Education, 334 F.2d 983 (5th Cir. 1964); Lee v.
Macon Cty. Bd. of Education, 231 F. Supp. 743 (M.D. Ala. 3-judge
ct. 1964); Armstrong v. Bd. of Education, 333 F.2d 47 (5th Cir.
1964); Davis v. Board of School Comm'rs, 333 F.2d 53 (5th Cir.
1964); Stell v. Savannah-Chatham Cty. Bd. of Education, 333
F.2d 55 (5th Cir. 1964); Northcross v. Bd. of Education, 333 F.2d
661 (6th Cir. 1964); Brown v. Cty. School Bd., 327 F.2d 655 (4th
Cir. 1964); Jackson v. School Bd., 321 F.2d 230 (4th Cir. 1963);
Goss v. Bd. of Education, 301 F.2d 164 (6th Cir. 1962), *rev'd on
other grounds,* 373 U.S. 683 (1963); Hill v. Cty. Bd. of Education,
232 F. Supp. 671 (E.D. Tenn. 1964); Monroe v. Board of Comm'rs,
229 F. Supp. 580 (W.D. Tenn. 1964). But cf. Miller v. Barnes,
328 F.2d 810 (5th Cir. 1964) (Gewin, J.; Tuttle, C.J., dissenting);
Rogers v. Paul, 232 F. Supp. 833 (W.D. Ark. 1964); Nesbit v.
Statesville Bd. of Education, 232 F. Supp. 288 (W.D. N.C. 1964);
Christmas v. Bd. of Education, 231 F. Supp. 331 (D. Md. 1964);
Brown v. Hendrix, 228 F. Supp. 698 (E.D. Tex. 1964). And see
Lockett v. Bd. of Education, 342 F.2d 225 (5th Cir. 1965).

60. Brief for the United States on the Further Argument of the Questions of Relief, p. 25, Brown v. Board of Educ., 349 U.S. 294
(1955).

61. See Mapp v. Board of Educ., 319 F.2d 571 (6th Cir. 1963);
Augustus v. Board of Pub. Instruction, 306 F.2d 862 (5th Cir.
1962); Christmas v. Bd. of Education, 231 F. Supp. 331 (D. Md.
1964); see U.S. Commission on Civil Rights Staff, *Public Education*
56-57 (1963).

62. See U.S. Comm'n on Civil Rights, *Education* 31 (1961).

63. Dillard v. School Bd., 308 F.2d 920 (4th Cir. 1962), *cert. denied,*
374 U.S. 827 (1963); Green v. School Bd., 304 F.2d 118 (4th
Cir. 1962); Dowell v. School Bd., 219 F. Supp. 427 (W.D. Okla.
1963); Davis v. Board of Educ., 216 F. Supp. 295 (E.D. Mo.
1963); Vick v. County Bd. of Educ., 205 F. Supp. 436 (W.D.
Tenn. 1962); Vickers v. Chapel Hill City Bd. of Educ., 196 F. Supp.
97 (M.D. N.C. 1961).

64. Goss v. Board of Educ., 373 U.S. 683 (1963); Mapp v. Board of
Educ., 319 F.2d 571 (6th Cir. 1963).

65. See Branche v. Board of Educ., 204 F. Supp. 150 (E.D. N.Y.
1962).

66. Taylor v. Board of Educ., 195 F. Supp. 231 (S.D. N.Y.), *aff'd,* 294
F.2d 36 (2d Cir.), *cert. denied,* 368 U.S. 940 (1961).

67. Evans v. Buchanan, 195 F. Supp. 321, 325 (D. Del. 1961).

68. Evans v. Buchanan, 207 F. Supp. 820 (D. Del. 1962).

69. U.S. Comm'n on Civil Rights Staff, *Civil Rights U.S.A.: Public
Schools, Cities in the North and West* 266, 267 (1962) [hereinafter

cited as *Public Schools in the North and West*]. See also U.S. Comm'n on Civil Rights Staff, *Public Education* 141 *et seq.* (1964).

70. *Public Schools in the North and West* 30.
71. *Id.* at 27, 29.
72. U.S. Comm'n on Civil Rights, *Education* 17 (1961); U.S. Comm'n on Civil Rights Staff, *Public Education* 112 (1964).
73. U.S. Comm'n on Civil Rights Staff, *Public Education* 144-45 (1963); see W. Maslow, "De Facto Public School Segregation," 6 *Villanova L. Rev.* 353, 354-55 (1961).
74. See note 66 *supra* and accompanying text.
75. See Clemons v. Board of Educ., 228 F.2d 853 (6th Cir.), *cert. denied*, 350 U.S. 1006 (1956).
76. See Flax v. Potts, 218 F. Supp. 254, 259 (N.D. Tex. 1963).
77. Evans v. Buchanan, 207 F. Supp. 820 (D. Del. 1962).
78. See Bell v. School City of Gary, 213 F. Supp. 819 (N.D. Ind.), *aff'd*, 324 F.2d 209 (7th Cir. 1963), *cert. denied*, 377 U.S. 924 (1964); Thompson v. County School Bd., 204 F. Supp. 620 (E.D. Va. 1962); Henry v. Godsell, 165 F. Supp. 87 (E.D. Mich. 1958); Sealy v. Department of Pub. Instruction, 159 F. Supp. 561 (E.D. Pa. 1957), *aff'd*, 252 F.2d 898 (3d Cir.), *cert. denied*, 356 U.S. 975 (1958). A gerrymander can be managed not only by tailoring a zone to a school, but also by locating a new school with the racial factor in mind. Where there is proof, this also can be enjoined. But see Cragett v. Bd. of Education of Cleveland, 338 F.2d 941, *affirming* 234 F. Supp. 381 (1964).
79. Cf. Gomillion v. Lightfoot, 364 U.S. 339 (1960).
80. Dillard v. School Bd., 308 F. 2d 920 (4th Cir. 1962), *cert. denied*, 374 U.S. 827 (1963).
81. Jackson v. School Bd., 321 F.2d 230 (4th Cir. 1963).
82. Goss v. Bd. of Education, 373 U.S. 683 (1963).
83. See, e.g., Davis v. Bd. of Education, 216 F. Supp. 295 (E.D. Mo. 1963).
84. McNeese v. Bd. of Education, 373 U.S. 668 (1963).
85. See McNeese v. Bd. of Education, 305 F.2d 783 (7th Cir. 1962), *rev'd*, 373 U.S. 668 (1963); Shepard v. Bd. of Education, 207 F. Supp. 341 (D. N.J. 1962).
86. Barksdale v. Springfield School Committee, 237 F. Supp. 543 (D. Mass. 1965); Blocker v. Bd. of Education of Manhasset, 226 F. Supp. 208, 229 F. Supp. 709 (E.D. N.Y. 1964); Branche v. Bd. of Education, 204 F. Supp. 150 (E.D. N.Y. 1962). And see Jackson v. Pasadena City School Dist., 59 Cal. 2d 876, 382 P. 2d 878 (1963).
87. Sec. 401(b), 78 *Stat.* 246 (1964).
88. Sec. 407(a)(2), 78 *Stat.* 248 (1964).
89. Bell v. School City of Gary, 324 F.2d 209 (7th Cir. 1963), *cert. denied*, 377 U.S. 924 (1964).

90. Downs v. Bd. of Education of Kansas City, 336 F.2d 988 (10th Cir. 1964), *cert. denied,* 380 U.S. 914 (1965).
91. See O. M. Fiss, "Racial Imbalance in the Public Schools: The Constitutional Concepts," 78 *Harv. L. Rev.* 564 (1965); H. Sedler, "School Segregation in the North and West: Legal Aspects," 7 *St. Louis U. L. J.* 228 (1963). But cf. J. Kaplan, "Segregation Litigation and the Schools—Part II: The General Northern Problem," 58 *Northwestern U. L. Rev.* 157 (1963).
92. *Public Schools in the North and West* 90-95; Taylor v. Bd. of Education, 221 F. Supp. 275 (S.D. N.Y. 1963).
93. See *New York Times,* Oct. 23, 1963, p. 32, col. 1.
94. *Public Schools in the North and West* 118.
95. *Id.* at 181, 266-67; U.S. Comm'n on Civil Rights Staff, *Public Education* 141 (1963).
96. *New York Times,* Oct. 23, 1963, p. 32, col. 1. See generally, U.S. Comm'n on Civil Rights Staff, *Public Education* 79 *et seq.* (1963).
97. *Public Schools in the North and West* 118.
98. H. Hill, *Changing Options in American Education* 59 (1958). And see J. B. Conant, *Slums and Suburbs* 30-31 (1961).
99. See, e.g., U.S. Comm'n on Civil Rights Staff, *Public Education* 113 *et seq.,* 87 *et seq.* (1963); *New York Times,* Sept. 7, 1964, p. 1, col. 1; Sept. 14, 1964, p. 36, col. 1; Mar. 8, 1965, p. 1, col. 8, p. 22, col. 1.
100. Morean v. Bd. of Education, 42 N.J. 237, 200 A.2d 97 (1964).
101. Balaban v. Rubin, 14 N.Y.2d 193, 199 N.E.2d 375 (1964), *affirming,* 250 N.Y.S. 2d 281 (1964), *cert. denied,* 379 U.S. 881 (1964).
102. Vetere v. Mitchell, 21 App. Div. 2d 561, 251 N.Y.S.2d 480 (1964); *aff'd sub nom.* Vetere v. Allen, 15 N.Y.2d 259, 206 N.E.2d 174 (1965).
103. Schnepp v. Donovan, 43 Misc. 2d 917, 252 N.Y.S.2d 543 (Sup.Ct. 1964).
104. Fuller v. Volk, 230 F. Supp. 25 (D. N.J. 1964).
105. See *supra* n. 102. See also Addabo v. Donovan, 22 App. Div. 2d 383, 256 N.Y.S. 2d 178 (1965); Strippoli v. Bickal, 21 App. Div. 2d 365, 250 N.Y.S. 2d 969 (1964).
106. Sec. 403, 78 *Stat.* 247 (1964).
107. *Ibid.*
108. Secs. 404, 405, 78 *Stat.* 247-48 (1964).
109. Sec. 407(a), 78 *Stat.* 248 (1964).
110. Sec. 301(b), H.R. 7152, 88th Cong., 1st Sess., Confidential Committee Print, Oct. 2, 1963.
111. Arizona Employers' Liab. Cases, 250 U.S. 400, 434 (1919).
112. See United States v. Williams, 341 U.S. 70 (1951); Williams v. United States, 341 U.S. 97 (1951); Screws v. United States, 325 U.S. 91 (1945).

113. 158 U.S. 564 (1895).
114. Sanitary Dist. v. United States, 266 U.S. 405 (1925); United States v. New Orleans Pac. Ry., 248 U.S. 507 (1919); Heckman v. United States, 224 U.S. 413 (1912); United States v. American Bell Tel. Co., 128 U.S. 315 (1888); United States v. Beebe, 127 U.S. 338 (1888); United States v. San Jacinto Tin Co., 125 U.S. 273 (1888).
115. Though the United States may not intervene in mere private controversies, "yet, whenever the wrongs complained of are such as affect the public at large, and are in respect of matters which by the Constitution are entrusted to the care of the Nation, and concerning which the Nation owes the duty to all the citizens of securing to them their common rights, then the mere fact that the government has no pecuniary interest in the controversy is not sufficient to exclude it from the courts." 158 U.S. at 586.

The objection to *Debs* and to government by injunction in labor cases generally was that federal courts were making law in an area where, either (a) there should be legislative, not judicial, law or (b) all that was in question was a breach of the peace that was itself either an independent executive responsibility or a state rather than a federal responsibility. The point, then, is that the federal courts should not have acted, not that the Attorney General was the wrong party to ask them to do so. See Z. Chafee, "The Progress of the Law, 1919-1920," 34 *Harv. L. Rev.* 388, 402-07 (1921); W. Dunbar, "Government by Injunction," 13 *L. Q. Rev.* 347 (1897). In the grant-in-aid cases, and the like, in which, as we shall see, the United States has more recently exercised the inherent power to sue in equity, there is little question of the propriety of judicial action; everyone is satisfied that the courts ought to apply the Fourteenth Amendment, and even the Commerce Clause, at the behest of private parties. The criticisms directed at *Debs* are hence not relevant, valid as they are in their own context.
116. See especially the discussion by Miller and Field, JJ., in United States v. San Jacinto Tin Co., 125 U.S. 273, 301 (1888).
117. See United States v. County School Bd., 221 F. Supp. 93 (E.D. Va. 1963); Simkin v. Moses H. Cone Memorial Hosp. 211 F. Supp. 628 (M.D. N.C. 1962), *rev'd*, 323 F.2d 959 (4th Cir. 1963), *cert. denied*, 376 U.S. 938 (1964); United States v. City of Montgomery, 201 F. Supp. 590 (M.D. Ala. 1962); cf. United States v. Wallace, 218 F. Supp. 290, 222 F. Supp. 485 (M.D. Ala. 1963); United States v. U. S. Klans, 194 F. Supp. 897 (M.D. Ala. 1961). But see United States v. Bossier Parish School Bd., 336 F.2d 197 (5th Cir. 1964); United States v. Biloxi Municipal School Dist., 219 F. Supp. 691 (S.D. Miss. 1963); United States v. Madison City Bd. of Educ., 326 F.2d 237 (5th Cir. 1964). See also United States v. City of Jackson, 318 F.2d 1, *petition for rehearing denied per curiam*, 320 F.2d 870 (5th Cir. 1963); United States v. City of Shreveport, 210

F. Supp. 36, 210 F. Supp. 708 (W.D. La. 1962); United States v. Lassiter, 203 F. Supp. 20 (W.D. La.), *aff'd*, 371 U.S. 10 (1962). See, generally, R. Dixon, "Civil Rights in Air Transportation and Government Initiative," 49 *Va. L. Rev.* 205 (1963); W. Taylor, "Actions in Equity by the United States to Enforce School Desegregation," 29 *Geo. Wash. L. Rev.* 539 (1961).

II. CIVIL RIGHTS: A NEW ERA OPENS, 1960-1962

2. Preview: The Presidency and Civil Rights

1. See P. M. Angle, ed., *Created Equal?—The Complete Lincoln-Douglas Debates of 1858* 23, 36, 56-58, 78, 333 (1958); R. P. Bosler, ed., *The Collected Works of Abraham Lincoln*, Vols. 2 and 3, pp. 495, 516, 255 (1953); A. M. Bickel, *The Least Dangerous Branch* 259-62 (1962).
2. U.S. Commission on Civil Rights, *With Liberty and Justice for All* 133 (1959).
3. 20 U.S.C. Sec. 1.
4. H. Wofford, Jr., "Notre Dame Conference on Civil Rights: A Contribution to the Development of Public Law," 35 *Notre Dame Lawyer* 328, 360 (1960).
5. U.S. Comm'n on Civil Rights, *With Liberty and Justice for All* 184-186 (1959).

3. Review: The Kennedy Record at Mid-term

1. Executive Order 11063, "Equal Opportunity in Housing," Nov. 20, 1962.
2. U.S. Comm'n on Civil Rights, *With Liberty and Justice for All* 133 (1959).
3. 20 U.S.C. Sec. 1.
4. The suit mentioned in the text is U.S. v. County School Bd. of Prince George County, 221 F. Supp. 93 (E.D. Va. 1963). Other cases were brought, with indifferent effect: U.S. v. Biloxi Municipal School District, 219 F. Supp. 691 (S.D. Miss. 1963); U.S. v. Sumter Cty. School Dist., 232 F. Supp. 945 (E.D. S.C. 1964); U.S. v. Madison Cty. Bd. of Education, 326 F.2d 237 (5th Cir. 1964); U.S. v. Bossier Parish School Bd., 336 F.2d 197 (5th Cir. 1964). The problem has been rendered moot by Title VI of the Civil Rights Act of 1964.
5. Simkins v. Moses H. Cone Memorial Hospital, 323 F.2d 959 (4th Cir. 1963), *cert. denied*, 376 U.S. 938 (1964).
6. 206 F. Supp. 700 (D.C. D. La. 1962).
7. 375 U.S. 399 (1964).

4. More on the Kennedy Judges

1. 294 F.2d 150 (5th Cir. 1961).
2. 214 F. Supp. 624 (E.D. La. 1963). See also Davis v. East Baton Rouge Parish School Bd., 219 F. Supp. 876 (E.D. La. 1963).
3. 217 F. Supp. 661 (E.D. La. 1963).
4. Hall v. West, 335 F.2d 481 (5th Cir. 1964). And see Hall v. St. Helena Parish School Bd., 233 F. Supp. 136 (E.D. La. 1964).
5. 321 F.2d 116 (5th Cir. 1963).

III. THE NEGRO PROTEST MOVEMENT AND THE CIVIL RIGHTS ACTS OF 1964 AND 1965

5. Civil Rights and Civil Disobedience

1. Hamm v. City of Rock Hill, 379 U.S. 306 (1964).
2. See Cox v. Louisiana, 379 U.S. 536 (1965), and cases cited.
3. Duplex Printing Press Co. v. Deering, 254 U.S. 443, 488 (1921).
4. Hamm v. City of Rock Hill, *supra* n. 1, 379 U.S. at 328.

7. The Limits of Effective Legal Action

1. Address Before the Pennsylvania Bar Association, June 27, 1916, 22 *Pa. B. A. Rep.* 221 (1916).
2. W. Lippmann, "Our Predicament under the Eighteenth Amendment," *Harper's,* vol. 154, p. 51.
3. National Prohibition Cases, 253 U.S. 350 (1920).
4. A. T. Hadley, "Law Making and Law Enforcement," *Harper's,* vol. 151, p. 641.

8. The Voting Rights Act of 1965

1. U.S. v. Atkins, 210 F. Supp. 441 (S.D. Ala. 1962). This suit was filed in March, 1961.
2. B. Marshall, *Federalism and Civil Rights* 10 (1964).
3. Alabama v. U.S. 304 F.2d 583, 584-85 (5th Cir. 1962), *aff'd,* 371 U.S. 37 (1962). See also U.S. v. Cartwright, 230 F. Supp. 873 (M.D. Ala. 1964); U.S. v. Parker, 236 F. Supp. 511 (M.D. Ala. 1964).
4. See, e.g., U.S. v. Ramsey, 331 F.2d 824 (5th Cir. 1964); U.S. v. Mississippi, 229 F. Supp. 925 (5th Cir. 1964), *reversed,* 380 U.S. 128 (1965); Kennedy v. Owen, 321 F.2d 116 (5th Cir. 1963). See also U.S. v. Duke, 332 F.2d 759 (5th Cir. 1964) (Clayton, J.).

5. U.S. v. Atkins, *supra* n. 1, *reversed*, 323 F.2d 733 (5th Cir. 1963).
6. See U.S. v. Blackburn, 9 *Race Rel. L. Rep.* 1350, 1792 (1964).
7. *Congressional Record*, May 3, 1965, p. 8953.
8. Lassiter v. Northampton Cty. Bd. of Elections, 360 U.S. 45 (1959).
9. Louisiana v. U.S., 380 U.S. 145 (1965).
10. U.S. v. Mississippi, 380 U.S. 128 (1965).
11. U.S. v. Mississippi, 339 F.2d 679 (5th Cir. 1964).
12. 302 U.S. 277.

IV. THE WARREN COURT: DEFENSES AND CRITIQUES

10. The Law Clerks

1. W. Rehnquist, "Who Writes Decisions of the Supreme Court?", *U.S. News & World Report,* Dec. 13, 1957, p. 74.
2. See A. Bickel, *The Unpublished Opinions of Mr. Justice Brandeis* 100, 116-18 (1957).

11. Curbing the Union

1. The text is most conveniently available in 36 *State Government* 10 (1963).
2. J. F. Byrnes, "The Supreme Court Must Be Curbed," *U. S. News & World Report,* May 18, 1956, p. 50.
3. See F. Frankfurter, *Law and Politics* 10-16 (E. Prichard and A. MacLeish eds., Capricorn edition 1962).
4. H.J. Res. 200, 84th Cong., 1st Sess. (1955).
5. H.J. Res. 678, 683, 686, 687 and 704, 87th Cong., 2nd Sess. (1962); H.J. Res. 30, 34, 162, 178, 223, 300, and 349, 88th Cong., 1st Sess. (1963); S.J. Res. 2, 89th Cong., 1st Sess. (1965); see *New York Times,* Feb. 9, 1965, p. 31, col. 2.
6. E.g., H.J. Res. 201, 86th Cong., 1st Sess. (1959).
7. E.g., H.J. Res. 476, 85th Cong., 2nd Sess. (1958); H.J. Res. 790, 87th Cong., 2nd Sess. (1962).
8. H.J. Res. 495, 84th Cong., 2nd Sess. (1956).
9. S.J. Res. 176, 87th Cong., 2nd Sess. (1962).
10. E.g., H.J. Res. 532, 83d Cong., 2nd Sess. (1954); H.J. Res. 587, 87th Cong., 1st Sess. (1961).
11. E.g., H.R. 13857, 85th Cong., 2nd Sess. (1958); H.J. Res. 91, 83rd Cong., 1st Sess. (1953); H.R. 11374, 84th Cong., 2nd Sess. (1956); H.J. Res. 453, 86th Cong., 1st Sess. (1959).
12. S. 2646, 85th Cong., 1st Sess. (1957); S. 3386, 85th Cong., 2nd Sess. (1958).

13. H.R. 3, 85th Cong., 1st Sess. (1957).
14. E.g., H.R. 1228, 85th Cong., 1st Sess. (1957).
15. E.g., S. 3759, 84th Cong., 2nd Sess. (1956); H.R. 4020, 88th Cong., 1st Sess. (1963).
16. B. Hindman, "1313's Mail-Order Laws," *American Mercury*, Jan. 1960, pp. 33, 37, 35, 39. For information on the structure and functions of the Council of State Governments, see 32 *State Government* 162 (1959); *The Book of the States* (1960).
17. See C. L. Black, Jr., "The Proposed Amendment of Article V: A Threatened Disaster," 72 *Yale Law Journal* 957 (1963).
18. Gomillion v. Lightfoot, 364 U.S. 339 (1960).
19. 157 U.S. 429 (1895).
20. J. Fordham, "The States in the Federal System—Vital Role or Limbo?", 49 *Va. L. Rev.* 666, 672-73 (1963).
21. See 32 *State Government* 60 (1959).
22. See F. Shanahan, "Proposed Constitutional Amendments," 49 *American Bar Association Journal* 631, 636, n. 4 (1963).
23. Frankfurter, *op. cit.*, *supra* note 3, at p. 3.
24. See Ker v. California, 374 U.S. 23 (1963).
25. Truax v. Corrigan, 257 U.S. 312, 344 (1921).
26. New State Ice Co. v. Liebmann, 285 U.S. 262, 311 (1932).

12. New Troops on Old Battlegrounds

1. Kennedy v. Mendoza-Martinez and Rusk v. Cort, 372 U.S. 144 (1963).
2. Perez v. Brownell, 356 U.S. 44 (1958); Trop v. Dulles, 356 U.S. 86 (1958).

13. Supreme Court Fissures

1. E.g., Reynolds v. Sims, 377 U.S. 533 (1964); Malloy v. Hogan, 378 U.S. 1 (1964); Gideon v. Wainwright, 372 U.S. 335 (1963).
2. Bell v. Maryland, 378 U.S. 226 (1964).
3. Aptheker v. Secretary of State, 378 U.S. 500 (1964).
4. Shelley v. Kraemer, 334 U.S. 1 (1948); Marsh v. Alabama, 326 U.S. 501 (1946) (Black, J.).

V. REAPPORTIONMENT AND LIBERAL MYTHS

14. First Round: Baker v. Carr

1. 369 U.S. 186 (1962).
2. E.g., Colegrove v. Green, 328 U.S. 549 (1946); MacDougall v. Green, 335 U.S. 281 (1948); South v. Peters, 339 U.S. 276 (1950).

3. Colegrove v. Green, *supra* n. 2.
4. 4 Wheat. 316, 421 (1819).
5. 7 *Harv. L. Rev.* 129 (1893).
6. E.g., Schware v. Board of Bar Examiners, 353 U.S. 232 (1957).
7. Wieman v. Updegraff, 344 U.S. 183 (1952).
8. P. Neal, "Baker v. Carr: Politics in Search of Law," 1962 *The Supreme Court Review* 252.
9. Gray v. Sanders, 372 U.S. 368 (1963).

15. Congress

1. Wesberry v. Sanders, 376 U.S. 1 (1964).
2. E. Goldman, *Rendezvous With Destiny* 291 (1952).

16. One Man, One Vote, More or Less

1. Reynolds v. Sims, WMCA, Inc. v. Lorenzo, Lucas v. The Forty-fourth General Assembly, Maryland Committee v. Tawes, Davis v. Mann, Roman v. Sincock, 377 U.S. 533, 633, 656, 678, 695, 713 (1964).
2. E.g., Hitchman Coal & Coke Co. v. Mitchell, 245 U.S. 229 (1917); Duplex Printing Press Co. v. Deering, 245 U.S. 443 (1921); American Steel Foundries v. Tri-City Central Trades Council, 257 U.S. 184 (1921); Bedford Cut Stone Co. v. Stonecutters' Ass'n, 274 U.S. 37 (1927).
3. Compare Smyth v. Ames, 169 U.S. 466 (1898), with F.P.C. v. Hope Natural Gas Co., 320 U.S. 591 (1944).

VI. RELIGION AND THE SCHOOLS

17. Federal Aid to Education

1. Everson v. Bd. of Education, 330 U.S. 1 (1947).
2. Rutledge, J., dissenting in Everson v. Bd. of Education, *supra* note 1, 330 U.S. at 28, 33.
3. 268 U.S. 510 (1925).
4. Meyer v. Nebraska, 262 U.S. 390 (1923).

18. The School Prayer Cases

1. Engel v. Vitale, 370 U.S. 421 (1962).
2. School Dist. of Abington v. Schempp and Murray v. Curlett, 374 U.S. 203 (1963).
3. Cf. McCollum v. Bd. of Education, 333 U.S. 203 (1948), with Zorach v. Clauson, 343 U.S. 306 (1952).

APPENDIX. The Original Understanding and the Segregation Decision

1. Brown v. Board of Education, 347 U.S. 483 (1954).
2. *Id.* at 489.
3. *Id.* at 492-93.
4. The Court's deliberate approach to these cases, clearly reflecting its awareness of their unique importance, is indicated in A. Sacks, "Foreword" to "The Supreme Court, 1953 Term," 68 *Harv. L. Rev.* 96 (1954).
5. See J. tenBroek, "Admissibility and Use by the United States Supreme Court of Extrinsic Aids in Constitutional Construction," 26 *Calif. L. Rev.* 287, 437, 664 (1938), 27 *Calif. L. Rev.* 157, 399 (1939).
6. See C. Curtis, "A Better Theory of Legal Interpretation," 3 *Vand. L. Rev.* 407 (1950); F. Frankfurter, "Some Reflections on the Reading of Statutes," 47 *Colum. L. Rev.* 527, 543 (1947).
7. 60 U.S. (19 How.) 393, 426 (1856).
8. 290 U.S. 398, 453 (1934).
9. Chief Justice Hughes, for the majority in the *Blaisdell* case, made his rejection quite explicit: "If by the statement that what the Constitution meant at the time of its adoption it means to-day, it is intended to say that the great clauses of the Constitution must be confined to the interpretation which the framers, with the conditions and outlook of their time, would have placed upon them, the statement carries its own refutation. It was to guard against such a narrow conception that Chief Justice Marshall uttered the memorable warning—'we must never forget that it is *a constitution* we are expounding' (*McCulloch v. Maryland,* 4 Wheat. 316, 407)." 290 U.S. at 442-43.
10. See, e.g., Dimick v. Schiedt, 293 U.S. 474 (1935). This opinion, delivered over the dissent of Justice Stone in which Chief Justice Hughes and Justices Brandeis and Cardozo joined, was by Justice Sutherland. But the view expressed in this case and in the passages quoted in the text is very strong medicine, indeed, and truly steadfast adherence to it is more than can be asked of any judge. See Village of Euclid v. Ambler Realty Co., 272 U.S. 365 (1926) (opinion by Justice Sutherland).
11. See, e.g., District of Columbia v. Clawans, 300 U.S. 617 (1937). See also United States v. Flores, 289 U.S. 137 (1933); *Ex parte* Grossman, 267 U.S. 87 (1925).
12. In Weems v. United States, 217 U.S. 349 (1910), the Court, per Justice McKenna, held that a punishment consisting of a fine plus lengthy imprisonment imposed under a Philippine statute for

corruptly making false entries in public records was cruel and unusual within the meaning of the Eighth Amendment and hence also
within the meaning of the Philippine Bill of Rights. Dealing with the
argument that the Court was applying the Eighth Amendment in
circumstances in which its framers might not have thought it
applicable, Justice McKenna said, in a frequently quoted passage:
"Time works changes, brings into existence new conditions and purposes. Therefore a principle to be vital must be capable of wider
application than the mischief which gave it birth." 217 U.S. at 373.
Justice White dissented. He noted that local conditions might well
have made appropriate the severity of this punishment. Then he
proceeded at length to demonstrate that the original understanding
of the phrase "cruel and unusual punishment" was grounded in the
excesses of the Stuart reigns and was restricted to inhuman bodily
punishments and arbitrary imprisonment without sanction of statute.
Justice White argued that the original understanding should not be
departed from. In this opinion he was joined by Justice Holmes.
217 U.S. at 382, 413.

In National Mut. Ins. Co. v. Tidewater Transfer Co., 337 U.S.
582 (1949), Justice Frankfurter, in dissent, took a distinction between "great concepts" such as "Commerce . . . among the several
States," "due process of law," "liberty," and "property," which, he
said, "were purposely left to gather meaning from experience," and
"explicit and specific" terms, such as the word "State" when used in
article III in the grant of the diversity jurisdiction. That word, he
stated, is governed by the original understanding and cannot be
broadened to include the District of Columbia. 337 U.S. at 646.
(Justice Reed joined in Justice Frankfurter's dissent. Chief Justice
Vinson and Justice Douglas, dissenting separately, also agreed with
this view. So did Justices Jackson, Black, and Burton of the majority,
though they were of the opinion that Congress could, under its
article I power, create federal jurisdiction in suits between a citizen
of the District of Columbia and a citizen of one of the states.)

13. This is especially true as regards the Fourteenth Amendment. In
Maxwell v. Dow, 176 U.S. 581, 601-602 (1900), counsel, taking as
his text the speech by Senator Jacob Howard of Michigan which
opened debate on the Fourteenth Amendment in the Senate, *Cong.
Globe*, 39th Cong., 1st Sess. 2764-65 (1866), see note 98 *infra*,
argued that the amendment made the entire Bill of Rights applicable
to the states. Proceeding from Howard's speech without more, the
argument is plausible. The Court dealt with it on the basis of the
plain meaning rule and a general proposition to the effect that historical materials such as debates are always ambiguous and of
dubious value. Twice subsequently the same argument was rejected,
though without examination of historical materials. Twining v. New

Jersey, 211 U.S. 78 (1908); Palko v. Connecticut, 302 U.S. 319 (1937). But Justice Black, speaking for a four-man minority, returned to the fray in Adamson v. California, 332 U.S. 46, 70 (1947). Finally, Professor Fairman demonstrated that the argument was based on a misreading and an incomplete reading of the original understanding. C. Fairman, "Does the Fourteenth Amendment Incorporate the Bill of Rights?", 2 *Stan. L. Rev.* 5 (1949).

Perhaps the most famous appeal to the Fourteenth Amendment's history came in the course of Roscoe Conkling's devious argument in San Mateo County v. Southern Pac. R.R., 116 U.S. 138 (1885). There is no doubt that Conkling overstated his case. See H. Graham, "The 'Conspiracy Theory' of the Fourteenth Amendment," 47 *Yale L. J.* 371, 48 *Yale L. J.* 171 (1938). The "conspiracy theory" of the amendment, according to which Conkling, John A. Bingham, and perhaps Reverdy Johnson and others, operating in a smoke-filled room, secretly contrived to extend the protection of substantive due process to corporations, has been pretty well exploded, whatever the effect it may have had on the adjudications of the Court in this field. See H. McLaughlin, "The Court, The Corporation, and Conkling," 46 *Am. Hist. Rev.* 45 (1940). And, in any event, it would be very questionable practice indeed, as Justice Black suggested, see Connecticut Gen. Life Ins. Co. v. Johnson, 303 U.S. 77, 87 (1938) (dissenting opinion), for the Court to deem itself bound by the uncommunicated, back-room purpose of a handful of men. One of the caveats applicable to the use of the legislative history of statutes is acutely relevant here. See Shapiro v. United States, 335 U.S. 1, 45-49 (1948) (Justice Frankfurter, dissenting); Curtis, *supra* note 6, at 411-12. But Justice Black, quoting some unguarded language from the opinion of the Court in the Slaughter-House Cases, 83 U.S. (16 Wall.) 36 (1873), went on to argue that it was inconsistent with the purpose of the Fourteenth Amendment, as revealed by its history and language, to extend the protection of the due process clause to corporations. Connecticut Gen. Life Ins. Co. v. Johnson, *supra*. See also Wheeling Steel Corp. v. Glander, 337 U.S. 562, 576 (1949) (Justice Douglas, dissenting). The historical materials give no more warrant for this view than for the so-called conspiracy theory. See Graham, *supra* at 171. But cf. L. Boudin, "Truth and Fiction About the Fourteenth Amendment," 16 *N.Y.U.L.Q. Rev.* 19, 67 (1938).

14. F. Frankfurter, *Mr. Justice Holmes and the Supreme Court* 76 (1938). For a shining and enduring demonstration, see the opinion of Justice Bradley in Boyd v. United States, 116 U.S. 616, 624-32 (1886). For a nonjudicial tour de force, see J. Thayer, "Legal Tender," 1 *Harv. L. Rev.* 73 (1887).

15. Justice Holmes in Gompers v. United States, 233 U.S. 604, 610 (1914).

16. 345 U.S. 972 (1953). The questions which concern us are as follows:
    1. What evidence is there that the Congress which submitted and the state legislatures and conventions which ratified the Fourteenth Amendment contemplated or did not contemplate, understood or did not understand, that it would abolish segregation in public schools?
    2. If neither the Congress in submitting nor the states in ratifying the Fourteenth Amendment understood that compliance with it would require the immediate abolition of segregation in public schools, was it nevertheless the understanding of the framers of the amendment
        (a) that future Congresses might, in the exercise of their power under section 5 of the amendment, abolish such segregation, or
        (b) that it would be within the judicial power, in light of future conditions, to construe the amendment as abolishing such segregation of its own force?
    3. On the assumption that the answers to questions 2(a) and (b) do not dispose of the issue, is it within the judicial power, in construing the amendment, to abolish segregation in public schools?
17. *Cong. Globe,* 39th Cong., 1st Sess. 1 (1865). The *Globe* for this session will hereinafter be cited *Globe;* its appendix, *Globe, App.*
18. *Globe* 3149.
19. Act of April 9, 1866, c. 31, 14 *Stat.* 27.
20. The bureau had been created by Act of March 3, 1865, c. 90, 13 *Stat.* 507.
21. *Globe* 318.
22. *Globe* 421, 742, 748.
23. *Globe* 688, 775.
24. Lovell H. Rousseau of Kentucky.
25. See R. Henry, *The Story of Reconstruction* 159 (1938); H. White, *The Life of Lyman Trumbull* 260 (1913); H. Hyman, *Era of the Oath* 90-91 (1954).
26. *Globe* 915-17, 943.
27. S. 9, 39th Cong., 1st Sess. (1865), introduced by Senator Wilson of Massachusetts. *Globe* 2, 39.
28. *Globe* 513. The amendment was never voted on directly. It was lost together with a substitute bill, in which it was incorporated and which proposed other changes not here relevant. *Globe* 654, 655, 688. Section 6 of the bill as it then stood and as finally passed, see E. McPherson, *History of the Reconstruction* 73 (1871), in any event empowered the bureau to provide or cause to be built suitable buildings for asylums and schools. *Globe* 210.
29. There is no doubt that Charles Sumner favored unsegregated

schools. See his argument in Roberts v. Boston, 59 Mass. (5 Cush.) 198, 201 (1849), and his draft of what, in amended form, became the Civil Rights Act of 1875, *Cong. Globe*, 42nd Cong., 2nd Sess. 383-84 (1872). His general remarks on this occasion may indicate that he would have liked to see unsegregated schools started in the South at this time. However, speaking specifically of the bill before the Senate, he used more guarded language. It proposed, he said, "nothing less than to establish Equality before the Law, at least so far as civil rights are concerned, in the rebel States." *Globe* 91.

30. Lovell Rousseau of Kentucky, the Conservative Republican who was to vote against the bill, criticized the Freedmen's Bureau for having taken over schoolhouses in Charleston for the benefit of colored children. The white children were thus deprived of instruction, unless—and this was put as a preposterous proposition—"they mix up white children with black." *Globe, App.* 71. This same action of the bureau was denounced also by John W. Chanler, Democrat of New York. *Globe, App.* 82.

The Democratic broadside was by John L. Dawson of Pennsylvania. He accused the Radicals who sponsored this bill of hugging to their bosoms "the phantom of negro equality." The Radicals, he said,

hold that the white and black races are equal. This they maintain involves and demands social equality; that negroes should be received on an equality in white families, should be admitted to the same tables at hotels, should be permitted to occupy the same seats in railroad cars and the same pews in churches; that they should be allowed to hold offices, to sit on juries, to vote, to be eligible to seats in the State and national Legislatures, and to be judges, or to make and expound laws for the government of white men. Their children are to attend the same schools with white children, and to sit side by side with them. Following close upon this will, of course, be marriages between the races. . . . *Globe* 541.

31. *Globe* 474, 475.
32. *Globe* 474-75, 476.
33. *Globe* 570.
34. See the remarks of Henry Wilson, the Massachusetts Radical, who was to be Grant's Vice-President. *Globe* 603. Trumbull, who closed, again and in the same terms laid stress on the bill's relatively narrow purpose. *Globe* 605. John Sherman of Ohio, a Moderate, speaking on Feb. 8 in justification of his votes in favor both of the Freedmen's Bureau and Civil Rights Bills, read section 1 of the latter bill as defining "what are the incidents of freedom, and [saying] that these men must be protected in certain rights, and so

careful is it in its language that it goes on and defines those rights, the right to sue and be sued, to plead and be impleaded, to acquire and hold property, and other universal incidents of freedom." *Globe* 744.

35. A number of Black Codes are collected in W. Fleming, *Documentary History of Reconstruction* 273-312 (1906), and in McPherson, *op. cit. supra* note 28, 29-44. The worst of them were vagrancy statutes and laws minutely regulating the master-servant relationship, which was taking the place of slavery but appeared in some respects to bear a striking resemblance to it. But there were also enactments such as an Alabama statute of Dec. 9, 1865, permitting Negro testimony in court and a Florida statute of Jan. 16, 1866, setting up schools of a sort for freedmen. Both of these are cited by Fleming. They are to be distinguished from an Arkansas statute of Feb. 6, 1867, printed in the same place, which was passed after the Civil Rights Act had become effective, and which more or less followed its pattern. One of the principal instruments used to popularize the Radical picture of the South, especially in Congress, was the Schurz Report. See text p. 217. In the election campaign of 1866 much use was made of records of hearings before subcommittees of the Joint Committee on Reconstruction. These, however, were not in print before Congress passed the Fourteenth Amendment. See notes 61, 77, 83, 97 *infra*. See also Henry, *op. cit. supra* note 25, at 108-10, 115-16.

36. There were in addition two violent harangues by Garrett Davis of Kentucky, a Democrat and a thoroughly unreconstructed one. The first was not unfairly characterized in an interruption by Senator Clark (Rep., N.H.). Said Mr. Clark: "[I]t only comes back to this, that a nigger is a nigger." Said Mr. Davis: "That is the whole of it." *Globe* 529. In the second, Davis argued that the bill discriminated against whites by creating special rights for Negroes. He drew from Trumbull the reply that "this bill applies to white men as well as black men. It declares that all persons in the United States shall be entitled to the same civil rights. . . . The bill is applicable exclusively to civil rights." *Globe* 599.

37. *Globe* 476-77.

38. *Globe* 500. Presumably the dire consequences Cowan feared would come about because the bill forbade discrimination in civil rights, and in Cowan's mind, as in Saulsbury's, and as in Reverdy Johnson's, see note 39 *infra*, that term was susceptible of a broad interpretation. But when, in closing, Trumbull turned on him asking whether, everything else being equal, Cowan was not in favor of extending "equal civil rights" to the Negro, Cowan, who had already said much and was to say yet more as the session progressed about the inferior place of the Negro in a society governed for and by

the Caucasian race, replied, "Certainly." *Globe* 605. In this instance, he evidently accepted the narrow meaning attributed to
the phrase by the majority.

39. *Globe* 505-506.
40. *Globe* 606-607. Reverdy Johnson was absent. So was James R.
Doolittle of Wisconsin, a Republican but a close friend of the
President. The veto of the Freedman's Bureau Bill and the definitive
public breach between President and Radical Congress, which it
signified, were still some two weeks away. But Thaddeus Stevens
in the House already spoke of the President in ominous tones.
Globe 536-37. And Conservative Republicans who considered the
Freedmen's Bureau Bill an appropriate concession to offer to the
Radicals, evidently felt quite differently about a statute which might
be applied in their constituencies.
41. *Globe* 1117, 1118.
42. The Black Codes were the evil to which the bill was directed in the
view of Burton C. Cook of Illinois, Russell Thayer of Pennsylvania,
and William Windom of Minnesota, Radicals all. *Globe* 1123-25,
1151, 1160. Thayer added that the bill simply declared "that all
men born upon the soil of the United States shall enjoy the fundamental rights of citizenship. What rights are these? Why, sir, in
order to avoid any misapprehension they are stated in the bill."
And the bill could not possibly be read to confer suffrage. *Globe*
1151. Windom pointed out that the bill did not confer either
political or social rights. *Globe* 1159. And John M. Broomall of
Pennsylvania, another Radical, said the bill secured rights denied to
the Negro in the South; he named these rights: speech, transit,
domicil, to sue, to petition, and habeas corpus. *Globe* 1263.
43. *Globe* 1120.
44. *Globe, App.* 134.
45. *Globe* 1121-22.
46. *Globe* 1157.
47. *Globe* 1162.
48. *Globe* 1268. It is not at all clear that the reference in the full
paragraph quoted in the text to attendance at common schools "with
the children of white men" means that Kerr thought the bill would
require establishment of unsegregated schools rather than separate
Negro schools, forming part of a state's educational system. Kerr's
further remark can be read to imply that he took the educational
objective of the bill to be segregated Negro schools, and that he
favored it, subject to his constitutional scruples. But he did go on
to express general apprehension concerning the meaning of the
term "civil rights": "What are [civil] rights? One writer says civil
rights are those which have no relation to the establishment, support, or management of the Government. Another says they are

the rights of a citizen; rights due from one citizen to another, the privation of which is a *civil injury* for which redress may be sought by a *civil action*. Other authors define all these terms in different ways. . . . Who shall define these terms? Their definition here by gentlemen on this floor is one thing; their definition after this bill shall have become law will be quite another thing." *Globe* 1270-71.

49. *Globe* 1120, 1266. To the same general effect, see remarks of Thomas T. Davis of New York. *Globe* 1265. But Davis, in the end, voted for the bill and to override the veto.

50. *Globe, App.* 156-58.

51. *Globe* 1266, 1271-72.

52. *Globe* 1290-93.

53. Wilson also said:

I find in the bill of rights . . . that "no person shall be deprived of life, liberty, or property without due process of law." I understand that these constitute the civil rights belonging to the citizens in connection with those which are necessary for the protection and maintenance and perfect enjoyment of the rights thus specifically named, and these are the rights to which this bill relates, having nothing to do with subjects submitted to the control of the several States.

Globe 1294-95.

54. *Globe* 1295. Commentators who have looked into the matter have tended to oversimplify Bingham's position. In the first work on the subject, he is represented as objecting to the bill "entirely upon constitutional grounds." See H. Flack, *The Adoption of the Fourteenth Amendment* 35 (1908). Similarly, in a recent article, Howard Jay Graham leaves the reader with the impression that the debate on the Civil Rights Bill in the House turned wholly on the issue of constitutionality, dealt, that is, entirely with means, not ends. The implication is that Wilson, on the one hand, and Bingham and those Republicans who held views similar to his, on the other, were all along in agreement concerning the ends which the Civil Rights Bill would attain and concerning their desirability. See H. Graham, "Our 'Declaratory' Fourteenth Amendment," 7 *Stan. L. Rev.* 3, 12-18 (1954). This may be true as applied to Raymond. It is true in so far as it indicates that Bingham and Wilson were at one in their understanding of the specific ends aimed at by section 1 in its final form, and that Bingham regarded the attainment of these ends by appropriate federal action as desirable. An assertion so limited is supported by a passage from Bingham's speech which, as quoted by Graham, starts as follows: "I say, with all my heart, that [the First Section] . . . should be the law of every State. . . ." *Id.* at 15. The reference in Graham's context is to "the First Section" as enacted. In the speech itself, it was to the first section

as it came from the Senate, but shorn of its first sentence. Bingham, who had just been urging the elimination of the civil rights provision in that first sentence, read the section to the House without it, and immediately thereafter declared himself as quoted. "I say, with all my heart that that should be the law of every State," he said with all his heart. *Globe* 1291. This is a poor foundation for the theory Graham erects on it. Graham ignores the form in which the bill came from the Senate, Bingham's motion, the rest of Bingham's remarks, and what happened to the bill.

John P. Frank and Robert F. Munro state that Bingham "opposed the Civil Rights Act solely because he thought it should await passage of the Fourteenth Amendment" and attribute to him also the opinion that "appropriate language should eliminate 'all discrimination between citizens on account of race or color in civil rights.' " J. Frank and R. Munro, "The Original Understanding of 'Equal Protection of the Laws,' " 50 *Colum. L. Rev.* 131, 142 n. 51 (1950). The brief quotation used by Frank and Munro is from the next to last paragraph of Bingham's speech, quoted and discussed in the text above. He does not in that passage in so many words express the opinion attributed to him, nor does he do so anywhere else, and in light of the full text of his speech and of his motion, it is doubtful that he held it.

Charles Fairman understands Bingham to have believed that his motion to recommit with instructions to strike the guarantee of civil rights in section 1 and to change the enforcement provision would, if adopted, have cured the bill's constitutional defect. Fairman, *supra* note 13, at 39-40. This was Delano's view and Wilson accused Bingham of holding it. Wilson must have made the same accusation in the cloakroom as well, for, as shown in the text, Bingham started right off by entering a disclaimer. His remarks calling for a constitutional amendment to embody that part of section 1 which he did not hesitate to say he approved reinforce the point.

55. *Globe* 1296.
56. *Globe* 1366-67.
57. But not without hearing one more violent speech by Garrett Davis, Kentucky's furious Democrat. *Globe* 1413-16; see note 36 *supra*.
58. *Globe* 1679-81.
59. *Globe* 1775-80, 1782-85, 1809; *Globe, App.* 181-85.
60. *Globe* 1861.
61. Representatives Stevens, Washburne of Illinois, Morrill of Vermont, Bingham, Conkling of New York, Boutwell of Massachusetts, and Blow of Missouri, Republicans, and Grider of Kentucky and Rogers, Democrats; Senators Fessenden of Maine, Grimes of Iowa, Harris of New York, Howard of Michigan, and Williams of Oregon,

Republicans, and Reverdy Johnson, Democrat. *Globe* 6, 30, 46-47. See B. Kendrick, *The Journal of the Joint Committee of Fifteen on Reconstruction* 133-54 (1914); Henry, *op. cit. supra* note 25, at 133-42.

62. The idea embodied in article B had been first suggested by James G. Blaine of Maine. *Globe* 136, 141-42. The House passed the proposal as reported by Stevens from the Joint Committee. *Globe* 538. Sumner attacked it heavily in the Senate, *Globe* 673-87, 1224-32, 1281-82, and the addition of his vote, and the votes of one or two other Radicals, to those of the Democrats and Conservative Republicans ensured its defeat there. *Globe* 1289.

63. Kendrick, *op. cit. supra* note 61, at 39, 45-47, 50-53, 55-58, 61-63. These citations cover the entire course of the Committee's deliberations so far described in the text.

64. *Globe* 1034.

65. Thus William Higby of California thought the amendment would simply give effect to parts of the Constitution which "probably were intended from the beginning to have life and vitality." *Globe* 1054. Frederick E. Woodbridge of Vermont said the amendment would enable Congress to "give to a citizen of the United States, in whatever State he may be, those privileges and immunities which are guarantied to him under the constitution." *Globe* 1088.

66. *Globe* 1057, 1062-63.

67. *Globe, App.* 133, 134, 135. Much of the rest of Rogers' time was taken up with the kind of political small talk—the Radicals loved to bait him—into which so many of his speeches were wont to degenerate. This, of course, cannot but detract from the weight of his remarks. Thus, Samuel J. Randall, Democrat of Pennsylvania and a future Speaker of the House, felt constrained, after Rogers had finished, to state: "I wish it to be understood that the gentleman from New Jersey does not speak for me." The House reacted with laughter. Rogers modestly said, "I speak for myself." *Globe* 1034; cf. note 44 *supra*.

68. *Globe* 1063-65.

69. *Ind. Const.* art. II, §§ 2, 5 (1851); see Fairman, *supra* note 13, at 31 n. 57.

70. *Ore. Const.* art. I, § 35 (1857); see Fairman, *supra* note 13, at 32 n. 58; Boudin, *supra* note 13, at 35 n. 13.

71. *N.Y. Sess. Laws* 1864, c. 555, tit. 10, provided: "Section 1. The school authorities of any city or incorporated village . . . may, when they shall deem it expedient, establish a separate school or separate schools for the instruction of children and youth of African descent, resident therein . . . and such school or schools shall be supported in the same manner and to the same extent as the school or schools supported therein for white children, and they shall be subject

to the same rules and regulations, and be furnished with facilities for instruction equal to those furnished to the white schools therein. "Section 2. The trustees of any union school district, or of any school district organized under a special act, may, when the inhabitants of any such district shall so determine . . . establish . . . separate schools for the instruction of such colored children . . . and such schools shall be supported in the same manner, and receive the same care, and be furnished with the same facilities for instruction as the white schools therein." *N.Y. Sess. Laws* 1894, c. 556, tit. 15, art. ii, §§ 28, 29, re-enacted the two sections of the 1864 statute quoted above. In 1900 segregation in Queens was upheld in People *ex rel.* Cisco v. School Bd., 161 N.Y. 598, 56 N.E. 81. Following this decision, the legislature passed an act "to secure equal rights to colored children." It did so by providing that "no person shall be refused admission into or be excluded from any public school in the state of New York on account of race or color" and by repealing § 28 of the Act of 1894 (§ 1 of the Act of 1864), which permitted segregation in cities and incorporated villages. But it left undisturbed § 29 of the same act of 1894 (§ 2 of the Act of 1864), which was the corresponding provision applicable to union school districts and districts organized under special acts, and which differed in that it permitted segregation only after a vote by the district's inhabitants. *N.Y. Sess. Laws* 1900, c. 492.

One hesitates to pass judgment with any feeling of confidence on this state of the New York law. But the legislative action of 1900 cannot simply be attributed to an oversight. In the face of this partial repealer, would the declaration that no person should be refused admission to "any school" on account of color have been given effect in school districts to which the unrepealed § 29 was applicable? It is noteworthy that while all of the act of 1864 was on the books, the legislature passed a civil rights act prohibiting trustees and other officers of "public institutions of learning" from excluding anyone on account of color "from full and equal enjoyment of any accommodation, advantage, facility or privilege." *N.Y. Sess. Laws* 1873, c. 186, § 1. Nevertheless, the New York Court of Appeals had no difficulty avoiding this statute and upholding school segregation in Brooklyn as provided for in the act of 1864. People *ex rel.* King v. Gallagher, 93 N.Y. 438, 455-56 (1883). Perhaps by 1900 segregation outside cities and incorporated villages was not a problem. Perhaps it never had been much of one. Yet here was a section dealing with it, and there just is no satisfactory explanation for what looks like a deliberate failure to repeal it. But cf. A. Sutherland, "Segregation by Race in Public Schools Retrospect and Prospect," 20 *Law & Contemp. Prob.* 169,

171 (1955). The section was at last stricken from the books by
N.Y. Sess. Laws 1938, c. 134.

72. *Globe* 1085, 1087.
73. *Globe* 1088, 1090-91.
74. *Globe* 1094.
75. *Globe* 1095.
76. *Ibid.*
77. The Committee considered a measure for the readmission of Tennessee, which was controlled by anti-Johnson forces and had a
special claim to Radical favor. For over a month it did not meet.
Subcommittees, however, were taking evidence on conditions in
the South. Kendrick, *op. cit. supra* note 61, at 63-81, 221-27.
78. *Id.* at 82, 252-55. Section 1 of Stewart's proposed amendment read:
"All discriminations among the people because of race, color or
previous condition of servitude, either in civil rights or the right
of suffrage, are prohibited; but the States may exempt persons
now voters from restrictions on suffrage hereafter imposed." *Globe*
1906.
79. Kendrick, *op. cit. supra* note 61, 83-84.
80. R. Owen, "Political Results from the Varioloid," 35 *Atlantic
Monthly* 660, 662-64 (1875).
81. Kendrick, *op. cit. supra* note 61, at 85-120.
82. Owen, *supra* note 80, at 665-66.
83. *Globe* 2265, 2286.
84. *Globe* 2433-34.
85. Owen, *supra* note 80, at 665.
86. *Globe* 537.
87. *Globe* 2459.
88. M. Russell Thayer of Pennsylvania: "As I understand it, it is
but incorporating in the Constitution . . . the principle of the
civil rights bill . . . [so that it] shall be forever incorporated."
Globe 2465. To the same effect, John M. Broomall of Pennsylvania, *Globe* 2498, and Thomas D. Eliot of Massachusetts, *Globe*
2511. Henry J. Raymond, who was going to vote for this amendment, also thought the "principle" of this proposal was that
embodied in the Civil Rights Bill, which he had opposed on
constitutional grounds. He was further of the opinion that the
same "principle" had been expressed by the Bingham amendment, concerning which Raymond had been silent and remained
so now. *Globe* 2502.
89. William D. Kelley of Pennsylvania: "There is not a man in
Montgomery or Lehigh county [the constituency of a Pennsylvania Democrat, Benjamin M. Boyer] that will not say those
provisions ought to be in the Constitution if they are not already
there." *Globe* 2468. George F. Miller of Pennsylvania: "As to

the first, it is so just . . . and so clearly within the spirit of the Declaration of Independence of the 4th of July, 1776, that no member of this House can seriously object to it." *Globe* 2510. John F. Farnsworth of Illinois: "This is so self-evident and just that no man whose soul is not too cramped and dwarfed to hold the smallest germ of justice can fail to see and appreciate it." *Globe* 2539. James A. Garfield, who discussed other parts of the amendment with his usual acuity, merely referred to "this first section here which proposes to hold over every American citizen, without regard to color, the protecting shield of law." *Globe* 2462.

90. E.g., Eliot of Massachusetts, *Globe* 2511; Farnsworth of Illinois, *Globe* 2539.

91. William E. Finck of Ohio: "Well, all I have to say about this section is, that if it is necessary to adopt it . . . then the civil rights bill . . . was passed without authority, and is clearly unconstitutional." *Globe* 2461. To the same effect, Charles A. Eldridge of Wisconsin, *Globe* 2506.

92. Boyer of Pennsylvania: "The first section embodies the principles of the civil rights bill, and is intended to secure ultimately, and to some extent indirectly, the political equality of the negro race. It is objectionable also in its phraseology, being open to ambiguity and admitting of conflicting constructions." *Globe* 2467. Samuel J. Randall of Pennsylvania: "The first section proposes to make an equality in every respect between the two races, notwithstanding the policy of discrimination which has heretofore been exclusively exercised by the States. . . . If you have the right to interfere in behalf of one character of rights—I may say of every character of rights, save the suffrage—how soon will you be ready to tear down every barrier? It is only because you fear the people that you do not now do it." *Globe* 2530. See also remarks by George S. Shanklin of Kentucky and Myer Strouse of Pennslyvania, *Globe* 2500, 2531.

93. Thus, James G. Blaine, Robert C. Schenck of Ohio, Green Clay Smith of Kentucky, a Conservative, Samuel McKee of Kentucky, Boutwell, Rufus P. Spalding of Ohio, John W. Longyear of Michigan, and Fernando C. Beaman of Michigan. *Globe* 2460, 2469-73, 2504-05, 2507-10, 2536-37.

94. *Globe* 2538.

95. *Globe* 2542-43.

96. *Globe* 2544-45.

97. *Globe* 2763. The House Democrat who had made a complaint similar to Sumner's was Charles A. Eldridge of Wisconsin. *Globe* 2506. A majority report was submitted by Fessenden in the Senate and Stevens in the House on June 8, and ordered to be

printed. *Globe* 3038, 3051. This was a political document written by Fessenden, though evidently strongly influenced by Stevens. It did not deal with § 1. Its conclusion stated that "your committee submit it [the Fourteenth Amendment] to Congress as the best they could agree upon, in the hope that its imperfections may be cured, and its deficiencies supplied, by legislative wisdom." See McPherson, *op. cit. supra* note 28, at 84-93; Kendrick, *op. cit. supra* note 61, at 320-26. A minority report, written by Reverdy Johnson and signed as well by Rogers and Henry Grider, was also submitted, and received and printed after an unedifying partisan hassle. *Globe* 3275, 3349-50, 3646-49, 3749-50, 3766-67. This report was rather an imposing paper, arguing for the reinstatement of the Southern states in their rights of representation in Congress. It made no mention of § 1. See McPherson, *op. cit. supra* note 28, at 93-101.

98. *Globe* 2765, 2766. This speech by Howard, together with a few less explicit remarks by Bingham, constitutes the principal reliance of those who purport to find an intention to incorporate the entire Bill of Rights in the Fourteenth Amendment. See note 13 *supra*; Fairman, *supra* note 13, at 65-68, 78-81.

99. *Globe* 2768-69, 2798-803; see note 78 *supra*.

100. *Globe* 2869.

101. *Globe* 2939; see Kendrick, *op. cit. supra* note 61, at 316.

102. *Globe* 2896, 2939, 2891-93.

103. *Globe* 2961.

104. *Globe* 3031, 3034-35.

105. *Globe, App.* 219. The Florida statute which Howe must have had in mind is the act of January 16, 1866, Fla. Laws 1865, c. 1475. It is printed in part in 1 W. Fleming, *Documentary History of Reconstruction* 277-79 (1906).

106. *Globe* 2896, 2939, 2891-93; *Globe, App.* 240. The same may be said of McDougall of California, also a Democrat, though not of the utterly unreconstructible Davis type. *Globe* 3030-31.

107. *Globe* 3026-30.

108. *Globe* 3041-42.

109. *Globe* 3144.

110. *Globe, App.* 229.

111. *Globe* 3148-49.

112. On the issues of the campaign of 1866, see H. Beale, *The Critical Year* (1930); with specific reference to § 1 of the Fourteenth Amendment, see Fairman, *supra* note 13, at 69-78. For a survey of ratification materials, see *id.* at 84-126. The state materials are most thoroughly reviewed in the appendix to the government's brief as amicus in the *School Segregation Cases*. Appendix to the Supplemental Brief for the United States on Reargument,

Nos. 1, 2, 4, 8, 10, at 160-393, Brown v. Board of Educ., 347 U.S. 483 (1954).

113. *La. Const.* art. 135 (1868); cf. *La. Const.* art. 224 (1879); *La. Const.* art. 248 (1898). *S.C. Const.* art. X (1868) *(semble)*; cf. *S.C. Const.* art. XI (1895).

114. See note 16 *supra*.

115. In 1871, in the course of the debate on the act of April 20, 1871 (Ku Klux Act), c. 22, 17 *Stat.* 13, Bingham argued the contrary. He contended that Congress had no less power to legislate under the Fourteenth Amendment than it would have had under his own earlier, rejected proposal. In other words, he attached no significance whatever to the defeat of that proposal. That is, of course, a rather arbitrary way to deal with the materials. As James A. Garfield had occasion to tell Bingham, "my colleague can make but he cannot unmake history." *Cong. Globe, App.,* 42nd Cong., 1st Sess. 83-86, 113-17, 151 (1871); see Fairman, *supra* note 13, at 136-37; Flack, *op. cit. supra* note 54, at 226-49. Bingham's view evidently prevailed in Congress, but the Supreme Court, without reference to the legislative history and dealing simply with the language of the Fourteenth Amendment on its face, saw it otherwise. United States v. Harris, 106 U.S. 629 (1883).

116. See note 112 *supra*.

117. See Thayer, *supra* note 14, at 75-78, and especially at 78 note 2.

118. See note 97 *supra*.

119. See note 13 *supra*.

120. Much has been made of the abolitionist antecedents of a number of men prominent in the 39th Congress, among them Stevens, and—a little more dubiously—Bingham. And it has been contended that terms similar to those used by Bingham in § 1 of the Fourteenth Amendment had been widely advertised abolitionist clichés, which were well understood by the country as embodying the fullness of the abolitionist doctrine. See J. ten-Broek, *The Antislavery Origins of the Fourteenth Amendment* (1951); H. Graham, "The Early Antislavery Backgrounds of the Fourteenth Amendment," 1950 *Wis. L. Rev.* 479, 610. Yet even among the abolitionists there were differences of view concerning the extent to which uncompromising egalitarian principles should be applied—suddenly and indiscriminately—to the Negro. See R. Nye, *Fettered Freedom: Civil Liberties and the Slavery Controversy 1830-1860* (1949). And it is always dangerous to assume that men—especially men of a revolutionary persuasion—who have achieved power act on principles they espoused while in violent opposition. Be that as it may, the abolitionist past of some Radicals can, in view of all the evidence, be relevant to

only one facet of the compromise they accepted; it helps to indicate not what they believed they were achieving immediately but what they hoped was open to future achievement.

121. Justice Cardozo in Palko v. Connecticut, 302 U.S. 319, 325 (1937).

122. E.g., Strauder v. West Virginia, 100 U.S. 303 (1880); Norris v. Alabama, 294 U.S. 587 (1935) (jury service). The Court has also, in the changed circumstances created by the Fifteenth Amendment, applied the equal protection clause of the Fourteenth to the right to vote. Nixon v. Herndon, 273 U.S. 536 (1927); cf. Smith v. Allwright, 321 U.S. 649 (1944).

Index

Acheson, Dean, 145
Airports, 58
Allgood, C. W., 69-71
Altgeld, J. P., 90
Apportionment. *See also Baker v. Carr*
  constitutional amendment proposed, 147, 153-156
  constitutional provisions, 193-194
  county-unit system, 187, 195, 196
  equal-representation principle, 191-195
  one-person-one-vote concept, 183, 185-187, 191, 196
  political implications, 180-190, 192
  Supreme Court decisions on, xi, 175-176, 180 ff, 191 ff
  questionable nature of, 196-198
Attorney General, 41-44, 102

Baker v. Carr, 147, 153-156, 175-176, 192
Baldwin, James, 4

Bentham, Jeremy, 142
Bible-reading. *See* Church and state
Bingham, J. A., 226-232, 235-242, 255, 258
Bingham amendment. *See* Bingham, J. A.; constitutional amendments
Birmingham demonstrations. *See* Negro protest movements
Black, Hugo, 168-172
Black Codes. *See* Slavery
Brandeis, L. D.
  and law clerks, 144-145
  on duty to community, 82
  on state government, 161
Brennan, W. J., 176-177
Bus terminals, 58

Carter, R. L., 8, 11-12
Chase, S. P., 135
Church and state
  Bible-reading in public schools, 209

293

Church and state (*continued*)
disestablishment clauses, 202, 205
in education, xi
school prayer cases, 205-210
Citizenship
denationalization of native born,
163-167
Fourteenth Amendment, 250
Civil disobedience. *See also* Negro
protest movements
generally, 13, 77
limits, 81-82, 88-90
local laws versus higher laws, 78-81
moral issues, 82, 87
protest movements as not constitut-
ing, 80
public order and, 81-82, 86
violence in streets, 80-81
Civil rights
education. *See* Desegregation; Education
legislative history, Fourteenth
Amendment, 219-258
presidential campaign platform, 57
presidential inaction, 58-59
presidential policies, 49-55
suffrage. *See* Voting Rights Act of
1965
transportation. *See* Transportation
Civil Rights Act of 1866, 215, 218-
231, 254-256
Civil Rights Act of 1964
Attorney General's power to bring
suit, 102
civil contempt clauses, 99
Civil Rights Commission, 102-104
communism, clauses on, 98
community relations service, 82
constitutionality, 107-108
criminal contempt clauses, 98-99
education clauses, 97, 102
federally assisted programs under,
102
history under President Kennedy,
92 ff

Civil Rights Act of 1964 (*continued*)
House changes, 96-98
housing clauses, 96-97
immediate effects, 105
"interstate commerce" under, 107-
108
juries in criminal contempt cases,
98-99
new objectives, 95
nondiscrimination clauses, 97, 102-
103
public accommodations clauses, 95,
100, 106
senate changes, 98-99
voting rights clauses, 99
literacy requirements, 100-101
Civil rights acts, federal power under,
37-45, 58-59
Civil Rights Commission, 63
extension under Civil Rights Act,
102-104
public education functions, 53
reports, 28-29
Civil Service Commission, 123
Clark, J. G., 119-120
Committee of Fifteen. *See* Joint Committee on Reconstruction
Community Relations Service, 96, 98,
104, 106
Conference of Chief Justices, 158-160
Congress of Racial Equality (CORE),
84-85
Conkling, Roscoe, 240-241
Connor, Eugene ("Bull"), 94
Constitution
as way of ordering society, ix-x
impact of politics upon, ix-xi
interpretation and construction, 176-
180, 211
amending clause, proposed changes,
146, 152-153
Constitutional amendments
analytical discussion, 154-161
Fourteenth Amendment: equal protection clause, x, 257

Constitutional amendments (*continued*)
Fourteenth Amendment: legislative history, 211-253
Fourteenth Amendment: narrow objectives, 256
proposals, 146-161
proposals, 1954 to date: 148-149
Constitutional Law
consensual nature, 11
enforcement, problems of, 42-45
Constitutionality, 31, 107-108, 177-178, 231-256
Council of State Governments, 146-161
Court of the Union, 147, 156-159
Cowan, Edgar, 220
Cox, W. H., 68, 73-74, 118

Dahl, R. A., 182
Davis, David, 136
De facto segregation, 4
constitutional questions, 43-45
definition, 43
in cities, 28, 32
New Jersey experience, 36-37
New York experience, 36-37
northern, 33 ff
Debs, E. V., 90
Delano, Columbus, 225-226
Deliberate speed formula
concept, 7-8, 10
purpose, 14
South Carolina study, 10
Demonstrations. *See* Negro protest movements
Department of Justice, civil rights division, 50, 54, 58-59
Desegregation
as rule of law, 5
community-school relations, 34
compliance, delays in, 7-10
compliance reports, 40-41
consent as vital, 41
coordination, lack of, 63

Desegregation (*continued*)
Decisions: Alabama, 18, 22
Arkansas, 18-19
Florida, 21
Georgia, 22-23
New Jersey, 37
New York, 36-37
North Carolina, 16
regressive rulings, 22
Supreme Court reversals, 23
Tennessee, 21, 24
Texas, 18
Virginia, 16-17
definition, 26, 31
enforcement, constitutional problems, 42-45
federal implementation, 38-45, 58 ff
Fourteenth Amendment; history, 217
impact, x
free choice principle, 27-28, 33, 39-41
"General Statement of Policies," 39-40
grade-a-year plan, 25
higher education, 14
integration differentiated, 4
Kennedy administration, 64
Little Rock, 15
Mississippi, 15
neighborhood school policy, 33 ff
New Rochelle, 28, 30, 33
Northern experience, 28 ff
Office of Education function, 63
opposition and non-compliance, 11 ff
permissive segregation in New York, 239
presidential assistance, 38
presidential inaction, 14-15
Princeton plan, 34
problems in decision-making, 34 ff
residential zoning plans, 24, 26-29
school pairing plan, 34
school segregation cases, 211 ff

Desegregation (*continued*)
    statistics, 5-6, 14-15, 28-29, 31, 34
    statistics, public accommodations, 109
    tokenism, 16-22
Deutsch, K. W., 146
Dirksen, E. M., 98
discrimination, Supreme Court recent decisions, 168-171
Doar, John, 59
Douglas, P. H., 53
Douglas, W. O., 170-172, 187, 207

Education. *See also* Desegregation; Vocational education
    free public education system, 53, 202-203, 208
    Negroes, history, 217
    presidential power, 53
    programs under President Kennedy, 61
    school personnel, 26
    unsegregated schools, 217
Education Act of 1965
    anti-discrimination effect, 39, 41
Eisenhower, D. D., 15, 50 ff, 58-59
Electoral College, 186
Elementary and Secondary Education Act. *See* Education Act of 1965
Elliott, J. R., 67
Ellis, F. B., 67-68
Employment
    anti-discrimination measures, 61-62
    equal employment opportunity, 106
    federal appointments under President Kennedy, 66-68
Equal Employment Opportunity Commission, 106
Equal protection. *See* constitutional amendments
Equal representation. *See* Apportionment
Expulsions, Negro school children, 69-70

Farmer, James, 86
Federal assistance to schools, 37-40
    effect of discrimination on, 65
    parochial schools, 201-204
Federal-state relations, 146-161
    local-state-federal laws, 78
Fessenden, W. P., 232-233, 243 ff, 249, 253-254
Field, S. J., 136
Fordham, J. B., 157
Fourteenth Amendment. *See* Constitutional amendments
Frankfurter, Felix
    effect of retirement on Court, 162
    on due process clause, 148
    on recall of judges, 159
    on the Constitution, ix, 1
Freedmen's Bureau Bill, 214-217, 254
Freedom of religion
    school prayer cases, 205-210
Freedom rides. *See* Negro protest movements

Goldberg, A. J., 162-167
Goldwater, Barry, 106
Government, consent to, ix-x, 184
Government contracts
    non-discrimination, 55
    presidential influence, 55
Grade-a-year plans. *See* Desegregation
Gradualism, 8

Hale, R. S., 237-238
Henderson, J. B., 251
Hill, Lister, 59
Holmes, O. W., 160-161
Hospitals, discrimination in, 65-66
Hotchkiss, G. W., 240
Housing
    anti-discrimination order, 65-66, 97
    federal assistance and integration, 54
    presidential influence, 54, 57
Howe, T. O., 251
Hughes, C. E., 136-138
Huxley, Aldous, 94

Integration
 action under President Kennedy, 64
 as next phase, 26
 legal approach, 4
 statistics, 28-29

Javits, J. K., 127
Johnson, F. M., 117
Johnson, L. B.
 Civil Rights Act of 1964, 104
 on voting rights, 120
Johnson, Reverdy, 221, 251
Joint Committee on Reconstruction, 232
 reconstruction plan, 241 ff
Judge-made law
 consensual nature, 11
 dissent and non-compliance, 11-13
 enforcement, 11-13
 limits of effectiveness, 87
Judges
 impact on Constitution, xi
 obstruction of civil rights by, 66-68
 political involvement, 134
 President Kennedy's appointees, 66-74

Kennedy, Edward, 128-129
Kennedy, John F., 49-51
 civil rights under, 52, 56 ff
 on equal representation, 182
 on public policy, 92
Kennedy, Robert F., 42
 civil rights under, 58-61
 on non-English literacy, 127
Kent, James, 222, 228
Kerr, M. C., 224
King, Martin L.
 Birmingham demonstrations, 69, 93
 opponents, 81
 Selma march, 116

LaFollette, Robert, 148
Latitudinarian construction, 231, 245, 255-256, 258
Law, definitions, 87, 88

Law clerks, xi, 140-145
Law enforcement
 limits of effective legal action, 110-112
 non-compliance and abandonment, 113
 persuasion, effect of, 114-115
Law reviews (journals), 143
Liberator, 81
Lippmann, Walter, 112
Literacy tests, 123-126
 non-English languages, 127

McKenna, Joseph, 42
McLean, John, 135
Magruder, Calvert, 145
Majority rule, 184-185, 196-197
Marshall, Burke, 59, 93
 on voting rights, 116-117
Marshall, John, 177-178
Marshall, Thurgood, 8, 11-12
Massive resistance, 16-18

Neal, P. C., 185-186
Negro protest movements
 Birmingham, 93-94
 bus boycotts, 94
 federal responsibilities, 81-84
 freedom rides, 79-80
 Harlem riots, 116
 labor movement compared, 90-91
 legality discussed, 77-78, 81-82
 Northern cities, 84 ff, 116
 Philadelphia riots, 116
 sit-ins, 78-79, 94
 sit-ins, Supreme Court decisions, 169-171
 Southern, 78-84
 stall-ins, 84
 the cause is just, 90-91
Negroes
 federal appointments, 66
 school personnel, 26
 teachers, 26
Office of Education
 functions and powers, 53, 63, 102

Office of Education (*continued*)
   general statement of policies, 39-40
   under Civil Rights Act, 38-45, 102
One-person-one-vote. *See* Apportionment
Owen, R. D., 242

Passports, 171-172
Poll tax, 128-129
Pound, Roscoe, 5, 111-112
Powell, T. R., 134, 144
Prince Edward County, "Private" schools, 17-18
Principled government, ix
"Private" schools, 17-18
Proclamations, civil rights, 53
Prohibition, 114
Proportional representation, 186
Protest movements. *See* Negro protest movements
Public accommodations
   Civil Rights Act, 95, 100, 106
   compliance, problems of, 110 ff
   desegregation statistics, 109
   Supreme Court decisions, 169
Punishment
   purposes, 164-165
   sanctions distinguished, 165-167
Pupil placement statutes, 18-24
Pupil transfers, constitutionality, 31
Pupil transportation, constitutionality, 31

Quint, H. H., 10, 12

Racial imbalance
   community activities, 34
   constitutionality question, 30-31
Railroad terminals, 58
Rationality, 177-181
Raymond, H. J., 225
Reapportionment. *See* Apportionment
Reconstruction plan, 241 ff
Representative democracy, 182-184
Reston, James, 88
Rice, W. G., 144

Riesman, David, 145
Rogers, A. J., 222, 236-237, 252
Rosen, S. J., 62

School prayers. *See* Church and state
Segregation
   abolition, history, 256-261
   constitutionality, 231-256
   "private" schools, 17-18
   public school segregation accepted, 256
Self-government, ix
Selma, Ala., 116, 119
Separation of powers, 51
Shanklin, G. S., 222
Sit-ins. *See* Negro protest movements
Slavery, 88
   Fugitive Slave Act, 113
   Negro Codes, 218-219, 251, 254
Stall-ins. *See* Negro protest movements
States' rights, 146-161
Stevens, Thaddeus, 232-234, 241 ff, 252-253, 259-260
Stewart, Potter, 207
Stewart, W. M., 241, 250
Student Non-Violent Coordinating Committee, 60
Suffrage. *See* Voting rights
Sumner, Charles, 249
Supreme Court
   attempted changes of, 148-149, 153-161
   constitutional amendments regarding, 153-161
   current relationships, 168-172
   decisions since 1962, 162-167
   law-making cycles, 147
   passive decision-making, 170-171, 175, 206
   political involvement, 133 ff
   school segregation cases, 211 ff

Taney, R. B., 135
Thayer, J. B., 178

Thomas, D. H., 118
Thompson, Smith, 136
Thornton, Anthony, 223
Tocqueville, de, ix, 134
Tokenism, 16-25
Transportation, desegregation history, 57-58
Trumbull, Lyman, 218-219, 253-254

Unwashed law, 12

Violence. *See* Civil disobedience; Negro protest movements
Vocational education, 62
See also Education
Voting rights, 58 ff
action prior to 1965, 116 ff
enforcement problems, 59-61
federal-state conflicts, 123
Fourteenth Amendment, history, 233-237, 241-242, 244-248, 250

Voting rights, (*continued*)
history, 58-59
literacy tests, 123-127
poll tax, 128-129
President Eisenhower's inaction, 50, 58-59
President Kennedy's action, 93
referee provision, 1960 Act, 118
registrars, use of, 188-119
statistics, 121-122
Voting Rights Act of 1965, 99
provisions, 121
Selma march, effect on, 120-121

Warren, Earl, xi, 133
Warren, R. P., 8, 15
West, E. G., 67-68, 71-73
White, B. R., 89, 145, 162
Williams, Aubrey, 8, 14
Wilson, J. F., 221-231
Wisdom, J. M., 67